The Psych 101 series

James C. Kaufman, PhD, Series Editor

Director, Learning Research Institute

California State University at San Bernardino

D0503432

Gerald Matthews, PhD, is Professor of Psychology at the University of Cincinnati, where he teaches courses on human performance, human factors, performance and information processing, and stress and cognition. Professor Matthews's main area of research interest is applying cognitive science models to human factors, individual differences, and stress, as well as the assessment and psychophysiology of personality and mood. More specifically, he is interested in personality and mood effects on attention and performance, stress and fatigue effects on performance, and the relationship between emotion and attentional processing. He has also researched the application of cognitive models of stress to individual differences in appraisal, coping, and stress outcomes. He is an associate editor of the journal *Personality and Individual Differences* and a consulting editor for the *Journal of Experimental Psychology: Applied*. He is currently Secretary-Treasurer of the International Society for the Study of Individual Differences.

Moshe Zeidner, PhD, is Professor of Human Development and Educational Psychology and Director of the Center for Interdisciplinary Research on Emotions at the University of Haifa, Israel. His research focuses on personality, the assessment of stress and emotion, coping with traumatic events, and emotional intelligence. Professor Zeidner received a Lifelong Achievement Award in July 2003 from the Society of Stress and Anxiety Research. His most recent book, *Emotional Intelligence: Science and Myth*, was accorded an Honorable Mention by the American Academic Publishing Society (2003). Professor Zeidner is a consulting editor for the *Journal of Educational Psychology*; *Personality and Individual Differences*; *Stress, Anxiety, and Coping*; *Psychology in the Schools*; and *Emotion*. He has co-authored or co-edited 10 books and has authored or co-authored over 200 articles and book chapters published in the scientific literature.

Richard D. Roberts, PhD, is a Principal Research Scientist in the Center for New Constructs in the Educational Testing Service's R&D Division, Princeton, NJ. A former National Research Council Fellow, he was also a Senior Lecturer at The University of Sydney, Sydney, Australia, from 1998 to 2003. His main areas of specialization are assessment and individual differences. He has published around 120 peer-review articles or invited book chapters on these topics in diverse subdisciplines (including education, psychology, military science, and wind engineering) and received significant grants and awards (from foundations, the military, and several governments). The editor of four books, with a fifth on the way, he has also co-authored two previous books with the current research team, *Emotional Intelligence: Science and Myth* and *What We Know About Emotional Intelligence: How It Affects Learning, Work, Relationships, and Our Mental Health*.

Emotional Intelligence 101

Gerald Matthews, PhD
Moshe Zeidner, PhD
Richard D. Roberts, PhD

SPRINGER PUBLISHING COMPANY

NEW YORK

Copyright © 2012 Springer Publishing Company, LLC

Springer Publishing Company, LLC
11 West 42nd Street
New York, NY 10036
www.springerpub.com

Acquisitions Editor: Nancy Hale
Composition: Newgen Imaging

ISBN: 978-0-8261-0565-3
E-book ISBN: 978-0-8261-0566-0

11 12 13/ 5 4 3 2 1

CIP data is available from the Library of Congress

Special discounts on bulk quantities of our books are available to corporations,
professional associations, pharmaceutical companies, health care organizations,
and other qualifying groups.

If you are interested in a custom book, including chapters from more than one of
our titles, we can provide that service as well.

For details, please contact:
Special Sales Department, Springer Publishing Company, LLC
11 West 42nd Street, 15th Floor, New York, NY 10036-8002
Phone: 877-687-7476 or 212-431-4370; Fax: 212-941-7842
Email: sales@springerpub.com

Printed in the United States of America by Hamilton Printing

To the new generation of emotional intelligentsia:
Ella, Shai, Tal, Matthew, and Caspian

Contents

Preface

Not long ago, psychologists interested in the differences between individuals thought they had a good handle on how to describe individual differences systematically. Differences in aptitude for performing mental and physical tasks belonged to the domain of *abilities*. The most famous of these is general intelligence (*g* or IQ), along with a host of other, more narrowly defined abilities. Differences in people's typical experiences of the world, along with characteristic behavioral styles, were part of *personality*. Multiple personality traits, such as extraversion and neuroticism, were discriminated. Individual differences in *motivation,* such as needs for achievement or affiliation with others, were sometimes seen as a third domain. This overall scheme for describing individual differences had its roots in the late 19th century, and, over more than a century, spawned a huge enterprise of psychometric test development, along with numerous lines of research on just what it is that is measured by these tests.

Developments in research and popular culture upset this settled view in the 1990s when the new concept of *emotional intelligence* (EI) came along. Broadly, EI refers to abilities for understanding and managing emotions, which may be especially important for relating constructively to others. EI may be different from conventional intelligence in that, in the realm of the emotions, success depends not so much on rational analysis but on being in tune with the enigmatic wisdom of the heart. In fact, EI chimes with current interest in psychology in "implicit" processes, which exert powerful but unconscious influences on our behavior.

EI differs from personality in that it is more than a temperamental quality, such as preferring one's own company, or being prone to being upset by little things. EI refers to adaptive traits that will help the person navigate the treacherous cross-currents of the emotions, turning challenges into opportunities, or at least providing the wisdom to accept the reverses of life.

This upstart construct thus threatened the established order of individual differences. Could it really be that psychologists had missed one of the major features of human nature? If so, standard accounts of individual differences in ability, personality, and motivation were severely lacking.

EI also had profound applied implications. Existing knowledge of individual differences supports an extensive testing and assessment industry, pursuing in modern times mostly worthy goals such as identifying academic and work potential, as well as supporting diagnosis, guidance, and therapy for those who might possess some problematic personal attributes. EI was introduced as a "street-smart" rather than a "book-smart" ability that was essential for dealing with the real world. There was a suggestion that academic psychologists, locked in their ivory towers, had failed to recognize these critical personal qualities. Understanding EI would then lead to practical benefits in educational, organizational, and clinical psychology, which simply could not be accomplished by working with existing personality and ability measures.

In 1999, the International Society for the Study of Individual Differences held its conference in Vancouver, Canada. The three authors of the present volume engaged in a wide-ranging discussion of EI, with the aid of a few liquid refreshments. Although our research backgrounds were rather different, we found we were in agreement. EI held the promise of being a major new idea in psychology, with far-reaching theoretical and applied ramifications. But the strong claims being made for its importance were not substantiated by adequate evidence—and some of the more extreme claims found in popular writings on the subject were simply ludicrous. Our discussion led to the first comprehensive critique of EI, our book *Emotional Intelligence: Science and Myth*, published by MIT Press in 2002.

In *Emotional Intelligence: Science and Myth*, we came to several general conclusions. Even in the scientific literature, the available evidence often failed to support researchers' claims for EI. Tests of EI often showed rather modest associations with objective outcome criteria, such as educational and job success. We also identified issues for the measurement of EI, which turns out to be a more challenging quality to assess than conventional ability and personality. In consequence, the promise of EI for enhancing individual and societal well-being was some way from being fulfilled.

Since that time, the fast pace of research on EI has kept us busy writing further books, journal articles, book chapters, and the odd conference presentation or two (in such settings, often with liquid libations close at hand to stimulate our critical thinking). Some of our initial concerns have been allayed by new evidence supporting the validity of scales for EI; other concerns still remain. In *Emotional Intelligence 101*, we aim to introduce critical perspectives on EI. That is, we aim to give the reader both an introduction to contemporary research on EI, in its various guises, and also a sense of the conceptual and empirical tests that must be satisfied before EI can be accepted as a major new aspect of individual differences. In the world of EI research, little should be taken at face value. The critic must clarify the claims made for EI, and examine carefully the evidence supporting those claims.

In Chapter 1 (Introduction), we introduce the concept, balancing its potential with our critical stance. Progress requires a clear and coherent theory-based conceptualization of EI, reliable and valid assessment instruments, and translation of basic research into practical interventions. One of the issues we identify is that two rather different strands of research have emerged, one concerned with EI as a true ability, the other seeing EI as more akin to a personality trait. Chapter 2 (EI as a Personality Trait) examines the role of personality traits in emotional functioning and considers whether questionnaire assessments of EI offer anything more than standard personality measures do. Chapter 3 (EI as a New Form of Cognitive Ability) considers strategies for assessing EI as an ability, using objectively scored tests. There are significant obstacles to overcome—not least how to create test items that may be scored as objectively right or wrong—but we identify some signs of progress in this field.

The next set of chapters looks at evidence on the implications and consequences of EI. What benefits might the emotionally intelligent person have in real life? What are the dangers of being low in EI? Chapter 4 (EI in Everyday Life) looks at studies of various outcomes that may be influenced by EI—our personal relationships, our health and well-being, and our capacity to cope with the vicissitudes of life. We show that tests of EI can predict a range of outcome measures, but argue also that the reader should be cautious in assuming that major benefits result from high EI. In practical settings, it may be as important to change personal qualities as to measure them. Chapter 5 (Training EI in Applied Settings) surveys training programs directed toward improving social–emotional functioning in two key real-life settings—the classroom and the workplace. We review both successes and failures and consider the improvements that need to be made to research methods to obtain solid evidence on the effectiveness of training EI. In Chapter 6 (Emotional Disorders: Pathology of EI?), we ask whether low levels of EI may contribute to psychopathology. There are several types of disorders in which emotional functioning appears to be abnormal or dysfunctional, including the classical emotional disorders, externalizing disorders expressed in impulsive or antisocial behaviors, and disorders that corrode social functioning, including schizophrenia and autism. We also examine the extent to which research suggests that a focus on EI may be useful in psychotherapy.

Chapter 7 (Conclusions) summarizes what psychology has gained from 20 years or so of research into EI, and what questions remain to be answered. We argued in our 2002 book that the term "EI" is often used rather loosely, to refer to a heterogeneous set of personal qualities that might well be separated from one another. We return to this idea by setting out some distinct EI constructs that may require their own theories, tests, and fields of application. To bring coherence to the field, it may be important to distinguish temperamental qualities, information-processing routines, emotion-regulation strategies, and context-bound emotional knowledge and skills. There is now evidence that relates various tests of EI to adaptive outcomes defined by criteria for social relationship quality, well-being and mental health, and performance in real-life settings (though associations may be of modest size). EI does indeed add to existing personality and ability constructs, though just how much will continue to be debated. Understanding the associations between EI and outcome measures found in empirical research—and capitalizing on them in applied settings—requires some diversification of multiple EI constructs. We finish the chapter with some views on promising new directions for research, within this multipolar perspective.

Armed with all of these facts, we trust that you the reader will have discovered some new facts about this most engaging of research domains, allowing you to reach your own conclusions about the current state of the art. For some the message will doubtless prove sobering, for others it might suggest a possible career in research to further scientific understanding. Either way, we would have accomplished our goals in penning this little compendium.

Finally, it is important to show that we each possess some modicum of EI. This book would not have been possible without the goodwill and patience of our respective spouses—Diana, Eti, and Cristina—who had to endure our endless emails, nerdy conversations, and late-night writings. We also thank Dr. James Kaufman and Nancy Hale, respectively, Psych 101 Series editor and acquisitions editor at Springer. Their guidance, feedback, and encouragement have been essential to the writing of this book. We also acknowledge support from our respective institutions: the University of Cincinnati, the University of Haifa, and the Educational Testing Service.

Enjoy!

Emotional Intelligence
101

Introduction

Science must begin with myths, and with the criticism of myths.
Popper, 1963, p. 50

A mark of success for a new idea in psychology is "going viral" in popular culture. At the time of writing, one ex-British premier (Tony Blair) has just chastised another (Gordon Brown) for having "zero emotional intelligence." Recent stories on a popular technology site, cnet.com, attribute emotional intelligence (EI) to a humanoid robot that may provide company to autistic children[1] and a lack of EI to Google engineers.[2] EI is certainly an idea that has caught the popular imagination.

The first systematic work on EI was conducted by psychologists Jack Mayer and Peter Salovey, who defined the concept in terms of superior emotion perception, assimilation of emotion into thought, emotion understanding, and constructive management of emotion. They also developed several tests for assessment of an individual's EI level which have become widely used in research and applied settings, as further discussed in Chapter 3. However, following on from Mayer and Salovey's early work, the book that put EI on everyone's lips and ignited worldwide interest was Daniel Goleman's (1995) *Emotional Intelligence*. This book has been translated into myriad languages and has become the best-selling popular book on psychology ever published. As tends to happen (e.g., intelligence, personality, emotion, stress), popular use of a concept is often a debased version of the original. Goleman's intent was not to give politicians a new generic insult. Instead, he had a vision of a remedy for human relationships that are too often shackled by limited emotional competencies. Too often, we fail to understand our own emotions and those of others. We can also do better in managing emotions, for example, in helping others cope with their grief and anger and in controlling our own emotional impulses. In short, we can learn from individuals, including gifted healers, teachers, and transformational leaders, who possess exceptional emotional gifts.

A central part of Goleman's (1995) thesis was that psychology has been blind to the importance of emotional competencies associated with the EI concept for too long. Studies of intelligence have fixated on cognitive (or academic) intelligence (so-called IQ), while neglecting emotional aptitudes. The stereotypical college professor has high IQ but low EI, and so fails to function well in normal society. One of the authors (Gerald Matthews) used to attend lectures in the Cavendish Laboratory in Cambridge. It is named after one of the most renowned chemists of the 18th century, Henry Cavendish (see Figure 1.1). According to one edition of the Encyclopaedia Britannica,[3] he possessed a "morbid sensibility" that led him to shrink from society. Being especially timid of women, he used to communicate with his female servants only by notes (a communication device predating emails). Intellectual gifts are no guarantee of normal social and emotional interaction, although Cavendish seems to have been sufficiently worldly wise to become one of the richest men in England.

H. Cavendish

FIGURE 1.1 Portrait of Henry Cavendish. A noted British scientist, he is remembered especially for his discovery of "inflammable air" (what we today call hydrogen). While considered a great intellect, it appears from various biographical accounts that he was emotionally challenged.

Understanding of EI may be especially important for various fields, including clinical, educational, and industrial–organizational psychology (Goleman, 1995). Organizations need employees who accomplish their formal work tasks efficiently and also foster team spirit, communicate well with others, and form an emotional commitment to the organization. People who get into needless arguments at work, or who fail to engage with

3

other employees, are not fulfilling their true potential. EI often overlaps with social competencies and skills. It is often supposed that EI can be more easily learnt than cognitive abilities, so that companies may boost both employee well-being and profits by training personnel in the necessary social–emotional skills.

The trainability of EI points toward a need for schools to instruct children in emotional competence, as well as in the academic curriculum. Children should learn how to understand and control their emotions, as well as empathizing with others. The seductive nature of child-friendly technologies including the Wii, Facebook, and iPad suggests a cultural shift toward modes of recreation and social interaction that involve very little face-to-face contact with other persons. Children may be slow to acquire social and emotional skills such as reading the facial expressions and body language of another, adding a sense of urgency to the need for emotional learning. Indeed, some schools have been experimenting with what commentators call "social–emotional learning" programs.

A focus on EI—or, rather on emotional illiteracy—may be important for clinical psychology as well. There is a loose parallel with the supposed over-emphasis of psychologists on IQ. EI should be important for many psychotherapists and mental health counselors who direct a lot of their practice on helping clients developing emotional competence. Many contemporary psychological treatments (as opposed to drug treatments) are based on the assumption that emotional problems primarily reflect faulty thinking, but it may also be important to enhance emotional understanding and competence directly, without overt cognitive mediation (Greenberg, 2011).

Goleman's (1995) book was successful for several reasons. It strikes a chord with popular beliefs. It is commonplace to observe people being led astray by emotions, and most of us can admit that there are times when we could have handled our own emotions better. We can also readily perceive the corrosive social effects of dysfunctional emotions. Beyond the disciplines of applied psychology, it seems evident that emotions play a role in crime, drug and alcohol abuse, and other social ills. At a less elevated level, we may also recognize Goleman's rhetorical gifts, for example, in playing on popular stereotypes of the intellectually gifted as bumbling, disenfranchised nerds and appealing to the "self-help" motivation so prevalent in the United States.

We have seen the appeal of EI, but one thing that psychologists have learnt is to be wary of popular beliefs that are not substantiated by scientific evidence. Lilienfeld, Lynn, Ruscio, and Beyerstein (2009) have published a list of 50 popular myths that have been disproved by scientific investigation. In the EI context, one popular belief is that it is desirable to express or vent pent-up negative emotions. In fact, to paraphrase the title of one of the key empirical studies (Bushman, 2002), venting anger actually seems to "feed the flame" and encourage aggression. Letting it all out, in the style of Oprah or Dr. Phil, is not necessarily healthy. We argued in a previous book that many of the claims made about EI are mythical, in that they are not substantiated by evidence (Matthews, Zeidner, & Roberts, 2002).

In this book, our purpose is to outline what psychological science tells us about emotional competencies, and whether we can meaningfully talk about "EI." Thus, our next section briefly sets out what kind of evidence is important for science, and some of the pitfalls that may trip up researchers in the area.

TOWARD A SCIENCE OF EI

To study some personal quality, we need at least an inkling of what it is that we are studying. In psychology, defining terms is often harder than it seems, as words like "personality," "stress," "anxiety," and indeed "intelligence" are often vague and fuzzy in meaning. Intelligence is a case in point. There is a sense in which an amoeba engulfing a bacterium with a pseudopod is "intelligent" in that it is adapting successfully to its environment. Professor Cavendish's design of an apparatus for isolating hydrogen gas was also intelligent, but in the rather different sense of reflecting insight and logical analysis. Figure 1.2 highlights the apparent disconnects between these two meanings.

It is also the case that psychologists rarely hit on a precise definition without a good deal of argument. Indeed, the definition of intelligence is still debated (for accessible discussions of debates on the definition of intelligence see *Intelligence 101* and *IQ Testing 101* in Springer's Psych 101 series). However, we need at least an initial working definition of "EI" to begin the research process. Without such a definition, ten different researchers may wind up working on ten different qualities.

Definitions of EI are a good example of the difficulties that one can encounter. Goleman (1995) adopted a scattershot approach of listing a wide variety of desirable character features, including self-control, empathy, and hope. There are two immediate problems here. The first is that it is unclear that these different attributes actually reflect any common underlying quality. Presumably, a psychopath, lacking any empathy for

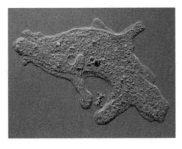

FIGURE 1.2 A symbol of human thought versus the amoeba's adaptive behavior. Are they in any way comparable?

fellow humans, could be hopeful for the success of his antiso-cial endeavors. Lumping together two quite different qualities under the heading of "emotional intelligence" simply leads to confusion. The second problem is that good character is not the same as intelligence. The "more intelligent" person is required to be objectively superior at some set of activities, compared to individuals of lesser intelligence. Many individuals of modest talents possess a range of desirable personal qualities, such as those listed by Goleman, but we do not need to call them "intel-ligent" to value their contributions. For example, the fictional Forrest Gump accomplishes financial and social success despite limited cognitive abilities. The capacity to experience positive feelings, such as hope, may support personal accomplishment on some occasions but hopes are not necessarily realistic. It does not seem that a kid who is 5'3, podgy, and uncoordinated is being emotionally intelligent in dreaming of basketball star-dom. Typically, psychologists address such definitional quan-daries through a focus on measurement. Rather than endlessly debating personal opinions about what is and what is not emo-tionally intelligent, we can try to develop a valid and reliable test of EI. This "operational" approach proved to be successful in intelligence research. It is unlikely that "IQ" really captures every facet of human intelligence (Sternberg, 2000). However, the success of standard intelligence tests in predicting real-life outcomes (e.g., work success) and measures of cognitive and brain processes shows that what the psychologist understands by "intelligence" is, at least, an important personal character-istic that should be studied. A test that measured at least some part of the individual's emotional competency with as strong validity as IQ tests would be equally important in psychology.

In fact, there are three necessary pillars of a science of EI (Matthews et al., 2002). As we have said, the first pillar is mea-surement, which means developing and then using standardized tests. Measurement requires at least a crude definition, but we expect that advances in measurement will sharpen definitions. At this point we need to introduce the idea of a *construct*, which is a key term from psychological measurement: "A construct is some postulated attribute of people, assumed to be reflected in test performance" (Cronbach & Meehl, 1955, p. 283). The point is that the construct is "postulated" or hypothetical—as opposed to a quality that we can directly observe, such as a person's height. As we shall see, there are many tests that purport to measure EI, but research is needed to show that whatever quality is measured by a test can be described as "EI."

Indeed, the second pillar is developing a theory of EI that explains the source of variation in test scores, and its consequences for behavior. Theory building and justification is perhaps the most essential characteristic of the scientific enterprise (Kerlinger, 1973). In short, what shapes a person's EI, and what difference does it make? This process is known as construct validation. It goes beyond simply showing that test scores predict the person's behavior in building an understanding of the nature of the psychological processes and structures that underpin our measurements of EI. For example, in conventional intelligence research we can investigate genetic and environmental influences on development of the brain areas that support reasoning and abstract thinking. We can also look at how the individual's level of intelligence influences their educational attainments, career success, and even health (e.g., Deary, 2000). Theory building in psychology is never finished. Successful research programs lead to the progressive theory refinement and modification, which in turn generates new directions for research.

With sound tests, and an understanding of what test scores actually mean, we can build a third pillar of our science, the application of research on EI to address real-life issues. It is plausible that wise men and women have been using their EI for good since the origins of the human species. The hope is that a scientific understanding of EI will allow a more systematic use of these competencies. Perhaps mediocre teachers, therapists, and managers may be trained in the skills that their emotionally gifted peers have developed spontaneously. A scientific approach is essential on several grounds—identifying key aptitudes, competencies and skills, creating procedures that will enhance them, and evaluating the outcomes of training programs that seek to enhance EI.

STRATEGIES FOR CONCEPTUALIZATION AND MEASUREMENT

We have suggested already that reliable and valid measurement is necessary for a science of EI. Measurement may be defined as a "rule for assigning numbers to objects in such a way as to represent quantities of attributes" (Nunnally, 1978, p. 3). In this case, the objects are people and the attribute is an EI level. To develop a valid EI test, we need a rule that describes how the response to a test item relates to EI. How to do this is not intuitively obvious. Our companion volume (*Anxiety 101*: Zeidner & Matthews, 2011) provides a more detailed account of issues in psychological measurement.

In practice, researchers have tried to use their best judgment in creating test items that may differentiate the emotionally intelligent individual from the person who is emotionally challenged. For example, we can set people "emotional puzzles" in which they must identify the best course of action for dealing with a difficult and emotive situation, such as calming a person experiencing a temper tantrum. This approach leads to an "ability-testing" philosophy of assessment. As with conventional ability tests, the idea is to find test items that are challenging, so that only the emotionally gifted can answer the majority correctly.

An alternative strategy, that owes more to personality than to intelligence research, is to rely on self-report items, making up a questionnaire. Rather than setting problems to be solved, the respondent describes their personal characteristics. If we have a working definition or conceptual EI model, we can ask questions directed toward each of the core components of EI.

Questions might probe qualities such as being aware of the emotions of self and others, having good control of one's own emotions, and being able to respond constructively when others becomes emotional.

In either case, we need a working conceptual model to guide item construction. As we have stated already, a laundry list of desirable personal qualities does not get us very far. Some of the definitions offered in the psychological literature are hardly better. For example, Bar-On (2000) states that "emotional and social intelligence is a multi-factorial array of interrelated emotional, personal, and social abilities that influence our overall ability to actively and effectively cope with daily demands and pressures" (p. 385). This is an over-inclusive definition which gives us little definite direction for test development. Next, we present three further definitions that may be more helpful.

Mayer-Salovey Model of EI. Jack Mayer and Peter Salovey (1990) published one of the landmark papers in research on EI, which represents a first attempt to set out a systematic model. They distinguished three types of adaptive ability: appraisal and expression of emotion, regulation of emotion, and utilization of emotions in solving problems. They also recognized subcategories within each of the three aspects of EI. For example, within "appraisal and expression" we might distinguish abilities related to self and others, and nonverbal and verbal abilities. A further paper (Mayer & Salovey, 1997) refined these categories somewhat, and added a fourth class of ability: understanding emotion. Figure 1.3 summarizes this influential "four-branch" model of EI. As we shall see shortly, it has provided the initial conceptual model both for questionnaires (e.g., Schutte et al., 1998) and for Mayer and Salovey's own work on developing ability tests for EI (Mayer, Salovey, & Caruso, 2000). It is further described in Chapter 3.

The Goleman Matrix. Although we have questioned the definitional clarity of Goleman's (1995) initial account, a later book (Goleman, 2001) provides a more coherent model of emotional abilities. Goleman divides emotional abilities

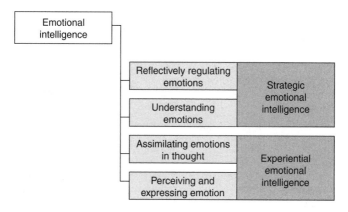

FIGURE 1.3 The four-branch hierarchical model of emotional intelligence (adapted from Mayer, Caruso, & Salovey, 2000, p. 269).

according to two dimensions, which may be presented as a 2 x 2 matrix, shown in modified form in Table 1.1. The first dimension is whether the ability refers to personal emotions or to dealing with the emotions of others. The distinction here echoes an earlier division between *intra*personal and *inter*personal abilities made by Gardner (1993). Gardner is famous for viewing intelligence as reflecting multiple, separate abilities, rather than a single factor of general intelligence or "IQ." The second dimension is whether the ability refers to identifying or acting on emotion (roughly, an input-output distinction). Knowing that oneself (or someone else) is unhappy is different from being able to do something about it. Each specific ability can then be slotted into one of the four cells shown in Table 1.1.

The Petrides-Furnham "Sampling Domain." Petrides and Furnham (e.g., Petrides, Furnham, & Mavroveli, 2007) examined early models of EI and related constructs, and tried to pick out the facets of EI that appeared in more than a single model, reasoning that these aspects of EI must be the most central ones. The list of facets they derived is shown in Table 1.2. Some of these facets, such as emotion perception and emotion regulation, are central to the Mayer-Salovey and Goleman

TABLE 1.1   A 2 × 2 MODEL OF EMOTIONAL COMPETENCIES,
WITH EXAMPLES OF EACH OF FOUR TYPES OF
COMPETENCY

	Self (Personal Competence)	Other (Social Competence)
Recognition	*Self-Awareness* • Emotional self-awareness • Accurate self-assessment • Self-confidence	*Social Awareness* • Empathy • Service orientation • Organizational awareness
Regulation	*Self-Management* • Self-control • Trustworthiness • Conscientiousness	*Relationship Management* • Communication • Conflict management • Teamwork and collaboration

models we have just illustrated. Other facets seem to cast the EI net wider, hooking in facets that seem indirectly rather than directly related to emotion, such as adaptability, assertiveness, and (low) impulsivity.

The contrast between models illustrates the difficulties of drawing clear boundaries around EI. Certainly, "adaptability" to changing circumstances is desirable. There are also occasions when adapting to change requires emotional competencies: managing fear of the unknown, for example. But, there is much more to adaptation than emotional response. Some people are more motivated than others to take up the challenges of change; we cannot say that someone who prefers a stable, quiet life is emotionally unintelligent. Managing change—for example, in taking up a new career—also requires cognitive skills that generalize across jobs. Again, we cannot simply assume that someone who has focused on specialized training for a specific career path, like a radiologist or anesthetist, is necessarily lacking in EI.

TABLE 1.2   **THE ADULT SAMPLING DOMAIN OF TRAIT EMOTIONAL INTELLIGENCE**

Facets	High scorers perceive themselves as...
Adaptability	...flexible and willing to adapt to new conditions.
Assertiveness	...forthright, frank, and willing to stand up for their rights.
Emotion perception (self and others)	...clear about their own and other people's feelings.
Emotion expression	...capable of communicating their feelings to others.
Emotion management (others)	...capable of influencing other people's feelings.
Emotion regulation	...capable of controlling their emotions.
Impulsiveness (low)	...reflective and less likely to give in to their urges.
Relationship skills	...capable of maintaining fulfilling personal relationships.
Self-esteem	...successful and self-confident.
Self-motivation	...driven and unlikely to give up in the face of adversity.
Social competence	...accomplished networkers with superior social skills.
Stress management	...capable of withstanding pressure and regulating stress.
Trait empathy	...capable of taking someone else's perspective.
Trait happiness	...cheerful and satisfied with their lives.
Trait optimism	...confident and likely to "look on the bright side" of life.

Challenges in Conceptualization and Measurement

We have seen the glimmerings of a path toward measurement of EI. First, we set out a working conceptualization of the various

13

qualities that contribute to being emotionally intelligent. Then, we use that model as a guide for either constructing problems for an ability test, or for self-report questions. Next, we consider what could go wrong.

There are some general criteria for test development that are standard in psychological measurement (also known as psychometrics), discussed at greater length by Zeidner and Matthews (2011). A test must be *reliable*, in the sense of being an accurate, consistent measuring instrument. We can calculate a statistic, Cronbach's alpha (i.e., α), that indicates, loosely, the extent to which the different test items are measuring a common, underlying quality. Because EI is supposed to be a stable, core quality of the person, we can also verify that tests have reasonably high test-retest reliability, that is, the extent to which the person's score remains similar across repeated measurement.

The scores from tests must also be *valid*, meaning that they do indeed assess the quality that they claim to. We need to be sure that a test for EI is truly measuring some set of emotional abilities, competencies, or skills, and not other, distinct qualities, such as being well-educated, or being motivated to please the researcher. One important form of validity is *criterion validity*, meaning that test scores correlate with some external criterion. Tests for EI might correlate with performance on an objective emotion perception task, for example. Testing criterion validity is part of the larger process of establishing construct validity, which allows correlations between the test and the criterion to be understood in terms of psychological theory.

Collecting data to evaluate reliability and validity is routine in developing psychological tests of all kinds. However, tests for EI pose some rather special problems that we will list next.

Is There Really Any Such Thing As EI? We cannot take it as a given that EI actually exists at all. From time to time, even knowledgeable individuals can come to believe in the existence of false realities, such as the lost continent of Atlantis, the canals of Mars, or that alien bodies are housed in Area 51. The human mind has a tendency to see meaning in random patterns, as in the well-known (but largely invalid) Rorschach inkblot test for psychopathology. Perhaps EI is illusory and no more than a product of the scientific imagination.

A red flag here is the number of rather different personal qualities that can be loosely described as "emotionally intelligent," such as an optimistic temperament, sensitivity to the feelings of others, and specific skills for handling social encounters (e.g., the skills of an interviewer). Perhaps these qualities all spring from a common source; equally, they may be unrelated. This is the kind of question that psychometrics is rather good at answering, for example, in relation to cognitive intelligence. It does take a long time and much data collection, though. The definitive work on the measurement of cognitive intelligence (Carroll, 1993) rests on over a century of work on intelligence testing. In the case of EI, researchers need to be able to examine the relationships between a plethora of different EI tests, using different measurement approaches. We have not yet reached the point where we can be sure whether there truly exists an overarching EI factor, akin to general intelligence, or whether human emotional functioning is supported by a multiplicity of unrelated qualities.

Another neglected issue is the role of *context*. Conventional intelligence is associated with abstract reasoning abilities that can be applied in a variety of different contexts or settings. If you are good at math, you can equally well work out the best bargains in a department store, which savings account offers the best return, or which project at work is most likely to pay off for the company. It is often assumed that EI is similar. If you are an emotional genius, you can equally well impress your parents with your wisdom, charm your fellow students into supporting you, and be a pillar of strength for your friends. This assumption may not be correct. We can certainly think of counterexamples, such as the caring doctor who beats his wife, or the politician that connects emotionally with voters but maintains a secret lover. Equally, having the perfect relationship with your

15

boyfriend or girlfriend may not guarantee emotional competence at college.

It is entirely possible that EI attaches to a specific setting such as the home, school, or work, without there being any general ability that is relevant to all contexts. Indeed, if we think of EI as being dependent on learnt skills, the possibility becomes likely, given that learning is context-specific. It follows that trying to test EI in an abstract way, separated from any real-life context, will not measure the emotional skills people use in everyday settings. A special case of context is culture. The emotional competencies that ease everyday social interaction may be very different in, say, the USA, Japan, and Azerbaijan. For example, as former President Bush's daughter Jenna discovered only too well, a jocular gesture of delight at her home school winning a football match in Texas did not win the Norwegians over (see Figure 1.4), but rather was interpreted as a sign of her endorsing devil worship.

FIGURE 1.4 Jenna Bush: Friend of Satan or Texas Longhorn fan?

Is EI Really an Intelligence? This seems like a ridiculous question (cf., Sullivan, 2007), but we can separate EI from conventional abilities. Petrides et al. (2007) see EI as a personality trait rather than a type of ability. That is, EI refers to styles of typical behavior rather than to some performance superiority (albeit, styles that tend to be adaptive). Petrides et al. (2007) use the term *trait EI* to refer to "emotion-related dispositions and self-perceptions measured by self-report" (p. 151). By contrast, Mayer and Salovey (e.g., Mayer et al., 2000) believe firmly in the ability model of EI. Like cognitive abilities, emotional abilities should be expressed in differences in performance in relevant tasks. Thus, while constructs such as "emotion perception" feature across the whole spectrum of EI research, there is a fundamental split between researchers in whether this construct refers to an objective ability or to a self-evaluation that may not be accurate. How the EI construct is conceptualized has far reaching implications for how EI is best measured, which, in turn, may impact on research findings and applications.

Is EI Distinct From Conventional Intelligence and Personality? One of the hazards of test development is reinventing the wheel. A test may check out to be reliable and valid—but then turn out to be measuring the same quality as some existing test. In this case, the new measure is redundant. We might just as well continue using the older test, which will have been more thoroughly researched. Tests for EI should be distinct from general intelligence; that is, finding the correct answers to the test questions should not just depend on abstract reasoning. However, we do not want EI to be too distinct from general intelligence! Contrary to the claims of multiple-intelligence theorists (Gardner, 1993), all mental abilities tend to correlate positively, at least to a moderate degree (Carroll, 1993). If EI is a true intelligence, it should show some relationship to cognitive abilities, without correlating too much.

The other issue is overlap between EI and personality. Contemporary personality theorists largely agree on the existence of five or more basic aspects or dimensions. The most popular model—the Five Factor Model (FFM: Costa & McCrae, 2008)—describes the "Big Five" dimensions of Openness, Conscientiousness, Extraversion, Agreeableness, and Neuroticism (conveniently recalled as OCEAN). Because we refer to these Big Five factors often in the book, we provide a brief capsule description of them in Table 1.3. We return to the FFM in Chapter 2.

TABLE 1.3 CAPSULE DESCRIPTIONS OF THE PERSONALITY FACTORS OF THE FIVE FACTOR MODEL, AND SAMPLE QUESTIONS DEFINING EACH CONSTRUCT

Personality Factor	Brief Description	Sample Questions
Openness (O)	Tendency to have intellectual and artistic interests, curiosity, unconventional values, and, in some accounts, emotional sensitivity. Low O tends to be conventional and down-to-earth.	Do you have a vivid imagination? Do you enjoy hearing new ideas? Do you like art?
Conscientiousness (C)	Reflects the individual's achievement striving, orderliness, organization, responsibility, and related behaviors. Low C tends to lack self-discipline, order, and strives less to achieve.	Do you work hard? Do you demand quality? Do you turn plans into actions?
Agreeableness (A)	Tendency to be cooperative, friendly, sympathetic, compassionate, and generous toward others. Low A tends to be distrustful, aloof, and less compliant.	Do you respect other people? Do you sympathize with others' feelings? Do you accept people as they are?

(Continued)

TABLE 1.3 **CAPSULE DESCRIPTIONS OF THE PERSONALITY FACTORS OF THE FIVE FACTOR MODEL, AND SAMPLE QUESTIONS DEFINING EACH CONSTRUCT (CONTINUED)**

Extraversion (E) vs. introversion	Tendency to be outgoing, social, talkative, assertive, and gregarious. Low E (introversion) tends to be characterized by less activity, quietness, and solitude.	Are you skilled in handling social situations? Are you the life of the party? Do you talk a lot?
Neuroticism (N) vs. emotional stability	Personality factor characterized by a chronic level of emotional instability, anxiety, proneness to psychological stress, and difficulty in coping with life's challenges. Low N persons (emotionally stable) tend to be unemotional, calm, resilient, and comfortable with themselves.	Do you panic easily? Do you have frequent mood swings? Do you worry about things?

Some of these dimensions seem like they could overlap with emotionally intelligent qualities (McCrae, 2000). For example, conscientiousness individuals may have more self-control, and agreeable persons may be more empathic toward others. We need to show that tests for EI are not simply picking up these well-known personality traits. The trait EI perspective (Petrides et al., 2007) described above can get confusing here, as it assumes that EI is part of personality. In this case, we would expect some correlation between questionnaires for EI and the FFM—but, again, the correlations should not be too large.

How Do We Decide What Behaviors Are EI? It is easier to describe a person's emotionally intelligent features than to state how they are expressed in measurable behaviors. Most people would agree that having good control over one's emotions is emotionally intelligent, but how can we determine a person's degree of control? There are experimental paradigms for measuring suppression of emotion (e.g., remaining calm following an unpleasant event), but emotional suppression is not always beneficial (Gross, 2002). Conversely, we could try to measure emotional expressivity, but sometimes excessive emotional expression is harmful. Clinical psychologists, for example, recognize histrionic personality disorder, whose symptoms include exaggerated, dramatic displays of emotion. In the case of emotional control, we can broadly assume that EI relates more to expression of an emotion that is appropriate to the person's circumstances. However, who is to decide what is "appropriate"? In addition, the variation of what is appropriate with "circumstances" makes it difficult to devise standard test items.

The problem is especially acute for the ability model of EI advocated by Mayer et al. (2000). If we want to measure EI with right-or-wrong questions, we need some means of deciding what is a "right" answer, which may not be at all clear. One of the tests for emotion perception developed by Mayer et al. requires the respondent to rate the emotions expressed in pictures and graphic designs. There hangs in the Louvre a painting by Géricault titled in English *The Raft of the Medusa* (see Figure 1.5). The overall mood of the painting is somber—some of the occupants of the raft have already expired—but hope remains. Those figures that still live also exude a certain tragic poise. In short, as with almost any worthwhile work of art, the force of the painting resides in its emotional complexities and ambiguities. (There is a reason the Mona Lisa does not have a cheesy grin.) As such, art appreciation does not lend itself to a multiple-choice EI test.

Similar difficulties attach to questions directed toward other abilities. How you should best deal with an angry

FIGURE 1.5 Théodore Géricault's "The Raft of the Medusa."

person, for example, might well depend on a host of factors such as the righteousness of their anger, how well you know them, whether they pose a physical danger, and whether you have any skills in anger management. Cultural factors may also be at play here. For example, trying to appease a colleague by inviting her out for an alcoholic drink may be perfectly acceptable in Australia but could get you into serious trouble in Saudi Arabia, where consumption of alcoholic beverages is against the law. In any case, none of the EI performance measures to date can be scored against truly veridical criteria (true-false or correct-incorrect), a real shortcoming if EI is to be considered a fully fledged ability.

Can We Believe Self-Reports? We cannot assume that people have perfect insight into their own emotional functioning. Regrettably, we cannot assume that they are honest either. Research on personality questionnaires (e.g., Paulhus, 2002) shows that people often unconsciously play up their character strengths, and minimize weaknesses. Especially in high-stakes situations, such as applying for a job, people may also

21

deliberately lie about their characteristics. There is little doubt that the characteristics listed in Tables 1.1 and 1.2, for example, are socially desirable, and so we cannot take self-reports at face value without corroborating evidence.

There is a further issue that self-awareness is at the heart of EI. All definitions—in line with the ancient injunction to "know thyself"—see insight into one's owns emotional functioning as a core attribute of the construct. However, answering questions accurately on a questionnaire for EI requires a similar level of self-knowledge. Thus, we have the "EI paradox" (Zeidner, Roberts, & Matthews, 2009), that the nature of self-assessments for EI precludes their being valid in those low in EI. Dunning, Heath, and Suls (2004) concluded from studies in the workplace that incompetent employees may be blissfully unaware of their personal failings. If you really are low in EI, how can you meaningfully respond to the questionnaire items? We will return to such issues in more depth in Chapter 2, when we examine questionnaire assessments of EI in greater detail.

Should We Focus on Measurement, Anyway? We have argued in several articles (e.g., Matthews, Zeidner, & Roberts, 2004) that measurement is essential for progress in on the field of EI. However, Oatley (2004) has presented a contrarian view, arguing that a fixation on measurement may lead us to neglect those aspects of EI that are difficult to test. Oatley also suggested some novel approaches to research, such as making more use of "experience-sampling" methods that require people to use a personal data assistant to report on their emotional experiences in everyday life. He also suggests that greater emphasis be placed on studying "experts" presumed to have high EI, especially in the fields of arts and literature. This perspective meshes with what is known as the *idiographic* approach in personality research, studying the individual human life in depth, as opposed to trying to find general principles applying to groups rather than individuals (*nomothetic* approach).

We have some sympathy with Oatley's (2004) critique of the psychometric approach. A theme we will develop is that what is emotionally intelligent depends on the context—and laboratory studies may not adequately capture the social and emotional contexts of real life. At the same time, we see limited prospects for a scientific account of EI arising from idiographic methods, which requires a systematic comparison of both test scores and emotional functioning across individuals (Zeidner, Roberts, & Matthews, 2004). We may also note that artists may possess a rather special type of EI. Whatever their gifts in understanding and communicating emotion, artists and writers tend to show elevated levels of abnormal personality traits (Batey & Furnham, 2006).

Strategies for Theory Building

We have spent some time talking about the measurement of EI and the obstacles that occur because of its fundamental importance. We will take rather less space to discuss theoretical issues, because there is a lack of theory-driven research on EI. The imbalance in research effort in part reflects the recency of EI as a topic area, and, naturally enough, researchers have been more preoccupied with how to assess this new construct than with finer points of theory. However, psychological testing is of limited use in the absence of a theoretical understanding of what the test scores actually mean. Here, we will briefly set out some of the directions for future theories of EI.

We need first to get a rough sense of what a theory of EI would look like. We need to be clear that descriptive schemes of the types set out in Tables 1.1 and 1.2 are *not* theories. A theory sets out to explain or account for observed phenomena, frequently by specifying cause-and-effect relationships, for example, how an abnormality of the neurons within a brain system for emotion produces unusual behaviors in an emotional situation. Lists of qualities or functions are theoretically ambiguous—that is, there are a variety of ways in which we could explain individual differences in emotional functioning. For example, what makes a person good at "emotion perception"?

There are various possible answers from theory (see Figure 1.6). There are brain circuits that are attuned to expressions of facial emotion, for example, in the amygdala. Perhaps, in some individuals, these circuits are especially finely attuned to facial stimuli. Encoding any kind of stimulus requires attention. An alternative hypothesis is that there are some persons who are especially good at attending to emotional stimuli, while ignoring other irrelevant ones. Reading the emotions of another is also easier if we know something about the person and their circumstances. Perhaps excellence in emotion perception resides in using background knowledge to make sense of clues to emotion, or in reasoning what the person is probably feeling given their recent experiences.

The general point is that simply listing "emotion perception" as a facet of EI does not tell us anything about the differences in processing emotional stimuli that determine the

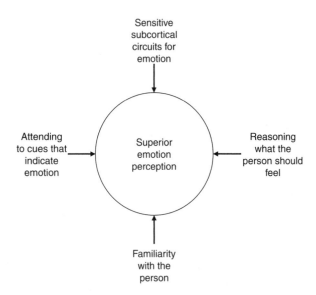

FIGURE 1.6 Multiple influences on emotion perception ability, in a real-life context.

individual's competency in this function. To understand emotion perception requires a theory of what drives the differences between individuals, and experiments to test predictions from the theory.

Thus far, we have referred to theories of how EI influences behavior and experience. Here, we are concerned with the short-term impact of EI in specific situations. Psychological experiments are typically concerned with just such short-term processes. For example, we could expose participants to a stressful situation, such as having to make a potentially embarrassing speech, and investigate how individuals high and low in EI respond. We also need to be concerned with theory of the longer-term development of EI. What are the factors that exert a causal influence on the aptitudes, competencies, and skills that make up EI (depending on our definition)? A study of EI over the lifespan would also tell us more about its role in the person's interactions with social environments. We could ask, for example, whether people high in EI make better choices of friends and life partners, whether they make good decisions for their children, and whether they are better at negotiating conflicts between work and domestic life. Over time, these life choices may feed back to influence EI. A teenager who chooses to join a gang, for example, may not be doing much to enhance his or her emotional functioning, for example.

Figure 1.7 shows a conceptual scheme for thinking about key constructs in development of EI during childhood and beyond (see Zeidner, Matthews, Roberts, & MacCann, 2003). We start with antecedents, such as genes for brain development, and the child's social environment, which influence EI over periods of months and years. These influences shape basic neural, emotional, and cognitive processes, beginning in infancy. For example, even young children show an emotional "temperament;" some are distress-prone while others have a more sunny disposition. In turn, these processing capabilities support learning of various kinds, often within a specific context. Learning includes conscious, explicit skills such as being

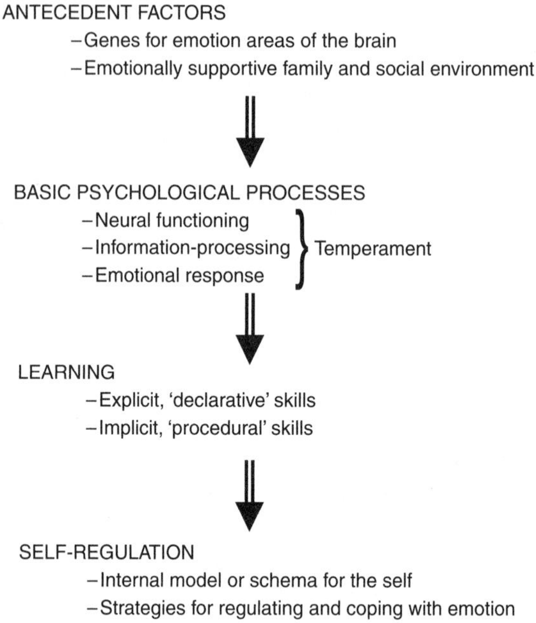

ANTECEDENT FACTORS
    −Genes for emotion areas of the brain
    −Emotionally supportive family and social environment

BASIC PSYCHOLOGICAL PROCESSES
    −Neural functioning
    −Information-processing } Temperament
    −Emotional response

LEARNING
    −Explicit, 'declarative' skills
    −Implicit, 'procedural' skills

SELF-REGULATION
    −Internal model or schema for the self
    −Strategies for regulating and coping with emotion

FIGURE 1.7 Some building blocks for a theory of EI (feedback loops omitted).

able to explain why another child is unhappy, and unconscious, implicit skills such as producing the nonverbal behavior that would tend to calm a friend who is upset. Explicit skills are sometimes referred to as "declarative" (i.e., verbally mediated), whereas implicit skills are "procedural" in that they depend on somewhat automatic information-processing procedures. During the school years, the child increasingly develops self-awareness (Sarni, 2000). Understanding of oneself, especially in relation to others, supports a capacity for self-regulation, and, ideally, of using self-knowledge to acquire effective strategies for handling emotion in self and others. EI is likely to develop over an extended period of time, shaped by a variety of emotional, cognitive, and social processes. Next, we will briefly outline in more detail some possible directions for theory.

Basic Processes in EI. A leading paradigm for psychology is provided by cognitive neuroscience. It is assumed that the person is an information-processor who encodes stimuli, builds some internal representation of the world in memory, and selects responses on the basis of that mental model. Studies of brain-damaged individuals, and advanced psychophysiological techniques such as imaging brain activity (e.g., with fMRI) allow researchers to localize processing functions such as perception, memory, and decision-making to specific brain areas. This approach also identifies specific brain areas that may support emotion, such as circuits connecting the amygdala to the cerebral cortex (LeDoux, 1996). There is also increasing interest in "social neuroscience" (Cacioppo, 2006), that is, in understanding the brain systems that control response to social stimuli.

Within this general paradigm, we can look for specific processes (i.e., specific brain areas) that contribute to EI. As we have already stated, we could imagine that individual differences in the functioning of the amygdala might contribute to the emotion perception ability. Another place to look is within the frontal lobe of the cortex. Clinical patients with damage to this area often show poor social decision making and emotional instability (recent work implicates a circuit including the amygdala and the ventromedial prefrontal cortex: Tranel & Bechara, 2009). Perhaps normal variation in the functioning of these brain areas feeds into observed EI.

We can also explore cognitive functioning without explicit reference to brain areas. The methods of cognitive psychology allow us to investigate how people differ in perception and attention to emotional stimuli, in recall of emotional memories, and in making decisions under stress. For example, Austin (2005) used an "inspection time paradigm" that required people to discriminate very-briefly presented facial emotion stimuli. Fellner et al. (2007) investigated the speed and accuracy with which people could locate a "target emotion" (e.g., an angry face) within an array of emotional faces. Ironically, neither study showed strong relationships between measures of trait EI and performance.

As well as looking at specific processes, we can treat temperament as a basic personal quality. It seems that children with certain temperamental qualities are prone to experiencing outcomes as adults that suggest a lack of EI later in life. A remarkable longitudinal study in New Zealand, the Dunedin Study (e.g., Koenen, Moffitt, Poulton, Martin, & Caspi, 2007), showed that temperament measured at age 3 predicted adult social and emotional problems. Poorly controlled toddlers were somewhat more likely to exhibit behavioral problems and even antisocial and criminal behavior in adolescence and adulthood. Inhibited children were prone to later emotional problems. An issue here is whether we really want to think of a basic temperament, perhaps associated with some biologically based sensitivity to rewarding or punishing stimuli (Corr, 2009), as being an "intelligence."

EI and Skill Acquisition. There is little doubt that at least some social–emotional skills may be learnt or even explicitly trained (see Chapter 6). Successful programs for skills such as assertiveness, anger management, and social problem-solving (Durlak & Weissberg, 2005) attest to the potential role of learning in EI. We might suspect that there is some relationship between basic aptitudes and skill acquisition; perhaps some people acquire social–emotional skills more readily than others. There is an analogous distinction in conventional intelligence theory between fluid intelligence—aptitude for abstract reasoning—and crystallized intelligence—specific intellectual skills fostered by education and being immersed in one's culture (Horn & Hofer, 1992).

To the extent that we think of EI as being "crystallized," it is worth considering what skill sets are critical. Many of the skills that come to mind are social in nature: understanding the emotions of others, displaying and communicating emotions effectively, and being able to manage the emotions of others for the benefit of self or others. We might also consider the more Machiavellian skills of using emotional displays to manipulate others. Such skills may be either explicit—having a good plan for negotiating in a business meeting—whereas others are implicit, such as displaying appropriate nonverbal behaviors. Often, these skills will be contextualized, such as those used in business, or the skills that a clinician might use to calm an anxious client prior to therapy.

One of the issues here is whether there is any real distinction between emotional and social intelligences. We have no simple answer, but we can envisage some skills that are more intra- than interpersonal. One of the branches of the Mayer et al. (2000) model is emotion understanding, in the somewhat academic sense of having knowledge about the sources of emotion, for example. A university course on emotion should train these skills. There may also be intrapersonal skills for mood-regulation—such as counting to ten in a crisis—but these are better considered under the heading of self-regulation.

El and Self-Regulation. There is a growing area of research on emotion-regulation (e.g., Gross, 2002) that is concerned with the strategies that people use to manage their own emotional state. It overlaps with the older and wider field of stress research and its focus on coping strategies (Zeidner & Saklofske, 1996). Yet another approach to the theory of EI is to suppose that the construct relates to more effective strategies for emotion-regulation and coping, as we discuss further in Chapter 4.

Necessarily, emotion-regulation requires at least two component abilities. First, the person must be able to identify and understand their own emotional state. Second, the person must be able to use that understanding to change their emotions in some constructive direction. Understanding why you feel anxious is a prerequisite to being able to calm yourself down. The process is also cyclical, in that the person needs to re-evaluate their emotional state following the effort at mood-regulation.

Because these processes involve little overt behavior, they are hard to study, but existing research provides some clues. Salovey et al. (1995) developed a questionnaire for assessment of mood-regulation called the Trait Meta-Mood Scale (TMMS). It includes two dimensions related to the "input" part of the cycle (Clarity and Attention), as well as an "output" dimension of Mood Repair. As always, some caution in interpreting self-reports is requisite, but validation evidence for the TMMS is encouraging. Broadly, it seems that individuals reporting insightful awareness of their emotions, and the ability to repair a bad mood are better able to regulate emotion and cope with stress constructively (John & Gross, 2007).

We can also get some insights into self-regulative skills from clinical studies that identify maladaptive styles of self-regulation (Wells & Matthews, 1994). For example, excessive brooding and rumination on emotional problems is implicated in anxiety and depressive disorders (e.g., Nolen-Hoeksema, Wisco, & Lyubomirsky, 2008). Wells (2000) has shown that meta-worry—worrying about one's own worries—and various other metacognitions of one's emotional state are also implicated in emotional disorders. Thus, one key skill seems to be "letting go" of one's concerns, at least temporarily, perhaps to focus on more action-oriented coping strategies.

Challenges for Theory. We will not discuss challenges to theory at length, because of the rudimentary nature of much of the theory concerned. As the reader may have noted, much of what we have set out under "theory" consists of findings from disparate areas of psychology that look like they could be incorporated into some more general theory of EI. We will briefly set out some general issues.

First, detailed theorizing is somewhat premature until we have better measurement models that tell us what it is we are trying to explain, although, equally, theory should refine measurement. Second, as with intelligence and personality, we will most likely need some multi-leveled theory. If EI is expressed in physical, neural processes, in learnt skills and in high-level self-regulation, it will be challenging to find some common theoretical framework that incorporates all of these multifarious processes.

Third, as with measurement, part of the challenge is to identify what is *unique* about EI, compared with other constructs. As we have already alluded, we can construct theories of clinical anxiety, for example, that identify abnormalities in information-processing and self-regulation that contribute to pathology (Wells & Matthews, 2005; Zeidner & Matthews, 2011). However, it is not clear how linking these abnormalities to EI advances understanding; theories of anxiety were doing just fine before EI came along. Similarly, it is unclear whether it is useful to separate theories of emotion-regulation from theories of stress and coping.

Fourth—and perhaps most profoundly—we need to establish that the attributes of EI are actually adaptive, that is, they help people to thrive and avoid harm in real life. This is not a given. We cannot assume that a person who is, for example, especially quick to identify emotions in photos of faces in the lab has any real advantage in living. Research on stress (Zeidner & Saklofske, 1996) offers a cautionary message. One of the questions here is which coping strategies are most successful, but, even after extensive research, it is hard to provide a clear answer. How well a strategy works depends on the source of stress, and how well the individual can implement the strategy.

Furthermore, significant life events usually have a range of outcomes so that it may be difficult to determine whether one set of outcomes is "better" than others. For example, employing Machiavellian strategies at work may provide short-term benefits but long-term harm (once coworkers figure out what you are doing). Other attributes of EI may also have a rather two-edged nature. Empathy may bring you closer to others but also impose the burden of their suffering on you. As the clinical literature shows (Wells, 2000), too much attention to one's own emotional states encourages rumination and keeps one's problems at the forefront of awareness. Thus, it is important not only to identify specific processes that are related to EI, but also to explore what the implications of those processes are for real-life well-being.

APPLICATIONS

A large part of the appeal of EI comes from its potential to contribute to solutions to personal and societal problems. The assumption here (e.g., Goleman, 1995) is that, individually and collectively, modern Western culture has tended to denigrate emotions in favor of high-brow intellectualism. We have cut ourselves off from emotionally fulfilling goals—typically, social in nature—and laid ourselves open to a host of emotional problems. Indeed, psychologists from a variety of research areas have voiced somewhat similar concerns. Twenge and Campbell (2009) argue that excessive narcissism (inflated self-image) has corroded communal ties and increased people's vulnerability to anxiety and other emotional disorders. Halpern (2006) has drawn attention to the increasing pressures on social well-being that result from escalating conflicts between work and family.

So, even though some popular accounts may be overblown, it is reasonable to look at what psychologists can do to address social issues by improving emotional functioning. The issue is whether understanding and even changing EI in real-life situations is the most productive strategy. We return to this issue in later chapters. For now, we will briefly highlight some of the potential challenges for application in the fields of occupational, clinical, and educational psychology.

Occupational Psychology

Views of work psychology often seem shaped by a 1930s-style production line mentality. Workers have a sharply defined job description, made up of a number of specific tasks. The main task for occupational psychologists is to align worker skills with task requirements. This can be done either by selecting and training workers so that all have the requisite skills and desired interests, or by designing tasks so that existing workers can do them proficiently and with sufficient motivation.

More recently, this mechanistic perspective on work has been challenged by an increased awareness of the importance of emotions (e.g., Pekrun & Frese, 1992). Most obviously, much may be at stake in the workplace, including financial security, and personal ambition and self-esteem. Not surprisingly, events such as promotions and job termination—or the anticipation thereof—may inspire strong emotions. How the employee handles situations, such as maintaining emotional engagement with work although layoffs are threatened, especially during times such as the current recession, may be important for both individual and organization.

The workplace is also an arena for the fulfillment of social motivations. Two of the basic social motivations (Wiggins, 2003) are (1) affiliation and communion with others and (2) dominance or agency. People often socialize with workmates, who may indeed provide social support. The workplace also has its competitive side as people strive for personal advantage. If we assume that fulfilling social motivations is critical for well-being (Oatley & Bolton, 1985), then the social successes and failures of the workplace assume an important role in life in general: job satisfaction overlaps with life satisfaction.

It is also the case that work activities themselves may place emotional demands on the person. There is increasing interest among industrial/organizational (I/O) psychologists in what is called "contextual performance" (Motowidlo, Borman, & Schmit, 1997), that is, activities that may not be part of a formal job description but are nonetheless critical for the success of the organization. These include providing informal support for other employees, communicating effectively with others, and generally being a good organizational citizen and teamplayer who is prepared to "go the extra mile." Again, social–emotional skills may be required.

The concept of *emotional labor* (e.g., Wharton, 2009) expresses the idea that expressing emotion may also be a quasi-formal job requirement. Persons working in service industries may be expected to be friendly and helpful to customers (whatever their true feelings). Occasionally, emotional labor becomes over-demanding. A JetBlue flight attendant named Steven Slater achieved a moment of fame in August 2010 by ditching the pretence of being nice to a particularly obnoxious passenger, and exiting the plane by the escape slide brandishing two bottles of beer. In fact, evidence shows that where emotional displays have to be consistently faked (known as surface-acting), psychological problems such as burnout and depression may ensue (Wharton, 2009).

Employees may also bring outside emotional issues to the workplace, called "spillover." It is not unknown for employees to engage in violence, theft, and substance abuse at work. In February, 2010, Amy Bishop, a professor of biology at the University of Alabama in Huntsville was denied tenure, a potentially career-ending event for an academic. She responded by bringing a handgun to a faculty meeting, killing three when she opened fire. It was revealed that she had a history of involvement in violent incidents ranging from the allegedly accidental shooting of her brother, to fighting inside an International House of Pancakes.[4] In cases such as this, abnormal personality contributes to dysfunctional emotional response.

Given the emotional dramas of the workplace, a case for the role of EI can readily be made. The emotionally intelligent employee finds both work and relationships with other personnel rewarding and fulfilling. She copes effectively with emotionally demanding work demands, and deals constructively with anxiety, disappointment, and anger in other areas of life. Indeed, she may offer support to other troubled employees. Two immediate courses of action are then available to organizations. They may seek to hire strong emotional paragons who will bring a range of benefits to the organization. They may also seek to train existing employees so that they are more likely to support each other and the organization, and less likely to go on a rampage with deadly weapons.

We will look at efforts of these kinds in more depth in Chapter 6. For now, we will briefly mention some of the challenges that arise. First, the benefits of a focus on EI are predicated on EI actually existing. If, as we have suggested may be the case, "EI" actually refers to a variety of different basic aptitudes and learned skills, then training specific skills may work better than trying to raise EI in some general sense. Second, we need valid tests of EI for any kind of practical application. An organization cannot select the most emotionally intelligent applicants for a job unless it can measure their EI accurately. Similarly, a test of EI is needed in order to evaluate whether or not training programs are successful in elevating EI. Third, it is imperative that organizational applications are supported by evidence. For example, use of an EI test to select job applicants is justified only if research has shown that test scores actually predict job performance (or other desirable workplace behaviors, such as absence of counterproductive workplace behaviors).

A final point here is to note the potential vulnerability of occupational psychologists to business fads. As Murphy and Sideman (2006) point out, the field of management is particularly susceptible to apparent panaceas that prove to be worthless, ranging from hand-writing analysis (which is still practiced in many businesses in France) to Total Quality Management. Self-help books that purport to provide simple paths to business success with plenty of "practical tips" and success stories have helped to feed interest in EI (Furnham, 2006). Before boom turns to bust, fortunes are made—not by managers, but by the purveyors of the books. As we shall see in Chapter 5, careful research is necessary to separate the real findings on EI from hype and even hucksterism.

Clinical Psychology

Our readers will need little persuading that emotions are important in treating mental disorders. Excessive negative emotion is a defining feature of anxiety and mood disorders, including depression. Negative emotions are also implicated in a variety of other disorders. For example, somatoform disorders (e.g., medically unexplained aches and pains) have been attributed to emotional stress. Eating disorders such as anorexia are often accompanied by depression, and may reflect anxieties concerning body image. Other disorders may tie in with facets of EI that go beyond simple vulnerability to negative emotion. One such facet is self-control, expressed in effective emotion-regulation and the avoidance of reckless, impulsive actions. Clinicians recognize several impulse control disorders including kleptomania (compulsive stealing), pyromania (firesetting), and the tongue-twister, trichotillomania (the compulsive urge to pull out one's own hair). Individuals with conduct disorders that lead them to commit violent acts also have issues with impulse control. Other disorders appear to overlap with the social disconnection that may also be a feature of low EI. A case in point is autism. In high-functioning autistic individuals, who may be diagnosed with Asperger syndrome, cognitive intelligence is normal, but the person has great difficulty in understanding and interacting with others. Henry Cavendish, whom we mentioned earlier, may have been autistic.

Loosely, then, we could say that a variety of individuals with mental disorders lack EI. The issue is how the new ideas about emotional functioning that EI represents may help the psychiatrist or clinical psychologist. Given that clinical psychology is currently dominated by psychobiological models of neural abnormality, and by cognitive-psychological models, perhaps we can again question whether emotions have been neglected. Conventional cognitive behavior therapy (CBT; Clark & Beck, 2010) sees emotions as a by-product of faulty thinking or information-processing. For example, depression is attributed to errors in thinking about the self such as supposing that one is worthless and that there is no hope for the future. The therapist's task is to look beyond emotions to identify the underlying cognitive mechanisms. By contrast, Greenberg (2006) has called for therapeutic approaches that are directly focused on emotions. The therapist should help the client experience distressing emotional experiences, and coach them toward positive transformations of emotion.

The case for EI might also refer to the role of emotion-regulation in certain mental disorders. Some patients appear to regulate their feelings of anxiety or distress in ways that are counterproductive, such as fruitless, repetitive rumination (Wells, 2000). Another example is provided by a condition called "alexithymia." This is not a mental disorder, but a trait that is quite common in range of disorders including autism, anorexia nervosa, and depression. Alexithymics have a range of emotional difficulties, including identifying and verbalizing their own feelings (Parker, 2000). Loosely, a common theme here seems to be difficulties in getting cognition and emotion "to talk to each other," corresponding to assimilating emotions into thought in the Mayer et al. (2000) model. The cognitive restructuring of emotions appears to be therapeutically beneficial. Intriguing studies conducted by Pennebaker (1997) showed that simply writing about a stressful event improves well-being. Psychotherapy for PTSD may also involve integrating memories of the event with normal cognitive and emotional processes (Foa, Keane, Friedman, & Cohen, 2008).

The first challenge here is to show that EI does offer something new. The ideas about emotion-regulation just discussed predate interest in EI, and so "emotion-focused" clinicians need to show that EI is more than just a relabeling of existing concepts. In addition, the various disorders we have described are highly diverse, and are typically seen as having different etiologies and outcomes. Attributing all of them to low EI may be too coarse-grained an approach. Again, the research needed to address such issues requires valid tests for EI, and demonstration that individuals with disrupted emotional functioning score lower on these tests than "normal" controls. There is a need also to document the underlying processes involved. At the same time, we should remain open to the possibility that work on EI may open up new therapeutic interventions, and we will return to these issues in Chapter 6.

Educational Psychology

In looking at the relevance of EI to education, we can pick up on previous themes. As in the workplace, a primary concern is the improvement of students' cognitive performance (in this case, learning) and grades. Given the large number of students who drop out of school all along the educational pipeline (estimates are as high as 60% in the United States), EI might also play a role in retention. The child's emotional issues may affect their attention and effort in the classroom, suggesting that better management of negative emotions may boost learning. In addition, school work is not necessarily intrinsically interesting, and students who are able to maintain positive attitudes will do better. Educators have increasingly moved on from the Victorian model of children as empty vessels into which the teacher pours knowledge. The child's active engagement with the learning process is critical. To this end, emotional skills such as self-motivation, self-control, and effective self-regulation become critical (Zins et al., 2007).

As in clinical psychology, educators are also concerned with abnormality in emotional functioning. According to Nastasi, Moore, and Varjas (2004), around a fifth of America's children and adolescents have diagnosable disorders that require some form of mental health treatment. Often, these disorders involve emotional dysfunction. Teachers may face two kinds of troubled students (Zeidner & Matthews, 2011). Children with "internalizing" disorders experience excessive negative emotion, similar to adult anxiety and depression. These conditions affect the child's ability to stay focused on learning in the classroom, and to use working memory in problem solving. By contrast, those with "externalizing" disorders are more likely to be immediately troublesome. Children with poor impulse control and aggressive tendencies are those that are most disruptive in the classroom, and most likely to fight with others.

Beyond improving grades and securing therapy where needed, educational and school psychologists also have wider concerns with the child's personal development. Children learn much more than academic content from school, perhaps most importantly social–emotional skills for getting along with other children and adults. Typically, such learning occurs informally in classroom and playground encounters. However, the education system may serve children better if the curriculum includes some more systematic training in such skills. In Chapter 5 we will look at programs that seek to enhance interpersonal skills, such as conflict resolution and self-regulative skills, such as resisting peer pressure to take drugs. The concern with the child's personal development as a fully rounded human being chimes with the growing "positive psychology" movement, which seeks to support personal growth and self-fulfillment.

The value of a science of EI now becomes clear. In principle, training programs that elevate the child's EI should improve grades, mitigate emotional disorders (through psychotherapy), and help the child to grow into adulthood capable of forming mature, constructive relationships with others. These laudable aims face the same general challenge that we have already mentioned, namely that the science and measurement of EI is still in its infancy. There are also potential barriers to progress that may be unique to education, including the difficulty of finding time for social–emotional learning in a crowded academic curriculum. Successful intervention is likely to require a sustained effort from administrators, teachers, and parents, and it may not be straightforward to secure the necessary commitment. This is the point where we can start to ask about the emotional literacy of the adults in the child's life and their willingness to support programs that may not produce an immediate payoff. As in business, there is also a danger from fads that may do more harm than good. For example, the movement to raise self-esteem, irrespective of the child's actual behavior, has been criticized as doing more harm than good (Twenge & Campbell, 2009).

SUMMARY AND CONCLUSIONS

There is no doubt that EI is potentially an exciting new frontier for both basic and applied psychologists. Despite its promise, we need to tread carefully in entering a territory where myths and legends abound. On the positive side, psychologists already have quite a good understanding of relevant topics, including emotion, abilities, and personality. The trick is to find the evidence that will show that EI is a distinctive ability that adds something to existing understanding. One of the barriers to this research enterprise is the role of emotion in pop culture. At worst, its siren song leads researchers astray into developing folksy but incoherent definitions of EI, junk questionnaires with no construct validity, and quick-fix self-help advice that is no more than a passing fad. Nonetheless, popular writers may be correct in identifying a neglect of emotional abilities and skills in psychological theory. The following points cover our conclusions about the path toward developing a psychological science of EI that is strong enough to support real-world applications.

1. *Reliable and valid measurement of EI is essential for any kind of research in the area.* Without standardized measurement tools, psychologists can do little more than trade opinions. Improving assessment of EI is also intimately related to the difficult task of finding a satisfactory definition and conceptualization of the construct. A coherent definition that says what is and what is not EI is necessary to take the first steps in building measurement instruments. Work on the psychometric properties of these instruments should in turn inform and refine definition. Currently, EI researchers are split into two camps. Those who see EI as a true ability gravitate toward developing objective tests, which, like conventional intelligence tests, have right-or-wrong answers. Those who see "trait EI" as closer to personality than to a true ability favor questionnaires that rely on self-reports of

emotional functioning. A general difficulty is that it remains to be established that there truly exists a general, overarching EI, as opposed to a variety of unrelated sources of emotional competency.

2. *Most accounts of EI are descriptive.* Many researchers state personal qualities that are associated with EI but simultaneously fail to dig any deeper into the neural, cognitive, and social processes that confer emotional competence. This is the task of psychological theory. We saw that theory must explain both the development of EI over the lifespan, and how EI impacts behavior over much shorter time spans of minutes or even seconds. There are several avenues that may lead us toward theoretical understanding. These include studying basic processes such as the operation of brain systems for emotion and cognitive processing of emotional stimuli. Another approach is to address learned skills for handling emotional encounters, skills that may be unconscious as well as conscious. Theory may also revolve around models of self-regulation. In each case, research needs to follow through the consequences of individual differences in emotion-regulation for adaptation to the pressures and opportunities of real life.

3. *Applications of EI are currently limited.* Fulfillment of the promise of EI for applied psychology requires stronger conceptualization, measurement tools, and theory. If researchers can build the theory, then real benefits will come. In the workplace, training for EI may help employees to work more productively, to form better relationships with coworkers, and to find greater personal satisfaction in work. In clinical psychology, understanding sources of pathological emotional illiteracy, such as alexithymia, may contribute to improving therapies for a range of disorders, including anxiety, depression, autism, and impulse control disorders. In education, social–emotional learning programs may help the child both to achieve academic success and to develop into a personally and socially well-adjusted adult. In all these domains

41

of application though, lack of rigorous research and the vulnerability of practitioners to passing fads remain a hazard. It also remains to show that EI is more than just a repackaging of existing concepts under a fancy new label.

NOTES

[1]Retrieved 9/10/10 from http://news.cnet.com/8301–17938_105–20013657–1.html?tag=mncol;4n

[2]Retrieved 9/10/10 from http://news.cnet.com/8301–1023_3–10396190-93.html?tag=mncol;1n

[3]Retrieved 9/10/10 from http://www.1902encyclopedia.com/C/CAV/henry-cavendish.html

[4]Retrieved 9/17/2010 from http://chronicle.com/article/Science Violence-The-C/64308/

Emotional Intelligence as a Personality Trait

As we saw in Chapter 1, there are several ways of thinking about emotional intelligence (EI) from a psychological science perspective. In this chapter, we explore the idea that EI is a part of the wider domain of personality. That is, EI refers to typical behaviors and ways of experiencing the world, rather than a true ability. Research on personality has already identified a variety of stable traits that describe the person's typical emotional life, such as extraversion and neuroticism. There are also well-validated models of the structure of personality that allow us to define and measure a variety of traits (de Raad, 2009; Matthews, Deary, & Whiteman, 2009).

If we want to talk about EI (or "trait EI") as part of this well-defined personality domain, then there are several steps to be taken. First, we need some working definition of EI that tells us which out of the many aspects of personality are relevant to emotional functioning. Second, having staked out some limited area of the personality domain as belonging to EI, we must determine how many specific traits or subdimensions are needed to capture the main features of trait EI. Third, we need to build assessment instruments that will measure these traits. In practice, this goal leads to development of questionnaires for trait EI, despite the potential problems of self-reports. Fourth, those questionnaires must be validated as predictors of behaviors and outcomes indicative of emotional competence, within the context of some underlying psychological theory. It is important too that these putative trait EI measures tell us something more about personality than we know already from standard personality assessments. There is no point in reinventing the wheel. Indeed, if we really do not gain any new insight into personality from studying the EI construct, then it leads us to wonder if we should even be studying EI at all.

In this chapter, we look at the research effort to develop valid questionnaires for trait EI. We begin with a short account of personality traits, as necessary background and context. Next, we look at the "trait EI" concept and some of the attempts made to develop questionnaires for it. We also briefly review evidence on the validity of trait EI questionnaires, and address the thorny problem of whether trait EI is really anything more than a slick repackaging of existing personality dimensions. We finish the chapter with a general critique of the trait EI perspective.

PERSONALITY AND EMOTION

Dimensional Models of Personality

As is often the case, what psychologists mean by "personality" is not quite the same as the everyday meaning of the word. Here, the idea is that we can describe personal attributes in terms of a set of quantitative dimensions that can be meaningfully applied to any individual person. The following assumptions are typically made (Matthews et al., 2009):

1. Personality dimensions are experienced along a continuum. We cannot, for example, divide the human race into one group of extraverts and a second group of introverts. Instead, each individual falls somewhere along a numerical scale for extraversion, and many people will be in the middle region of the scale, showing some extraverted and some introverted qualities.

2. Personality dimensions are not set in concrete, in that personality changes over time; normally slowly but occasionally quite fast (e.g., following a traumatic event). Typically, personality attributes are quite stable over periods of many years. Here we have a tension between seeing "trait EI" as a part of personality and the idea that EI is amenable to improvement.

3. The individual's personality is shaped by interactions between genes and environmental factors, so that personality corresponds in part to individual differences in brain functioning. There has been interest in neurological bases for EI, but again it seems that EI may be something more than a collection of learned social-emotional skills.

4. Individual differences in behavior reflect both stable personality traits and situational factors. If a party is wild enough, then even introverts may be talkative and sociable. Similarly, specific instances of emotionally intelligent behavior may reflect both the person's underlying behavior, and situational influences that make it more or less easy to show emotional competence. In the 2006 soccer World Cup, French player Zinedine Zidane notoriously headbutted an opponent, who had apparently taunted him about his sister, and was expelled from the game. Was this instance of emotional stupidity a consequence of Zidane's temperamental hotheadedness, or of intolerable provocation, or, most likely, some interaction of the two?

5. Traits are related to consequential life outcomes; that is, they have a real impact in shaping the course of the individual's life. Traits have been shown to relate to vulnerability to stress, to mental and medical illness, to job performance and work satisfaction, and to educational outcomes. At the same time, personality is not destiny. Although traits have far-reaching influences, they are often only modestly correlated with outcomes. As just noted, trait effects often depend on environmental influences.

The best-known personality model developed on these principles is the Five Factor Model (FFM: McCrae & Costa, 2008; see also the forthcoming *Personality 101* in Springer's Psych 101 series). As the name suggests, it proposes five major traits—openness, conscientiousness, extraversion, agreeableness, and neuroticism—which we listed previously in Table 1.3. The FFM is a *hierarchical* factor model. That is, each major or higher-order factor is defined as a cluster of correlated lower-level factors or facets. For example, extraversion captures a common element to traits such as assertiveness, sociability, and positive emotionality. Importantly, each lower-level facet has some uniqueness. Some of the variation in assertiveness, for example, cannot be attributed to extraversion. Potentially, trait EI might also be understood using a similar hierarchical model—a general factor of EI defined by several lower-order EI traits, which are correlated but distinct from one another. The NEO-PI-R questionnaire developed by McCrae and Costa (2008) includes six facet scales for each higher-order factor (see Table 2.1 for a listing of these facets by the five major traits).

Reasons for the widespread (though not universal) acceptance of the FFM include extensive psychometric evidence supporting the reliability and validity of the "Big Five," evidence for partial heritability and neurological correlates of the traits, cross-cultural generality, and applications in fields, including clinical, organizational, and educational psychology (McCrae & Costa, 2008). The evidence suggests "consequential validity"

TABLE 2.1 FACETS OF THE FFM AS ASSESSED BY THE NEO-PI-R QUESTIONNAIRE

Openness (O)	Conscientiousness (C)	Extraversion (E)	Agreeableness (A)	Neuroticism (N)*
Fantasy	Competence	Warmth	Trust	Angry hostility
Aesthetics	Order	Gregariousness	Straightforwardness	Self-consciousness
Feelings	Dutifulness	Assertiveness	Altruism	Anxiety
Actions	Self-discipline	Activity	Compliance	Impulsiveness
Ideas	Deliberation	Excitement-seeking	Modesty	Depression
Values	Achievement	Positive emotions	Tender-mindedness	Vulnerability

*Emotional stability is represented by *low* scores on the six facets of neuroticism.

(McAdams & Pals, 2006); that is, personality composition as defined by the Big Five influences various aspects of the individual's life trajectory.

Emotional Competency And the FFM

What does the FFM have to say about individual differences in emotional functioning? In fact, quite a lot! The extraversion (E) and neuroticism (N; or low emotional stability) dimensions are quite reliably related to positive and negative emotions, respectively (Lucas & Diener, 2000). There has been some debate over the extent to which positive emotionality is central to extraversion, and negative emotionality is at the core of neuroticism (Ashton, Lee, & Paunonen, 2002). There may also be a variety of mechanisms that produce the typically happy moods of extraverts, and the anxiety and unhappiness characteristic of individuals high in neuroticism. Matthews et al. (2009) list the following:

1. *Basic temperament.* Extraversion and neuroticism are linked directly to brain systems that control the relevant emotions; for example, being happy is intrinsic to extraversion. A variant of this mechanism is the emotional reactivity hypothesis. Personality is associated with the sensitivity of brain systems controlling immediate emotional response to events (Corr, 2009). Thus, extraverts are not necessarily happier than introverts in all circumstances, but when some positive, potentially rewarding event is perceived, the stimulus activates the reward system of the brain more strongly in extraverts than in introverts. Similarly, a brain system for handling punishment stimuli is more reactive in high neuroticism persons relative to those low in neuroticism.

2. *Cognitive appraisal and coping.* Personality is known to relate to different styles of interpreting the world, and of coping with its many demands and pressures. These cognitive processes of appraisal and coping strongly influence emotional response (Lazarus, 1999), and may indeed contribute to

EI (Scherer, 2007). Extraverts tend to interpret demanding events as challenging. They are also inclined to use direct, problem-focused coping strategies. This pattern of cognitive processing tends to maintain positive emotions, even in adverse circumstances (Shaw et al., 2010). Similarly, the tendencies of highly neurotic individuals to appraise events as threatening and outside of personal control, coupled with often-maladaptive, emotion-focused coping strategies such as self-criticism, are apt to produce negative emotion (Connor-Smith & Flachsbart, 2007). Critically, appraisal and coping are highly flexible processes that primarily reflect the nature of situational pressures, and the person's store of knowledge about the situation and their own functioning in that context (Wells & Matthews, 1994). The implication is that there is more to extraversion and neuroticism than basic temperament; traits correspond to different modes of understanding the world and one's own place in it. In a sense, the unhappiness of the highly neurotic person reflects an existential insecurity that feeds negative self-beliefs and emotions.

3. *Mood-regulation.* Appraisal and coping are often directed towards external events; good, bad, and indifferent. People also monitor their internal emotional states and attempt to control or regulate them; for example, to snap out of a negative mood, or to damp down feelings of elation in order to focus attention. Logically, mood-regulation must depend on both insight into one's current emotional state, and also on the effectiveness of the strategies used to modify mood. Researchers on EI have been much concerned with individual differences in mood-regulation. For example, clinical patients with mood disorders often display "alexithymia"— difficulties in recognizing, labeling, and understanding their emotions (Parker, 2000). However, individual differences in mood-regulation are also a feature of personality traits, including extraversion and neuroticism. Extraverts appear to be better than introverts at maintaining positive moods

and repairing negative moods (Lischetzke & Eid, 2006). Individuals high in neuroticism tend to worry excessively and ruminate unproductively on problems, perpetuating or even amplifying negative moods (Matthews & Funke, 2006).

4. *Environmental interactions.* Cognitive theories of emotion (Lazarus, 1999) emphasize the importance of the dynamic interplay (or *transaction*) between person and environment. We cannot divorce the effects of personality on emotion from the environments to which individuals of various personality characteristics gravitate (consciously or unconsciously). Extraverts enjoy more active and varied social lives, and social engagement is known to elevate positive mood. Thus, the happiness enjoyed by extraverts may in part reflect greater social exposure (Lucas, Le, & Dyrenforth, 2008). Similarly, highly neurotic persons tend to get themselves into various kinds of trouble, including interpersonal conflicts, which in turn elevates negative mood (e.g., Ormel & Wohlfarth, 1991).

While extraversion and neuroticism are the traits most strongly linked to emotional response, other traits of the FFM may play more subtle roles. Conscientious individuals appear to be more likely to employ task-focused coping strategies in performance contexts, which may confer most positive moods in that setting (Matthews et al., 2006). Recent studies also support a similar stress-protective role for conscientiousness in life generally (Bartley & Roesch, 2011), not to mention recent research showing that C significantly predicts longevity (Friedman, Kern, & Reynolds, 2010). Agreeableness may tend to confer more pleasant moods in cooperative settings, but lead to emotional stress in situations that promote disagreements between people (Coté & Moskowitz, 1998). The emotional side of Openness is little-known, but we might imagine that the artistic and intellectual enjoy some frisson of pleasure through creative endeavor. Table 2.2 summarizes some of the parallels that exist between the FFM and various facets of EI (see de Raad, 2005; McCrae, 2000).

It follows that any distinctive contribution made by EI research must be placed within this pre-existing body of work on personality. If we can straightforwardly link positive emotion to extraversion and negative emotion to neuroticism, then what more can EI add to the picture?

Another issue is that associations between EI and emotion found in research might reflect multiple underlying processes, not all of which are genuinely "emotionally intelligent." A case in point is the role of brain systems in emotionality. If some people possess a highly reactive brain reward system, then they will tend to enjoy greater happiness, but it is hard to say that they are more emotionally intelligent. Conceptualizations of EI imply insight and understanding of emotion, which is a different quality. Conversely, there may be a stronger case for attributing high EI to people who can appraise situations constructively, who can regulate their moods to meet immediate

TABLE 2.2   CORRESPONDENCES BETWEEN THE FFM AND FACETS OF TRAIT EI

Openness	Creative thinking
	Aesthetic appreciation of emotion
Conscientiousness	Task motivation
	Perseverance
	Impulse control
Extraversion	Positive affect
	Optimism
	Social skills
	Adaptive regulation of others' emotions
Agreeableness	Empathy
	Interpersonal relationships
	Altruism
Emotional stability	Low levels of negative emotion
	Freedom from clinical anxiety and depression
(low N)	Stress resistance
	Adaptive self-regulation of emotions

needs, and who can choose to engage in life-enhancing situations and activities.

ASSESSING EI BY QUESTIONNAIRE

As several commentators (e.g., O'Sullivan, 2007) have pointed out, measuring an ability by questionnaire is a rather strange enterprise. Self-reports of conventional intelligence correlate only modestly (around 0.3) with objective measurements using validated tests (Paulhus, Lysy, & Yik, 1998). Why would we suppose that people have any better insight into their own emotional competence? There are also some immediate reasons for skepticism about self-report. Even assuming that people do their best to answer the questionnaire truthfully, they may simply lack knowledge of how their abilities compare with those of other people. Indeed, answering questions on one's EI requires one to have sufficient EI to be able to respond accurately. It is thus difficult to see how a low-EI person can provide meaningful responses. As mentioned in Chapter 1, this conundrum has been termed the "EI paradox" (Zeidner, Matthews, & Roberts, 2009).

Empirical studies also provide pause for thought. Dunning (e.g., Dunning, Heath, & Suls, 2004) has shown that people's ratings of their own emotional and social competence often bear little resemblance to their actual functioning. On occasion, people of very limited job competence may believe that they are really indispensable to their organization. There is also a long-established research literature on conscious and unconscious distortions of self-evaluations on personality scales (see Ziegler, MacCann, & Roberts, 2011). We will look later at evidence on the vulnerability of EI questionnaires to such distortions.

Questionnaires for EI—The First Wave

In fact, there may have been a variety of motives for the initial attempts at questionnaire development. Interest in how people regulate their own emotional states predates the concept of EI (e.g., Koriat, Melkman, Averill, & Lazarus, 1972), and has inspired a number of questionnaires. For example, Thayer, Newman, and McClain (1994) developed a scale that distinguished strategies for improving mood, including talking to someone else, controlling thoughts, exercise, and listening to music. There is also a clinical-psychological literature on measures of counterproductive strategies such as excessive rumination on problems and attempting to suppress negative thoughts and feelings (e.g., Wells & Davies, 1994). Salovey, Mayer, Goldman, Turvey, & Palfai (1995) published the Trait Meta-Mood Scale (TMMS), which is comprised of scales for attention to one's moods, clarity of thinking about moods, and repair of negative moods. The TMMS appears to be quite effective in predicting well-being and even some psychophysiological indices of stress, with this relationship holding after personality factors are controlled (Extremera & Fernández-Berrocal, 2005; Salovey, Stroud, Woolery, & Epel, 2002). However, although a useful research instrument, the TMMS does not seem to be sufficiently broadly based to provide a general assessment of EI.

The early science-based studies of Mayer and Salovey (e.g., Salovey & Mayer, 1990) together with Goleman's (1995) popular book inspired a wave of interest in developing more comprehensive scales. For example, Schutte et al. (1998) developed a questionnaire that includes subscales corresponding to the different branches of EI in the Mayer–Salovey conceptual framework. Bar-On (2000) presented a different rationale for using a questionnaire to assess social and emotional abilities. He proposed a "mixed-model" conceptualization of EI. In this model, EI is made up of both objectively definable competencies, as well as broader personality characteristics that facilitate expression of EI. Like other personality models, the Bar-On model is hierarchical in nature; higher-level aspects of EI are defined by several more specific lower-level facets. His EQ-i scale includes 15 subscales, grouped into five broader dimensions referring to intrapersonal, interpersonal, stress management, adaptability, and general mood. In common with other scales, the subscales are intercorrelated so that an overall "general factor" of EI may be assessed. Bar-On calls this EQ, by analogy with IQ. Other questionnaires too numerous to list followed these initial efforts, including some designed expressly for use in the business context (e.g., Sala, 2002).

The early questionnaires were certainly successful in inspiring research. We will present a more detailed evaluation of research outcomes below, but for now we will briefly note some highlights of research during the late 1990s and early 2000s. On the positive side, the better questionnaires met some standard psychometric criteria. Most scales and subscales proved to have good internal consistency, indicating reliable, accurate measurement (of whatever it was that was being measured). They also proved to have some "criterion validity." That is, questionnaire scores correlated significantly with other, independent measures of emotional functioning. Schutte et al.'s (1998) original article reported correlations between EI and a variety of relevant measures, including optimism and impulse control. More recent work has also substantiated the association between questionnaire-EI and well-being. As will be discussed in Chapter 4, recent meta-analyses show that self-report measures of EI correlate significantly with subjective self-reports of well-being.

We note at this point that to appreciate the relevant research findings, readers will need an appreciation of the Pearson correlation coefficient (abbreviated as r). It expresses the strength of linear association between two variables, that is, the extent to which they tend to "go together." The size of a correlation varies between 0 and 1, and can roughly be interpreted as follows:

1. nonexistent or trivial (absolute value of $r = 0.00$–0.09);
2. small (absolute value of $r = 0.10$–0.29);
3. moderate or medium (absolute value of $r = 0.30$–0.49);
4. large (absolute value of $r = 0.50$–0.69); or
5. very large (absolute value of $r = 0.70$–1.00).

Correlations may be negative as well as positive. A negative correlation indicates that larger values of one variable are associated with smaller values of the other (e.g., conscientiousness is negatively correlated with laziness).

Limitations of First-Wave Questionnaires

As part of establishing the credibility of a measure, scores should tend to intercorrelate highly with other similar measures, suggesting that there is a common underlying quality to them all. These early questionnaires tended to intercorrelate with one another (Brackett & Meyer, 2003), which provides evidence for "convergent validity." A meta-analysis (where correlations are averaged across studies; see Van Rooy, Viswesvaran, & Pluta, 2005) reported that scales correlate among themselves at 0.71, a value that suggests considerable overlap.

At the same time, some cracks in the questionnaire-assessment edifice began to appear. At a psychometric level, it proved difficult to reproduce the factor structure of the scales in detail. Psychologists use a technique called factor analysis to separate and identify multiple dimensions that may be measured by a scale or test. Bar-On (1997) claimed that the 15 subscales of the EQ-i were grouped into five higher-level dimensions, as previously described. However, Matthews, Zeidner, & Roberts (2002) re-analyzed Bar-On's (1997) own data and found most of the variance in the subscales could be explained using just three dimensions: self-esteem, interpersonal sensitivity, and impulse control. Similar difficulties were found in reproducing the four dimensions of EI claimed by Schutte et al. (1998) (see e.g., Austin, Saklofske, Huang, & McKenney, 2004). The issue here is that the components of EI as assessed by questionnaire remain unclear.

Limits on the validity of EI scales also became apparent. As we have seen, the questionnaires predict a variety of criteria. However, most of these criteria are themselves defined by questionnaire assessments (e.g., of subjective well-being or social skills). A skeptic might argue that both the EI scale and the well-being criterion simply reflect the person's positive opinion of himself/herself, which may not be reflected in objective measures of competence. Adding to such concerns is the problem that some of the conceptually weaker measures (e.g., the EQ-i) include subscales for positive mood and related qualities such as optimism. If the EI score itself reflects positive mood, then it is not surprising that the score is associated with higher well-being (this problem is known as "criterion contamination").

Improving Validity

There are two ways in which we might find stronger evidence for validity than by correlating EI questionnaires with other questionnaires. The first is to run laboratory experiments in which we test whether EI predicts objective measures of emotional competence, such as performance on tasks in which the person must process emotional stimuli. For instance, accurate emotion perception is typically seen as core element of EI (e.g., Mayer, Salovey, & Caruso, 2000). Thus, EI questionnaires should predict better performance on tasks that require the person to identify emotion; for example, whether a person accurately identifies a happy face as being "happy."

There are, in fact, reasonably valid tests of facial emotion recognition, based on well-established emotion theory (Scherer, 2007). Fellner et al. (2007) investigated recognition of brief "micro-expressions" of facial emotions, lasting only 200 ms, in video sequences constructed by Paul Ekman (2003), a leading emotion theorist. Several EI questionnaires were included in the study, including the Schutte et al. (1998) scale. None predicted emotion recognition. Ironically, an intelligence test (based on solving analogy problems) was a superior predictor of performance on the emotional task. Fellner et al. (2007) also tested whether EI was associated with superior attention to facial emotional stimuli, by having participants search arrays of faces for target emotions, including happiness and anger. Again, EI was unrelated to speed and accuracy of search, but conventional intelligence related to better performance.

We have described just one study. Other researchers have occasionally found small but significant associations between EI questionnaires and performance measures (e.g., Austin, 2005), so we should not entirely dismiss the utility of the scales as predictors of objective measures. However, as we have explored in various reviews of the evidence (e.g., Zeidner et al., 2009), the overall impression that comes from these studies is that questionnaire-EI is just not that good a predictor of performance on tasks that require the processing of emotional stimuli.

A second validation strategy is to assess whether questionnaire measures correlate with meaningful real-life outcomes, such as being formally diagnosed with a mental illness, being promoted at work, or attaining high grades at school or university. Here, the evidence is mixed. Some studies do indeed show that various emotionally disturbed groups tend to obtain low questionnaire scores. To give just one example, Riley and Schutte (2003) administered clinically validated screening measures for drug and alcohol users along with the Schutte et al. (1998) scale. Substance abusers obtained low scores for EI, consistent with the view that drug use may be influenced by poor emotional self-regulation. Schutte et al. (1998) had already shown that drug abusers were less emotionally intelligent than psychotherapists, a finding that must have come as a relief to that profession. We will note in passing that not all such studies have provided such supportive outcomes. Hemmati, Mills, and Kroner (2004) gave the EQ-i to 119 male offenders in a US federal prison, convicted of crimes including assault and robbery. The offenders obtained *higher* scores than expected on the basis of norms. Perhaps the emotional ingenuity of the criminal fraternity has been under-estimated, although Hemmati et al. (2004) preferred the explanation that questionnaire items have different meanings for offenders and non-offenders.

Evidence for the validity of the EQ-i in the occupational context came from a study of managers working for a major British retail company (Slaski & Cartwright, 2002). They found a small (but significant) correlation of 0.22 between EI and ratings of performance made by the respondent's immediate line-manager. Validating questionnaires in the educational context has proved harder. A relatively early study (Newsome, Day, & Catano, 2000) found that the EQ-i correlated at only 0.01 with grade point average in Canadian college students. With some exceptions (see Parker, Saklofske, Wood, & Collin, 2009), later research has generally found questionnaire assessments of EI to be unrelated to academic attainment (Tok & Morali, 2009). Nonetheless, there is sufficient evidence to make a prima facie case for the relevance of EI to real-life emotional functioning.

Reinventing the Wheel: EI Overlaps With Personality

We now turn to perhaps the most striking shortcoming of EI questionnaires: their overlap with standard personality dimensions. In psychological assessment, a distinction is made between *convergent* and *discriminant* evidence. Broadly, a scale should correlate substantially with related measures (convergent validity evidence) but it should correlate weakly or not at all with measures of other, distinct qualities (discriminant validity evidence). Conventional intelligence tests meet these criteria for validity with ease. In most contexts, it is not critical whether intelligence is measured with the Wechsler, Stanford-Binet, or Kaufman tests (all leading IQ tests; see Kaufman, 2009). If you score as a genius on one, then it is highly likely that you will attain an exceptional score on the others as well. In addition, intelligence is modestly correlated with personality scales, at most; it overlaps only a little with the Big Five (Austin et al., 2011).

Thus, alternate EI measures should correlate with one another (convergent validity evidence) but only to a small degree with personality (discriminant validity evidence). As we have seen, different *questionnaire*-EI measures do indeed correlate with one another (Van Rooy et al., 2005). However, this same meta-analysis found that the correlation between "questionnaire-EI" and EI measured by ability tests was only 0.12. The two kinds of test are measuring essentially different constructs. A striking failure of convergence was obtained by Zeidner, Shani-Zinovich, Matthews, and Roberts (2005). They compared academically gifted and non-gifted high school students in Israel on a popular questionnaire for EI, the Schutte Self-Report Inventory (SSRI: Schutte et al., 1998), and the Mayer-Salovey-Caruso Emotional Intelligence Test (MSCEIT) ability-based test (Mayer, Salovey, Caruso, & Sitarenios, 2003). The gifted group scored higher than the non-gifted on the MSCEIT but lower on the SSRI. The answer to the question of whether academic talent is accompanied by higher or lower emotional competence depends entirely on whether a questionnaire or ability-based measure of EI is used.

We might also wonder whether EI converges to any degree with general intelligence. Whether it should depends on one's perspective. The view that there are multiple, separate intelligences (Gardner, 1983) suggests independence of emotional and cognitive ability. Goleman's (1995) rhetorical device of highlighting the supposed high IQ but low EQ of absent-minded professors might even suggest a negative correlation. There is, however, a long established principle in ability research (which some call the first law of intelligence) that states that different abilities will correlate positively. On this basis, EI should be distinct from IQ, but somewhat correlated with it (Mayer, Caruso & Salovey, 1999). In fact, the evidence is clear that questionnaire measures of EI are largely unrelated to cognitive ability (Van Rooy et al., 2005). Whether this finding suggests a problem with the validity of the measures depends on whether one believes that EI should, like other specialized abilities, correlate with general intelligence, or if it is an exception to the general rule. As a science though, going against a law is usually conceived of as a highly problematic practice.

Turning to personality studies, it soon became apparent that the newly-minted scales for EI were highly correlated with existing personality measures (Barchard & Hakstian, 2004). An influential study by Dawda and Hart (2000) found that scores on the EQ-i were substantially correlated with low neuroticism, extraversion, conscientiousness, and agreeableness. In fact, neuroticism correlated strongly with EQ in both men ($r = -0.62$) and women ($r = -0.72$). Seemingly, EI in large part reflects an emotionally stable temperament. In similar vein, Newsome et al. (2000) found a very strong negative correlation between the EQ-i and trait anxiety ($r = -0.77$), suggesting that these two measures are largely opposite poles of the same dimension. In fact, most of the variation in scores on the EQ-i is predictable from the FFM of personality (Matthews et al., 2002), so that it really does little more than mush together the more attractive personal qualities assessed by the FFM. This is a predictable outcome to the extent that the specific qualities assessed by the EQ-i and other EI questionnaires show a great deal of conceptual overlap with the FFM (de Raad, 2005; see Table 2.2).

The EQ-i represents a spectacular failure of divergence from personality. Other pioneering questionnaire scales have fared somewhat better. For example, in Saklofske, Austin, and Minski's (2003) study of the Schutte et al. (1998) questionnaire, the highest correlation with the Big Five was 0.51, for extraversion, with lesser correlations for the remaining personality dimensions. There is still quite a lot of overlap, suggesting poor discriminant validity, but the questionnaire seems to measure some personal qualities beyond the Big Five (Saklofske et al., 2003).

Failings of the Early Questionnaires

The work we have described should suffice to show that the efforts at developing EI questionnaires were really quite thorough, involving multiple research labs, and extensive data collection. The primary payoff from these initial efforts was evidence that the scales concerned did a pretty good job of predicting subjective well-being, and, to a lesser degree, some other real-world criteria such as ratings of job performance (Slaski & Cartwright, 2002). However, the studies also highlighted two serious limitations of the scales. First, they failed to correlate reliably with objective performance measures in controlled experimental studies. This lack of evidence in turn made it difficult to articulate theoretical accounts of the cognitive and emotional processes that might mediate effects of EI on behavior. Indeed, a common criticism is that the "theory" attached to questionnaires is little more than a laundry list of desirable personality characteristics (Matthews et al., 2002).

Second, the leading questionnaires were substantially correlated with existing personality dimensions, notably the Big Five. Their predictive validity may then be a consequence of this overlap. A scale such as the EQ-i that correlates at around 0.70 with the major personality dimensions of neuroticism and trait anxiety will necessarily tend to correlate with all the multifarious criteria associated with these traits. It is well-established that neuroticism relates to poorer mental health, interpersonal conflict, and low job satisfaction (Matthews et al., 2009). The overlap between questionnaire-EI and neuroticism comes close to guaranteeing that EI will correlate with a similar range of criteria.

REVIVING EI BY QUESTIONNAIRE: "TRAIT EI"

Findings on the first wave of scales suggested a need to re-evaluate what EI questionnaires were actually measuring. It became difficult to sustain the argument that they assess emotional ability or competency in the light of the following observations:

- Self-reports are not well-suited to measuring ability in the first place.
- Questionnaire-EI relates more strongly to personality than to other abilities, including the Mayer et al. (2003) ability tests for EI.
- There is little evidence that questionnaire-EI is strongly associated with superior emotional competency in laboratory or real-life settings, once overlap with personality is taken into account.

Petrides and Furnham (2003) took the radical step of defining EI-as-measured-by-questionnaire as part of the personality domain, rather than an ability. They coined the term "trait EI" to refer to individual differences in typical experiences and behaviors. They suggested that various dimensions of trait EI, such as those comprising the EQ-i, might be integrated into a broader conception of personality. That is, trait EI is a lower-level personality construct that contributes to several of the higher-order Big Five (Petrides et al., 2007). Like standard personality traits, trait EI may then relate to objective emotional competence in some circumstances, just as extraverts may on occasion exhibit superior social skills to introverts (Uziel, 2007). However, it is not expected that trait EI exerts the systematic effect on performance in emotional settings that standard intelligence exerts on cognitive competence.

What does this new perspective on EI have to offer? An immediate issue is that we are now in the strange position of labeling a personality trait (or collection of traits) as an "intelligence," which seems terminologically inept (O'Sullivan, 2007). Indeed, the definitional problem is even worse, since intelligence is also a trait; so one could easily paraphrase the new terminology as "trait emotional trait." Assuming we can get over these definitional conundrums, the trait EI approach provides some immediate relief for the problems of questionnaire-EI just listed:

- The use of questionnaire measures is well-accepted in personality research, and so we can assess trait EI in this way just as we can assess other traits such as those of the FFM. (Of course, new trait measures still have to be validated against relevant outcomes and criteria.)
- If trait EI is part of the personality domain, and not a true ability, then its pattern of associations with personality traits (strong) and abilities (weak) makes much more sense.
- Standard personality traits also show complex patterns of association with behavioral criteria (Matthews, 2009). Validating trait measures typically requires careful attention to research methods and the context in which personality is studied. Thus, it now comes as no surprise that questionnaires for EI are often weak predictors of relevant criteria. We can hope that further work will uncover contextual factors that determine whether or not trait EI is predictive of emotional functioning.

We now have some reasons for pursuing research on trait EI in principle. It still has to be established through research that the approach does in fact enhance understanding of individual differences in emotional competency. The issue is still whether trait EI measures do any better than standard personality traits in predicting measures of emotional functioning in laboratory and applied settings.

Developing Scales for Trait EI

A starting point for examining the "added value" of trait EI scales is to examine their overlap with standard personality traits. The higher the overlap, the less trait EI measures are likely to radically change our views on personality and emotion. We have seen already that the pioneering attempts at questionnaire assessment were flawed by excessive overlap with personality. We might reasonably hope that more recent scale development exercises would learn from the past and go to some lengths to avoid high intercorrelations between trait EI and existing personality dimensions.

Petrides and Furnham (2003) developed the first questionnaire that was explicitly shaped by the concept of trait EI as a part of personality. They called it the TEIQue (Trait EI Questionnaire—pronounced "Take-way"). In its current form, it is made up of 15 correlated scales. Thirteen of these can be grouped together to define four higher-order factors of emotionality, self-control, sociability, and well-being, as shown in Table 2.3. These scales can also be aggregated to estimate overall trait EI. The factor structure of the TEIQue seems quite robust. In fact, it has been reproduced not just in the original English language version but also in other languages, including German (Freudenthaler, Neubauer, Gabler, Scherl, & Rindermann, 2008), French (Mikolajczak, Luminet, Leroy, & Roy, 2007), and Dutch (Petrides et al., 2010).

The obvious question is how distinct the TEIQue is from the FFM. Table 2.4 shows correlations between the Big Five and the four TEIQue higher-order factors in a sample of 632 US and Canadian respondents (Vernon, Villani, Schermer, & Petrides, 2008). They completed the "gold standard" for the Big Five,

TABLE 2.3   DEFINITION OF FOUR HIGHER-ORDER TEIQUE FACTORS BY LOWER-LEVEL TRAIT EI SCALES

Well-being	Self-control	Emotionality	Sociability
Self-esteem Trait happiness Trait optimism	Emotion regulation Stress management Impulsiveness (low)	Emotion perception (self and others) Emotion expression Relationship skills Empathy	Social competence Emotion management (others) Assertiveness

TABLE 2.4 CORRELATIONS BETWEEN FOUR HIGHER-ORDER TEIQUE FACTORS AND THE PERSONALITY TRAITS OF THE FFM

	Well-being	Self-control	Emotionality	Sociability	Total EI
Neuroticism	-.60**	-.74**	-.18**	-.30**	-.61**
Extraversion	.49**	.09*	.31**	.57**	.51**
Openness	.25**	.01	.29**	.31**	.32**
Agreeableness	.28**	.35**	.27**	-.14**	.32**
Conscientiousness	.34**	.48**	.22**	.25**	.47**

Note: *$p < .01$, **$p < .05$

65

Costa and McCrae's (1992) NEO-PI-R questionnaire. Three of the four trait EI factors are quite highly correlated with Big Five dimensions. Neuroticism was strongly related to lower well-being and poorer self-control, as well as to lower overall trait EI. Other substantial correlations linked extraversion to greater well-being and sociability, and conscientiousness to higher self-control. These two FFM traits also related to higher trait EI. Other studies, including those cited in the preceding paragraph, have obtained similar findings.

One message we can take from Table 2.4 is that over-lap between questionnaire-EI and the Big Five remains problematic. Correlational data of the kind shown can be further analyzed using techniques such as multiple regression to estimate the total percentage of variation in overall trait EI that can be predicted from the Big Five. Reviewing the studies of the TEIQue, Petrides et al. (2007) conclude that the Big Five explains 50–80% of the variation in the scale—quite a lot!

However, Table 2.4 suggests that the problem of overlap depends on which of the four more specific factors we look at. Well-being and self-control seem to be rather strongly related to the Big Five, whereas emotionality shows a smaller set of correlations (the largest is 0.31). On the face of it, the distinctiveness of emotionality seems surprising. As previously discussed, we have seen already that temperamental emotionality is central to neuroticism (negative emotions) and to extraversion (positive emotions). The answer to the puzzle is that what Petrides et al. mean by "emotionality" is different to the more typical use of the term. (Note to reader: labels for personality scales may be misleading!). Returning to Table 2.3, we see that emotionality in the TEIQue does not refer to the intensity of emotional experience per se. Instead, the common elements to its four defining scales seem to be perceiving, understanding, and sharing emotions in social contexts. Here then, we have a set of personal qualities that refer to emotional functioning that are quite distinct from the FFM. Whether people with high scores on this social "emotionality" factor are genuinely superior in perceiving, understanding, and sharing emotions is an open question to be addressed by research.

As with the first wave of EI questionnaires, it remains unclear how to best describe the subdimensions of overall trait EI. The Petrides et al. factor models for the TEIQue seem to work well for that particular instrument. However, other and different factor models for trait EI have been advanced. Tett, Fox, and Wang (2005) also performed a fairly thorough, systematic questionnaire-development exercise arriving at 10 correlated scales for various facets of trait EI. As always, a general trait EI factor could be defined. However, they also showed that there were three higher-order factors. Self-orientation and other-orientation factors were defined by scales including recognition and regulation of emotion in self and others, respectively. The third factor, emotional sharing, was defined by scales for empathy, nonverbal expression, and mood-redirected attention. These factors do not seem to align in any simple way with the four higher-order TEIQue factors ("emotionality," self-control, sociability, and well-being). The lack of agreement is troubling.

Faking and Social Desirability

Another problem with trait EI, and self-reports of EI more generally, is the "little problem of faking" (Ziegler et al., 2011). Suppose you wish to enter the job of your dreams and you are confronted as part of the selection process with the following question: "Are you good at controlling your emotions when a colleague yells at you?" Even if you have a long and checkered history of yelling back at colleagues, what chance is there that you would answer this question completely honestly, either because you wanted to get the job or because you did not wish to appear too bad in other people's eyes? In short, self-report measures of EI seem particularly vulnerable to faking and socially desirable responding. A wide range of studies have shown faking and social desirability to severely compromise the validity of self-report measures of EI (e.g., Day & Carroll, 2008;

Grubb & McDaniel, 2007; Kluemper, 2008). In one particularly striking study, Grubb and McDaniel (2007) showed that respondents improved their scores on the EQ-i by nearly a full standard deviation if instructed to fake. Findings of this kind suggest that while trait EI might be of interest to researchers, practitioners may find it more problematic, especially if being used to make important (sometimes called high-stakes) decisions. Note this problem does not seem to occur with ability-based EI measures (Day & Carroll, 2008).

Validating Scales for Trait EI

If scales for trait EI do give us something more than standard personality traits, then it should improve over the FFM in predicting criteria for emotional competence. Here, the evidence is mixed. Generally, trait EI questionnaires are good predictors of questionnaire measures of well-being. A recent meta-analysis (Martins, Ramalho, & Morin, 2010) calculated the average correlation between trait EI and mental well-being as 0.36, across 67 separate studies. The SSRI, TEIQue, and TMMS were all shown to predict well-being. Of course, we would expect these questionnaires to correlate highly with well-being because of their overlap with temperamental factors that relate to negative and positive emotions, that is, neuroticism and extraversion. However, several studies have shown that trait EI predicts well-being over and above the FFM (Petrides, Furnham, & Mavroveli, 2007), at least to some degree (see Day, 2004 for a contrary view).

Certainly, there is sufficient evidence to justify using trait EI scales in studies of personality predictors of mood and emotion. However, a couple of cautionary notes are needed. First, the TEIQue measure includes well-being (defined by scales for happiness and optimism) as itself one of the major factors contributing to overall EI. If the TEIQue is in part itself a well-being measure, then it is not surprising that it predicts well-being criteria! Again, we have a "criterion contamination" issue. Examination of the different TEIQue factors may provide a more nuanced picture. Unfortunately, several of the studies concerned (e.g., Petrides, Pérez-González, & Furnham, 2007) simply use the overall EI score, so that the role of the subfactors is unclear.

A second issue is that in comparing trait EI scales with the FFM, we are not necessarily comparing like with like. The Big Five are broad-based dimensions that bundle together a variety of somewhat distinct characteristics, which may be differentially related to emotion. For example, Morrone-Strupinsky and Lane (2007) found that the assertiveness component of extraversion related more to positive emotion response than to its social warmth component. It may just be that trait EI scales are giving us a more fine-grained description of traits related to emotionality, in which case their ability to improve over the broader Big Five is not so surprising.

Many well-being studies are concerned only with correlating different sets of questionnaires. More powerful validation techniques require the use of objective measures. Here too the data are mixed. Some of the more persuasive evidence has been obtained by Moïra Mikolajczak at the University of Louvain in Belgium. In one study, an experimental stressor was used – having to give a public speech (Mikolajczak, Roy, Luminet, Fille, & de Timary, 2007). Stressors of this kind tend to elevate secretion of a hormone called cortisol. The study showed that individuals high in trait EI showed a smaller cortisol response (implying less stress). Furthermore, the effect held up with the Big Five controlled, suggesting that trait EI was uniquely predictive of one component of the physiological stress response. Another study (Mikolajczak, Roy, Verstrynge, & Luminet, 2009) showed that one of the four broad TEIQue factors—self-control—was related to attention and memory performance. As is typical in personality research, the associations were complex, varying with stress and emotional content.

By contrast, Fellner et al. (2007) failed to find any significant associations between perception and attention to emotional stimuli and the TMMS, Schutte et al. (1998) scale, and "emotionality" scales of the TEIQue. A further study failed to establish any relationship between questionnaire measures of EI and the ability to use emotional cues in learning to discriminate different categories of individual (terrorists vs. non-terrorists). It seems that trait EI is not related to any general superiority in processing emotive material. However, there may be some circumstances under which trait EI (or more correctly, selected facets of EI) are associated with specific cognitive processes.

WHAT HAVE WE LEARNT FROM RESEARCH USING EI QUESTIONNAIRES?

What is the payoff from the fairly extensive questionnaire-based research that we have briefly reviewed? Are scales for EI no more than rebranded personality traits? Or can we use EI questionnaires to tell us something about the person's emotional functioning we could not ascertain from existing personality measures? Research is still ongoing and hence there are no definitive answers to the questions that we have posed. But we can summarize some interim conclusions, as follows:

1. *Personality influences emotion (but we knew that already)*. Much of the work done using questionnaire scales for EI reiterates existing knowledge of personality and emotion. It is well established that traits, in conjunction with situational factors, influence emotion. It should come as no surprise that scales for EI that overlap with personality traits such as extraversion and emotional stability (low neuroticism) are likewise related to various measures of emotional state, well-being, and resilience under stress.

2. *Be skeptical about EQ*. Typically, questionnaires allow the computation of an overall EI score of the kind described by Bar-On (2000) as EQ. Typically, "EQ" is an amalgam of extraversion and low neuroticism, perhaps with some

agreeableness and conscientiousness thrown in. The trouble is that mixing established traits in this way discards some of the key insights of emotion research, notably that positive and negative emotionality are separate dimensions. Being happy is not the same as freedom from negative emotion. EQ seems to have little psychological meaning except as a crude overall indicator of traits contributing to different forms of well-being.

3. *Trait EI may contribute to a more fine-grained understanding of personality and emotion.* In hierarchical models of personality (de Raad, 2009), broad factors such as the FFM are defined by multiple facets or lower-order traits. One of the contributions of trait EI research is to identify some specific facets, and clusters of facets, that may add to understanding of individual differences in emotional functioning. In particular, the TEIQue "emotionality" cluster (e.g., emotion perception) and several of the lower-order facets found by Tett et al. (2005) are only modestly related to the FFM. Some psychometric difficulties remain in realizing the potential of these trait EI dimensions. First, it is unclear what the definitive factor structures should be; note the differences between the Petrides, Furnham, & Mavroveli (2007) and Tett et al. (2005) dimensional models. Second, it is unclear how the lower-order EI dimensions align in detail with the FFM. Some dimensions can be straightforwardly assigned to specific factors (e.g., empathy is one element of agreeableness). The alignment of others is less clear.

4. *Questionnaire-EI predicts experience better than behavior.* EI scales predict various subjective indices of well-being quite effectively, and in some cases improve over the FFM. They tend to perform much worse in predicting both real-life outcomes such as job performance (Van Rooy & Viswesvaran, 2004), objective behavior, and task performance. Trait EI is most definitely not associated with any across-the-board advantage in dealing with emotive stimuli or situations. However, as with personality measures, generally, reliable

objective correlates of trait EI measures may be found with careful experimental design (Mikolajczak, Roy et al., 2007).

5. *Questionnaire-EI measures should not be used to make high-stakes decisions.* Currently, there is pretty compelling evidence to suggest that questionnaire measures of EI are susceptible to faking and other response biases. Procedures exist for limiting or taking into account faking; for example, forcing respondents to choose between two or more equally attractive alternatives (Ziegler et al., 2011). Until such time as these techniques are implemented into these questionnaires and studied using instructed faking designs, we believe questionnaire measures of EI should only be used in low-stakes (e.g., self-help) and research settings.

SUMMARY AND CONCLUSIONS

Quite a lot of what we might loosely call "emotional intelligence" is captured by the existing personality dimensions of the FFM. Extraversion relates to positive emotion and social competency, emotional stability to calmness (low negative affect) and resilience, agreeableness to empathy and interpersonal sensitivity, conscientiousness to self-motivation and impulse control, and openness to artistic expression of emotion. However, it is misleading to relate any of these traits to some general EI, because each is associated with a complex pattern of strengths and weaknesses.

Efforts at developing questionnaires for trait EI face two formidable obstacles. The first is to demonstrate that self-reports provide valid measures of ability, in the face of much contrary evidence. This barrier appears to be insuperable. Several contemporary questionnaire developers have redefined questionnaire-EI as "trait EI," assigning the construct firmly to the personality rather than to the ability domain. It is, to say the least, terminologically confusing to refer to personality traits as "intelligence." The second obstacle is the need to show that trait EI measures add usefully to existing personality scales, such as those for the FFM, in spite of much overlap between measures.

We arrived at a mixed appraisal of the usefulness of trait EI scales. On the negative side, the meaningfulness of overall EI or trait EQ is questionable, the dimensional structure of trait EI is uncertain, many specific dimensions seem largely redundant with existing personality dimensions, and criterion validity for objective and real-life criteria is often unimpressive. On the positive side, researchers have identified some dimensions that correlate only modestly with the FFM, and may add something new to our understanding of the role of personality in emotional competencies. Some researchers are starting to demonstrate that these new facets of personality may be more predictive than existing constructs.

There appear to be two requisites for future research. First, the dimensional structure of trait EI and its relationship to the FFM needs to be clarified. We appear to have some dimensions that are poorly captured by existing FFM scales, but it is unclear exactly what they are. It would help too if questionnaire developers were more forthright about what is new and what is recycled in trait EI measures.

Second, to pick up a theme from Chapter 1, progress remains limited by a lack of theory in the field. Models of trait still appear to be shaped primarily by the researcher's subjective personal impressions of what traits should be sampled, rather than a coherent theoretical framework. We saw that existing personality research establishes individual differences in several qualitatively different emotion processes, including brain circuits for emotion, cognitive appraisal and coping processes, and mood-regulation and environmental interactions. Trait EI researchers have accomplished disappointingly little in linking trait EI to specific mechanisms of these kinds. On the positive side, some of the research we have reviewed suggests good prospects for theory-driven research, especially if researchers focus on specific competencies rather than some nebulous EQ. For example, enough theories exist in fields such as mood-regulation, interpersonal communication, and impulse control to refine the trait EI constructs relevant to these fields. A focus on more specialized trait measures may yield more than the futile pursuit of some global EQ.

Emotional Intelligence as a New Form of Cognitive Ability

Like all young men I set out to be a genius, but mercifully laughter intervened.

Lawrence Durrell, 1960

As we saw in Chapters 1 and 2, there are several ways of conceptualizing emotional intelligence (EI) from the perspective of psychological science. In Chapter 2, we explored the idea that EI is a part of the wider domain of personality; in this chapter, we focus on Jack Mayer and Peter Salovey's idea that EI is a new form of intelligence (or cognitive ability) (e.g., Mayer, Caruso, & Salovey, 1999). Our exposition here addresses whether EI refers to a true ability rather than typical behaviors and ways of experiencing the world through emotions. Research on cognitive ability has already identified disparate dimensions that describe a person's cognitive capacities, such as verbal comprehension, quantitative reasoning, fluid ability, and the like. There are also well-validated models of the structure of intelligence that allow us to define, classify, and measure a wide variety of cognitive skills (see e.g., Carroll, 1993; Kaufman, 2009; McGrew, 2005; Roberts & Lipnevich, in press).

If we wish to consider EI (or "ability EI") as part of this well-defined domain of cognitive abilities, then there are, as we argued in Chapter 2, several steps to be taken. First, we need some working definition of EI that informs us of the many components of intelligence that are relevant to emotional functioning and to both interpersonal and intrapersonal success. Second, having demarcated the domain comprising "ability EI," we must determine how many specific dimensions are needed to capture its main features. Third, we need to develop reliable assessments that will measure these cognitive abilities. In practice, this goal leads to the development of objective, performance-based assessments. (Imagine how easy it would have been to get into college if you merely had to self-report on your cognitive skills!) Fourth, these assessments must be validated as predictors of behaviors and outcomes indicative of EI. As for personality, this must be achieved within the context of some underlying psychological theory or pertinent classification of cognitive skills. Ability EI measures should also tell us something new about cognitive abilities that we did not already know from standard assessments of intellectual capacity. Similar to the case we made when discussing self-assessments of EI and personality, there is no point in reinventing a well-oiled, fully functioning, wheel.

In this chapter, we examine research efforts to develop valid performance-based assessments of ability EI. As necessary background and context, we begin with a short account of cognitive ability models. Next, we look at the "ability EI" construct and various attempts to develop objective indicators of this concept. We also briefly review evidence surrounding the validity of performance-based EI tests. The chapter concludes with some proposed issues that the ability EI perspective might address in the future to arrive at a more compelling scientific model.

HUMAN COGNITIVE ABILITIES

We begin by taking a look at what is known about the measurement of cognitive abilities, and how EI might fit into contemporary models. It is sometimes useful to describe ability in terms of a single, general factor, which may be crudely labeled as "IQ." However, contemporary researchers distinguish a large number of more specifically defined abilities. Research on psychological measurement (*psychometrics*) aims to describe precisely what the various dimensions of ability are, and how they are related to one another. A model of this kind is referred to as a *structural model*.

Contemporary structural models are arranged in layers that represent different levels of "grain-size" in describing ability. Depending on the context, we may work with either a rather large set of finely differentiated abilities (e.g., foreign language learning ability), or with a coarser-grained account of only a few, more broadly defined abilities such as crystallized intelligence. Once we have such a multi-leveled model we can try to find a place in it for both general EI (presumably a somewhat broad ability), as well as the more narrowly defined specific abilities that constitute EI, such as emotion perception.

Structural Models of Cognitive Ability

As is often the case, what specialists mean by "intelligence" is not quite the same as the everyday meaning of the word. The available myriad online dictionaries variously define intelligence as "the capacity to acquire and apply knowledge," "the ability to deal with new or trying situations," and "understanding; intellect; mind." By contrast, over the years, many famous psychologists have attempted to provide a more focused definition. Boring (1923) defined intelligence as "what intelligence tests test." Spearman (1923, 1927) took it to be "the eduction of relations and correlates" (note this is not a typographical error, eduction is related to deduction, and means the drawing out of something that is latent or hidden). Wechsler (1974), who developed some of the most popular measures of intelligence (e.g., the Wechsler Adult Intelligence Scale and the Wechsler Intelligence Scale for Children), defined the concept as "the aggregate or global capacity of the individual to think rationally, to act purposefully, and to deal effectively with his/her environment." Each of these definitions, as well as several others offered as alternatives, have limitations. For instance, in Spearman's (1927) account, it is considered unscientific to presuppose the existence of some force that lies behind or explains behavior (Ryle, 1949). We have moved beyond the idea of a homunculus, that little person in our heads who controls our behavior, no matter how intriguing the concept was to early humans. The operational definition is also unsound, since it begs the question: What is an intelligence test?

This definitional controversy can be resolved if one accepts the existence of not one, but several, relatively independent types of intelligence (Roberts & Lipnevich, in press). This argument is buttressed by various surveys of the ordinary person in the street. Across many different cultures, such surveys indicate that people believe intelligence is composed of anywhere between three to six broad classes (i.e., verbal ability, problem-solving ability, interpersonal intelligence, intrapersonal intelligence, intellectual self-promotion, and intellectual self-effacement) (e.g., Sternberg, Conway, Ketron, & Bernstein, 1981; Yang & Sternberg, 1997). This argument is also consistent with a major summary of the available literature conducted by Carroll (1993), where he re-analyzed nearly 500 studies. Carroll's re-analysis of each data set led him to a model having three levels (or strata). On the first layer are a variety of narrowly defined primary mental abilities, such as verbal comprehension and number facility. On the second level are broad cognitive abilities, such as fluid and crystallized intelligence and factors tied to memory and perceptual processes (see e.g., Cattell, 1963, 1987; Horn & Hofer, 1992; Horn & Noll, 1994; Roberts & Stankov, 1999). Finally, at the highest level is a single, general intelligence factor. Figure 3.1 depicts these levels (in what specialists call a hierarchical model).

This model may be best understood by reference to Figure 3.1, in concert with materials presented in Table 3.1. This table provides definitions of the major components of the theory, as well as sample tests, which should give the reader a flavor for the processes underlying each cognitive factor. Note that, in the interests of space, the first level of concepts is not defined. There are a large number of primary mental abilities (Carroll discusses approximately 66 of them), and researchers continue to uncover still further factors (e.g., abilities tied to sensory processes, especially smell and touch). Generally, however, factors at the bottom of this hierarchy are also of lesser importance than those higher up. The model is roughly equivalent to the periodic table in chemistry: One can consult it to ascertain the composition of a particular form of intelligence or to assemble a battery of tests to ensure coverage of relevant cognitive skills (see Flanagan McGrew, & Ortiz, 2000). For example, general intelligence, or g, is comprised, to varying extent, of constructs measured by each of the broad cognitive (i.e., Stratum II) abilities. By contrast, fluid intelligence is comprised of a much more limited set, including most especially reasoning concepts and measures designed to assess reasoning skill with verbal, pictorial, and numeric contents.

The importance of three-stratum concepts extends to educational interventions, public policy on testing, and sociological issues. For example, Carroll pointed out that the achievement gap probably does not apply to all of the broad cognitive abilities, while there is compelling evidence that crystallized intelligence can be enhanced more readily than fluid intelligence (Kyllonen, Roberts, & Stankov, 2008). Carroll's model has also proven

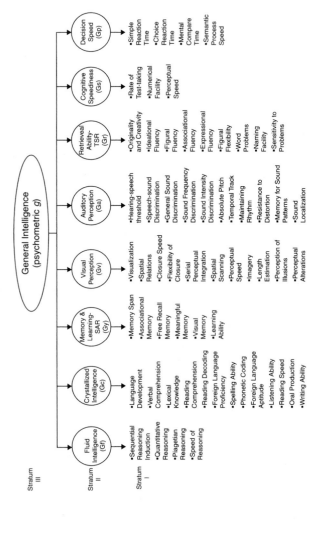

FIGURE 3.1 The Structure of Human Cognitive Abilities (after Carroll, 1993).

TABLE 3.1 DEFINITIONS OF THE MAJOR CONSTRUCTS OF THREE-STRATUM THEORY, ALONG WITH REPRESENTATIVE PRIMARY MENTAL ABILITIES IDENTIFIED BY CARROLL (1993), AND SAMPLE TESTS AND ITEMS (ADAPTED FROM ROBERTS & LIPNEVICH, IN PRESS)

Construct	Definition	Sample Tests and Item
Stratum III		
General Intelligence (*g*)	A factor emphasizing the level of difficulty that can be mastered in performing induction, reasoning, visualization, and language comprehension tasks.	In principle, all reliable and construct validated test scores serve to measure *g* to varying degree. There is a natural ordering of Stratum II constructs with respect to the general intelligence factor, such that Gf is closer to *g* than Gc, which in turn is closer than Gy and so forth.
Stratum II		
Fluid Intelligence (Gf)	A cognitive ability that depends minimally on formal learning and acculturation.	*Induction:* What are the next two numbers in this sequence: 2 9 4 7 6 5 8 3 10 1 ? ? (i.e., 12, -1) *Nonsense Syllogisms:* Is the following argument true or false? All vegetables are whales. All whales are computers. Therefore, all vegetables are computers. (i.e., True) *Symbol Sets:* Find the group of letters that does not belong with the others? (e.g., ABCD, GHIJ, DERS, UVWX, MNOP).

(*Continued*)

81

TABLE 3.1 DEFINITIONS OF THE MAJOR CONSTRUCTS OF THREE-STRATUM THEORY, ALONG WITH REPRESENTATIVE PRIMARY MENTAL ABILITIES IDENTIFIED BY CARROLL (1993), AND SAMPLE TESTS AND ITEMS (ADAPTED FROM ROBERTS & LIPNEVICH, IN PRESS) (CONTINUED)

Construct	Definition	Sample Tests and Item
Crystallized Intelligence (Gc)	A cognitive ability reflecting the influences of formal learning and acculturation (including education).	*Vocabulary:* What is the meaning of the word, "cantankerous?" (i.e., difficult or irritating to deal with) *General Knowledge:* The author of the book "Moby Dick" was? (i.e., Herman Melville) *Anagrams:* Rearrange the following letters to make a word: "g-r-e-s-n-i-a-o-n" (i.e., reasoning) *Analogies:* Einstein is to physics, as Zeidner is to? (i.e., psychology☺)
Memory and Learning (Gy)	A cognitive ability involved in any task involving retention of material over a short period of time (usually less than 30s).	*Digit Span Forwards:* The test administrator presents a series of digits with a one-second delay between each. The participant recalls the digit string (Stimuli: 2 4 6 7 5 9). *Digit Span Backwards:* Test as above, although this time the participant is required to recall the numbers in reverse (i.e., 9 5 7 6 4 2).
Broad Visualization (Gv)	A cognitive ability involved in any task that requires the perception of visual forms.	*Paper Folding:* Drawings illustrate two or three folds made in a square sheet of paper. A hole is also punched into the paper. The participant chooses from among a series of other drawings how the sheet would appear when fully opened. *Hidden Figures:* The task is to decide which of five geometrical figures is embedded within a complex pattern.

Broad Auditory Reception (Ga)	A cognitive ability involved in any task or performance that requires the perception of, or discrimination of, auditory patterns of speech or sound.	*Auditory Closure:* Words are presented orally, but with some sounds omitted. The task is to complete the word (e.g., stimuli: "door/ep" [doorstep]). *RST Test:* A sequence of the letters R, S, and T is heard (e.g., "R-S-S-T-R-T-R-S-R"). The participant indicates how many times each letter appeared (i.e., 4-Rs, 3-Ss, 2-Ts). *Words in Noise:* Write words spoken against a background of simulated aircraft noise.
Retrieval Ability (Gr)	A cognitive ability involved in any task involving retention of material learned in the distant past.	*Ideational Fluency:* In two minutes list the members of a broadly defined class, with the score being the number of things listed (e.g., "Fluids that burn"?) *Topics:* In four minutes, write as many ideas as possible about a given topic (e.g., "reality television").
Broad Cognitive Speed (Gs)	A cognitive ability involved in any task that requires rapid cognitive processing of information.	*Number Comparison:* Indicate whether or not the two digit strings are the same or different (e.g., "36795438 1937—36795438 1937"). (Note, time, rather than accuracy, is the variable of interest.) *Finding As:* Find all the "A's" in a large passage of text, given only 90 s.
Broad Decision Speed (Gp)	An ability involved in any task that requires rapid processing of basic sensorimotor stimuli.	*Card-sorting:* Sort a deck of playing cards into colors, suits, or number. *Posner Task:* Indicate whether two letters have the same meaning (e.g., Aa—Yes) or are physically the same (e.g., Aa—No).

influential in the development of intelligence and achievement tests. Thus, recent revisions to well-known measures such as the Stanford-Binet, Wechsler, Kaufman, and Woodcock-Johnson intelligence scales have used this framework (see Kaufman, 2009). The uniqueness of Carroll's model is that virtually all models of cognitive abilities may be subsumed under its broad umbrella. While coverage of all such models is outside the scope of the present chapter (see, however, Kaufman, 2009), we give specific features of these models in Table 3.2, along with how each aligns with what is sometimes called (for obvious reasons) the three-stratum model.

Empirical evidence from several lines of inquiry supports the distinctions between the major dimensions of this theory. Thus, data have shown:

1. *The constructs are replicable across diverse populations using factor analysis.* Factor analysis is a statistical technique for identifying underlying dimensions in multivariate data sets. In exploratory factor analysis (EFA) statistical "rules-of-thumb" are used for exploring the data. By contrast, in confirmatory factor analysis (CFA), the researcher tests a specific hypothesis about underlying dimensions against the data. Both EFA and CFA support the existence of each of the cognitive ability constructs given in Table 3.1. The ensuing model derives from analysis conducted in no fewer than 20 countries, with data collected since 1925, involving anywhere from 6 to 100 variables per study, on populations that include university, community college, and K-12 students; military enlistees and officers; gifted individuals; community volunteers; prison inmates; hearing impaired; and many other types of special populations (see Carroll, 1993). Since the completion of Carroll's opus, numerous studies have replicated the general structure encapsulated by this theory using CFA techniques with large, representative (or carefully selected) samples spanning the age range from 6 to 90 years (see e.g., Roberts, Goff, Anjoul, Kyllonen, Pallier, & Stankov, 2000;

TABLE 3.2 A SUMMARY OF PROMINENT MODELS OF INTELLIGENCE AND THEIR RELATIONSHIP TO CARROLL'S (1993) THREE-STRATUM MODEL, ALONG WITH PROSPECTS FOR INCLUDING EI IN THEIR FRAMEWORK

Theory	Prominent Researcher	Correspondence with Carroll	Key Notion	Prospect for EI
General Intelligence (g)	Spearman (1923)	Stratum III only	Two factors underlying mental test performance: A general factor (g, which is common to all intellectual tasks) and specific factors (s, which are unique to any cognitive test).	*Problematic*: EI requires the presence of at least one other intelligence (e.g., rational intelligence) for the qualifier (i.e. emotional) to have currency.
Primary Mental Abilities	Thurstone (1938)	Stratum I only	Seven primary mental abilities (Verbal Comprehension, Verbal Fluency, Number Facility, Spatial Visualization, Memory, Inductive Reasoning, Deductive Reasoning, Practical Problem-Solving, and Perceptual Speed), collectively comprise intelligence.	*Plausible*: Constructs such as Emotion Perception and Emotional Management could be added to a list that already exceeds 66 since Thurstone's original formulation.

(Continued)

85

TABLE 3.2   A SUMMARY OF PROMINENT MODELS OF INTELLIGENCE AND THEIR RELATIONSHIP
TO CARROLL'S (1993) THREE-STRATUM MODEL, ALONG WITH PROSPECTS FOR
INCLUDING EI IN THEIR FRAMEWORK (CONTINUED)

Theory	Prominent Researcher	Correspondence with Carroll	Key Notion	Prospect for EI
Structure of Intellect (SOI)	Guilford (1967, 1988)	Stratum I (but not for all constructs)	Every cognitive task involves 3 facets: 5 operations, 5 types of content, and 6 forms of product. The SOI has been symbolized as a rectangular prism composed of 150 smaller prisms, each representing a primary mental ability.	*Present:* A related construct—behavorial knowledge (social intelligence) is part of the SOI model.
Multiple Intelligences	Gardner (1983)	Stratum II (but not for all constructs)	Seven independent types of intelligence: linguistic, spatial, logical-mathematical, musical, bodily-kinesthetic, intrapersonal, and interpersonal.	*Present:* Inter- and intrapersonal intelligence involves understanding people, behavior, motive, and/or emotion.

Taub & McGrew, 2004; Tirre & Field, 2002; Tulsky & Price, 2003).

2. *Meaningful differential relations with cognitive processes.* Each of the factors has unique underlying cognitive processes and functions associated with them. For example, fluid intelligence has been tied to working memory (Kyllonen & Christal, 1990); while crystallized intelligence has been related to long-term working memory (e.g., Horn, 2008; Horn & Masunaga, 2000).

3. *Differential test-criterion relations.* Each of the factors shares different predictive validities for a number of outcomes, such as job and academic performance, quality of life, long-term employment status, and psychological well-being (e.g., Lee, 2008). This includes the prediction of mortality, which some commentators consider ultimate validity (see O'Toole & Stankov, 1992).

4. *Differential sensitivity to training and other forms of intervention.* Each construct is differentially sensitive to various forms of intervention (e.g., Eilander et al., 2010; Kyllonen, Roberts, & Stankov, 2008; Stankov, 1986), including those based on nutrition- and health-related factors (Benton, 2008). In general, over the life span, fluid intelligence is less suscep-tible to intervention than the crystallized intelligence, as are many of the cognitive factors tied to perceptual processes. However, there are periods, especially prior to adulthood, where these factors appear more malleable.

5. *Different learning, developmental trajectories, and genetic com-ponents.* The various factors of the three-stratum model also appear subject to different learning and genetic influences (e.g., Horn & Hofer, 1992; Horn & Noll, 1994). Evidence also suggests the various cognitive abilities have distinct under-lying neurological and physiological mechanisms (Stankov, Danthiir, Williams, Gordon, Pallier, & Roberts, 2006). Particularly important to the fields of human development and gerontology (i.e., the study of aging), has been the very consistent (and near lawful) finding that fluid intelligence

improves fairly quickly over the formative years on up until the late-twenties. It then shows a reasonably slow, but steady decline over the life span. By contrast, and somewhat heartening to the three authors of the current book, crystallized intelligence continues to improve until very, very old age.

El and Broad Cognitive Abilities

The three-stratum model is analogous to the Big Five model covered in Chapter 2, in that it is a consensual model. That is, just like the Big Five is considered the most efficacious model for understanding and systematizing the body of facts surrounding human personality, the three-stratum model is considered the current state-of-the-art in intelligence research. It is therefore important to note that Carroll (1993) did make a number of relevant comments concerning the concept of EI in his synthesis of the psychometric literature. In particular, Carroll (1993) argues that there is evidence for a domain of behavioral knowledge, which is relatively independent from the other constructs of his model. This domain includes assessment of a range of abilities that appear important in the decoding and processing of social and emotional content. Carroll also suggests that the domains encapsulated by behavioral knowledge require more careful and systematic exploration than had been accomplished up to the time of his writing. In short, three-stratum theory leaves open the possibility for new forms of intelligence that have hitherto not been identified by previous research.

Indeed, although many commentators rightfully claim that systematic study of EI can be traced back to the early 1990s (see Chapter 1), EI appears as a construct that has certainly been entertained in almost all extant cognitive ability models. To highlight this feature, consider again Table 3.2, and especially the final column. Here we have indicated whether or not a given popular intelligence model could entertain (or in fact, include) EI.

Strikingly, with the exception of Spearman, all of these models could plausibly include an EI factor, a finding that will doubtless not only surprise the casual reader, but has confounded more than a few self-proclaimed experts. Indeed, with the added exception of Thurstone, many models have included specific constructs that closely resemble EI. And even Spearman may have had his doubts. Thus, in 1947, Spearman sponsored a doctoral dissertation in his laboratory at the University of London, which did give consideration to a concept bearing close similarities to contemporary notions of EI; something termed "the psychological ability." This construct was thought to involve the "ability to judge correctly the feelings, moods, [and] motivations of the individual" (Wedeck, 1947, p. 133). Wedeck (1947) operationalized "the psychological ability" through a number of tests, which look remarkably similar to contemporary performance-based measures of EI (e.g., pictures portraying the facial expressions of laughter, doubt, confusion, etc.). Based on a large-scale study, Wedeck argued that "the psychological ability" exhibited some distinctiveness from verbal and nonverbal intelligence tests.

In short, unlike the case with personality, where emotions already appear subsumed by many of incumbent constructs (see Chapter 2), there seems both precedent and scope for expanding the three-stratum model to include emotional abilities. Viewed from this perspective, research aimed at uncovering the structure and correlates of EI is vindicated, providing that tests meeting the highest standards can be devised to capture this construct. It is thus to a consideration of the measurement of ability EI, and its related research program, that we now turn.

ASSESSING EI USING MAXIMUM PERFORMANCE APPROACHES: THE FIRST WAVE

Ability models, in general, consider EI as a form of intelligence that is best assessed by maximum performance tests (i.e. tests that assess the upper limits of the individual's performance). Such tests contain items that have correct and incorrect answers and attempt to determine how proficient an individual is by examining one's best performance on a test, as with a standard intelligence test. Therefore, it allows for the measurement of an individual's actual ability rather than one's belief in his or her ability. Abilities related to both intra- and interpersonal phenomena may be assessed (e.g., predicting one's own emotional responses to an event versus predicting the responses of someone else). Maximum performance tests assess an individual's capability to, for example, perceive emotions in others via nonverbal (e.g., facial expressions, posture) and verbal (e.g., voice pitch, tone) cues. Correct answers to these types of items can be said to exist, for example, due to evolutionary and culturally engendered consensus relating to emotional information (Mayer, Salovey, & Caruso, 2000).

In this section, we review the best-known ability test for EI, developed by Jack Mayer, Peter Salovey, and their colleagues. We survey its validity, focusing especially on whether the test scores actually predict measures of emotional functioning. We will also consider some of the weaknesses of this approach.

The Mayer-Salovey-Caruso Emotional Intelligence Test (MSCEIT)

The four-branch model of EI, which we introduced in Chapter 1 (see Figure 1.3), is generally used as the basis for defining emotional abilities (see Mayer & Salovey, 1997; Mayer, Caruso, Salovey, & Sitarenios, 2001). Under this framework, EI consists of four branches of abilities that increase in complexity from the first to fourth branch. The component abilities in the higher branches depend or build on abilities in the lower branches. At the simplest level (Branch 1), EI is the perception and expression of emotions (Perception). Branch 2 consists of the integration of emotions in thought processes (Facilitation). Branch 3 includes the understanding of emotion labels, relations between emotions, associations between emotions and circumstances, and transitions among emotions (Understanding). Finally, the highest branch involves managing emotions to moderate negative, and enhance positive, emotions (Management). The first two branches are collectively defined as Experiential EI (expression, perception, and generation of emotions) and the last two as Strategic EI (the understanding and management of emotions; e.g., Mayer, Salovey, & Caruso, 2002).

Using the above framework, Mayer and colleagues have developed the Mayer-Salovey-Caruso Emotional Intelligence Test (MSCEIT; Mayer et al., 2002). Table 3.3 provides a brief capsule description of the tests comprising the MSCEIT, as well as how each task matches to the theoretical constructs described above. As for cognitive abilities, the branches are ordered from left to right, such that Emotional Management is thought to be closer to the general EI factor than is Emotional Understanding, and so forth. As the task descriptions may be rather cryptic, we also give the reader a feeling for an operational item in Figure 3.2. Recently, a youth version (the MSCEIT-YV) has also been developed to assess the four branches (Mayer, Salovey, & Caruso, in press), although published literature on it remains rather sparse at present.

Evidence for the Four-Branch Model

Whenever researchers grapple with measurement issues in the physical sciences, an attempt is made to develop a set of standards. The issue is no different for psychological and educational testing, which gain rigor by having standard procedures for test development, administration, interpretation, and use. These standards are known as *The Standards for Educational and Psychological Tests* (American Educational Research Association, American Psychological Association, & National Council on Measurement in Education, 1999). In concert with a careful examination of these standards, current researchers have

TABLE 3.3 OVERVIEW OF THE FOUR-BRANCH MODEL ALONG WITH TESTS COMPRISING THE MSCEIT (ADAPTED FROM MAYER ET AL., 2002)

Level	Abilities and Indicators		
General	Emotional Intelligence (EI)		
Areas	"Strategic EI" assesses ability to understand and manage emotions without necessarily experiencing the feelings of emotion		"Experiential EI" is the ability to perceive, respond, and manipulate emotional information without necessarily understanding its meaning
Branches	"Managing Emotions" by using feelings to create better outcomes	"Understanding Emotions" and how they change over time	"Facilitating Thought" through cognitive processing of emotions and decisions	The ability to "Perceive Emotions" in faces and pictures
Tasks	*Management:* Participants rate how effective an action is to manage mood *Relations:* Participants rate how effective various responses are to emotion-laden situations	*Blends:* Participants answer questions assessing which combinations of emotions form complex emotions *Changes:* Participants answer questions assessing which emotions are related to particular situations	*Sensations:* Participants make judgments about the similarity of an emotion to a physical sensation *Facilitation:* Participants rate the helpfulness of three different moods	*Faces:* Participants rate the presence of emotions in photographs of faces *Pictures:* Participants rate the presence of emotions in pictures of art and nature

Indicate how much of each emotion is expressed by this face?

No Happiness	1	2	3	4	5	Extreme Happiness
No Anger	1	2	3	4	5	Extreme Anger
No Fear	1	2	3	4	5	Extreme Fear

FIGURE 3.2 Example of the MSCEIT Item Format (this example would assess the Emotional Perception Branch).

established specific criteria for evaluating the validity of maximum performance EI tests (see Matthews et al., 2006; Mayer et al., 1999; Roberts, Zeidner, & Matthews, 2007). Specifically, there appear to be three major evaluative criteria. Briefly, these are:

1. EI scores should show moderate, positive correlations with other tests of cognitive ability, including standard intelligence tests. The existence of positive correlations among intelligence tests is a universal finding throughout Carroll's (and other scientists') research; measures of EI should be no different. At the same time, these correlations should not be so high as to suggest that EI measures exactly the same type of construct (or constructs) that other cognitive ability tests already assess.

2. Maximum performance EI scores should relate to personality in the same manner that other tests of intelligence tend to do; that is, have a correlation (r) that is equal to .30 or less (Ackerman & Heggestad, 1997; Ashton, Lee, Vernon, & Jang, 2000).

3. EI scores should be meaningfully related to important outcomes valued by society, such as mental health, grade point average, and relationship satisfaction. Conceivably, these scores should relate to indicators of social (e.g., social support, networking skills) and emotional (e.g., happiness, quality of life) functioning especially highly, indicating that EI operates in the domain of the emotions.

Maximum performance tests of EI need to meet these criteria. In particular, constructs assessed with EI measures must not duplicate existing intelligence constructs. And yet scores on EI tests should converge to some degree with results from other cognitive tests if EI is to qualify as a new type of intelligence. In addition, for EI to be a useful concept, it ought to meaningfully relate to some real-world outcomes not already predicted by existing ability and personality tests. The following passages review available evidence from the MSCEIT concerning each of these evaluative criteria.

1. *Relationships of EI with other measures of intelligence.* Available findings concerning the MSCEIT suggest that this measure assesses a new form of intelligence. Data relevant to this assertion are provided in Table 3.4. This table provides correlations from a large number of independent research studies conducted around the globe, with the results distilled using meta-analysis. (Meta-analysis is a statistical technique that averages findings from multiple studies, taking into account various statistical features of the data analyzed.) The studies covered by this table have typically measured each of the EI branches and either fluid (Gf) or crystallized (Gc) intelligence. Of note, the Emotional Understanding branch shares the highest relationship with Gc, but this correlation is not so large as to suggest that it is simply a repackaging of crystallized intelligence with a fancy new, PC-friendly label. Correlations with Gf are also universally lower than Gc, which appears consistent with

TABLE 3.4 META-ANALYTIC CORRELATIONS BETWEEN MSCEIT SCORES AND FLUID AND CRYSTALLIZED INTELLIGENCE FACTORS (ADAPTED FROM ROBERTS, SCHULZE, & MACCANN, 2008)

	Fluid Intelligence (Gf)	Crystallized Intelligence (Gc)
Emotional Perception	.08 Trivial	.13 Small
Assimilating Emotions	.09 Trivial	.15 Small
Emotional Understanding	.19 Small	.38 Moderate
Emotional Management	.13 Small	18 Small
Total score	.18 Small	.31 Moderate

Note: The descriptors below the numbers (whose hypothetical range is between −1.00 and 1.00) correspond to the terminology discussed in Chapter 2 for interpreting correlation coefficients.

various claims about the importance of acculturation (and training) to EI.

These studies have not typically examined the relationship of the MSCEIT to other cognitive ability factors, such as those listed in Table 3.1. In a recent study (Roberts, Betancourt, Burrus, et al., 2011) we did just this, administering cognitive measures of fluid and crystallized intelligence, broad visualization, broad retrieval ability, and a variety of other measures (e.g., quantitative reasoning), along with the MSCEIT. In this study, which sampled both university and community college students, the highest correlations remained with Emotional Understanding and crystallized intelligence. However, there were some other important findings. For example, broad visualization measures, which index visual processes, shared a moderate, positive correlation with the Emotional Perception branch of the MSCEIT, which also requires visual processing. As testament to the validity of the MSCEIT, some of the weakest correlations (i.e., approaching zero) between these subtests and cognitive measures were those assessing quantitative skills. In a separate study (MacCann et al., submitted) we performed EFA and CFA of the MSCEIT, along with these cognitive ability measures. The results suggest that Emotional Perception, Understanding, and Management (but not Emotional Facilitation) operate as though primary mental abilities. Above these is broad EI, which not only resembles Stratum II abilities, but also is independent from other broad cognitive factors.

2. *Relationships of EI with personality.* Table 3.5 summarizes evidence from a meta-analysis linking MSCEIT scores to the Big Five personality dimensions. Generally, scores from each of the respective MSCEIT branches are not strongly related to the various personality dimensions. Indeed, only Emotional Management shows moderate correlations, relating to Agreeableness around 0.30, and to a lesser extent with Openness at nearly 0.20. Given that intelligence tasks do tend to correlate with Openness (at around 0.30; Ackerman & Heggestad, 1997) and EI is a form of intelligence, a relationship of medium strength with Openness can be expected.

Exactly why Emotional Management, but not the other branches, relates meaningfully to personality factors is worth considering. Mayer et al. (2001) state that all branches assess cognitive abilities but that Management must also "balance many factors including the motivational, emotion, and cognitive" and has an "interface with personality and personal goals" (p. 235). Although all branches of EI require processing of information concerning emotions, Management is the only one that involves judgments that clearly fall outside the realm of the intelligence domain. For example, whether one cares if other people experience negative emotions is a type of judgment that influences responses to Management tasks. A person very low on Agreeableness may not consider a crying or angry college

TABLE 3.5 META-ANALYTIC CORRELATIONS BETWEEN MSCEIT SCORES AND THE BIG FIVE PERSONALITY FACTORS (ADAPTED FROM ROBERTS, SCHULZE, & MACCANN, 2008)

	O	C	E	A	N
Emotional Perception	.04 Trivial	.01 Trivial	.00 Trivial	.08 Trivial	−.08 Trivial
Assimilating Emotions	.08 Trivial	.07 Trivial	.01 Trivial	.13 Small	−.10 Small
Emotional Understanding	.14 Small	.05 Trivial	.02 Trivial	.11 Small	−.06 Trivial
Emotional Management	.18 Small	.12 Small	.10 Small	.27 Small-Moderate	−.09 Trivial
Total score	.12 Small	.11 Small	.11 Small	.26 Small-Moderate	−.14 Small

Notes: O = Openness, C = Conscientiousness, E = Extraversion, A = Agreeableness, N = Neuroticism
The descriptors below the numbers (whose hypothetical range is between −1.00 and 1.00) correspond to the terminology discussed in Chapter 2 for interpreting correlation coefficients.

classmate to be particularly disturbing or problematic, whereas someone high on Agreeableness might view this as a serious disturbance.

The correlation patterns among EI and the Big Five personality factors are quite unlike the patterns found for self-reports of EI. For the latter, the strongest relationships were with Extraversion and Neuroticism (see Chapter 2). Standing in stark contrast, Extraversion and Neuroticism show the weakest correlations with the MSCEIT. Note too that the significant correlations between Agreeableness and Emotional Management and total EI, albeit of theoretical interest, are not too high. Clearly, variables assessed with the MSCEIT are distinctive enough from personality factors to suggest they are outside the realm of the Big Five model of personality.

Given our previous comments concerning the large overlap between personality and trait EI in Chapter 2, one further finding is worth mentioning. The correlation between the MSCEIT and trait EI seldom exceeds 0.20, and in some studies is even negative in sign (Zeidner, Matthews, & Roberts, 2009). This set of findings suggests that trait EI measures and the MSCEIT are largely unrelated. In turn, this suggests that the label "emotional intelligence" can be reserved for one, but not both, constructs. We assume from our exposition thus far that the astute reader might be aware on which form of measurement we are hedging our bets.

3. *Relationships of EI with valued outcomes.* One of the possible advantages associated with EI is the prediction of valued criteria in formal academic and workplace environments, as well as areas of life where understanding emotions and their management may be more important than reasoning or knowledge (e.g., Bastian, Burns, & Nettelbeck, 2005; Roberts, Schulze, Zeidner, & Matthews, 2005; Roberts, MacCann, Matthews, & Zeidner, 2010). Space precludes a detailed discussion of all such relations, though they have been the topic of recent reviews (e.g., Mayer, Roberts, & Barsade, 2008; Zeidner et al., 2009). Some representative findings between EI and criteria covered by these commentators include:

   (i) *Relationship satisfaction.* Brackett, Warner, and Bosco (2005) found that couples where both partners were low on EI reported (a) lower relationship depth, (b) lower support and positive relationship quality, and (c) higher conflict and negative relationship quality. We address the conceptual meaning of these correlations in Chapter 4.

   (ii) *Social interaction.* Lopes et al. (2004) found that the Emotional Management predicted self-reports of positive interactions with friends. Emotional Management also correlated moderately with reports by friends of positive and negative interactions and emotional support. After controlling for the Big Five personality factors and gender, almost all relationships remained significant.

(iii) *Giftedness.* Zeidner, Shani-Zinovich, Matthews, and Roberts (2005) found a group of gifted students scoring higher on the MSCEIT than did a group of age-matched controls. Mean differences were especially high for Emotional Understanding and Management, while both Emotional Perception and Facilitation resulted in negligible differences between the groups.

(iv) *Teacher ratings of social and emotional competence.* In one of the few published studies with the MSCEIT-YV, Rivers et al. (in press) found that the higher the student's MSCEIT-YV scores, the fewer externalizing, internalizing, school, and behavioral problems reported by the teacher.

(v) *Emotional labor.* Emotional labor has been defined as the extent to which workers are expected to express positive emotion as part and parcel of the job (Grandey, 2003). In a recent meta-analysis, Joseph and Newman (2010) found that MSCEIT (and especially the Emotional Management branch) predicted job performance in high emotional labor occupations (e.g., sales and marketing), but showed a zero correlation with job performance in low emotional labor occupations (e.g., research scientists [which is again fortunate for the three folks who penned the current book]).

(vi) *Coping with stress.* Gohm, Corser, and Dalsky (2005) found significant relationships between MSCEIT subscale scores and coping styles. Emotional Understanding and Management were moderately, negatively correlated with behavioral disengagement and denial (the negative sign is expected, because these are problematic behaviors). At the same time, Emotional Management also correlated positively with seeking emotional and instrumental social support. In another study, MacCann, Fogarty, Zeidner, and Roberts (2011) found that coping styles and a combination of Emotional Understanding and Management explained 28% of the variation in grade point average for a group of community college students.

(vii) *Self-control.* Brackett, Rivers, Shiffman, Lerner, and Salovey (2006) found that MSCEIT total scores correlated moderately and negatively with constructive/destructive responses after controlling for the Big Five personality factors, psychological well-being, empathy, life satisfaction, and Verbal SAT (again, negative correlations are expected because of the nature of the criteria). Notably, these relations were found only for the male participants, which may not surprise many of our female readers.

(viii) *Drug and alcohol use.* In another series of studies, total EI scores correlated negatively with self-reported use and intention to use tobacco and alcohol products (Trinidad & Johnson, 2002; Trinidad et al., 2005). Strategic EI has also been found to correlate negatively with self-reported illegal drug use (Brackett, Mayer, & Warner, 2004).

(ix) *Presence of psychopathology.* EI also appears related to a number of psychopathological syndromes, as further discussed in Chapter 6. For example, Hertel, Schütz, and Lammers (2009) administered the MSCEIT to patients diagnosed with major depressive disorder, substance abuse disorder, or borderline personality disorder, as well as a matched nonclinical control group. Findings showed that all clinical groups differed from controls with respect to their overall EI score, with Emotional Understanding and Emotional Management best distinguishing between the various groups. Aguirre, Sergi, and Levy (2008) found similar results for persons high in schizotypy, while Kee et al. (2009)

observed analogous results in a group of individuals diagnosed with schizophrenia.

In summarizing the available evidence with the MSCEIT, the Management branch and, to a lesser extent, Understanding appear to be key predictors of outcomes valued by society. On this basis, research directed toward the branch level appears more promising than efforts targeted at the general EI factor. Instead of a discussion of what EI predicts, it might be more informative to couch research questions in terms of what Emotional Management or Emotional Understanding predict, as these two constructs appear to be the most promising on the basis of the available evidence relating EI to outcomes. Indeed, such findings augur well for the importance of considering each of various strata of EI, rather than a single, general "ability" EI factor.

Problematic Features of the MSCEIT

It is a principle of good scientific writing to provide a warts-and-all account of any construct, and its associated measurement. Providing a one-sided account is fine for a debate or a journalistic, editorial, or opinion piece, but not scientific discourse. In short, there are problematic features of the MSCEIT that researchers are trying to grapple with in order both to improve measurement and to further the field. In the passages that follow, we cover two such features currently associated with the four-branch model. The first concerns the way that scores are derived from responses to the MSCEIT, and the second, various findings that have accrued with the instrument that are currently difficult to reconcile with both theory and practice.

1. *Scoring maximum emotional ability measures is different from traditional cognitive ability tests.* In traditional cognitive ability, aptitude, and achievement tests such as arithmetic, hidden figures, or vocabulary, organized systems such as mathematics, geometry, or semantics determine the correct answer

logically. There are no equivalent systems for determining the correct answer to measures that assess EI (Roberts, Zeidner, & Matthews, 2001; Zeidner, Matthews, & Roberts, 2001). This problematic state-of-affairs is the case because tasks from the Strategic Area (and especially Emotion Management) present situations that are designed to mirror the complexity of real-life situations (Roberts, Schulze, & MacCann, 2008). With such complexity, unambiguously applying a set of rules about Emotion Management would appear difficult, even if such a set of rules were available. Systems grounded in psychological, philosophical, legal, and/or other theories are not used as a basis for scoring the MSCEIT. This is true even for Emotion Perception, where this is demonstrably possible through various procedures (e.g., see Ekman, 2004; Matsumoto et al., 2000; Scherer, Banse, & Wallbott, 2001), which we take up later in this chapter. Instead, solutions to the problem of determining the correct answer are undertaken in two main ways: (1) expert-scoring and (2) consensus-scoring. A discussion of these scoring rubrics follows:

(i) *Expert-scoring.* This form of scoring uses a panel of experts who determine the correct answer. Expert-scoring does not solve the problem of finding a unique correct solution to the problems presented in EI tests; it simply pushes the specification of the correct answer one step back, into the specification of criteria for expertise. Academic study of the psychology of emotions certainly leads to enhanced knowledge in this domain and can therefore be considered as a reasonable criterion for expertise. (Although we acknowledge, along with many of the readers, some professors simply do not appear to be in touch with their own emotions, or for that matter, those of their students). However, as Roberts et al. (2001) proposed, there might be multiple domains of expertise, of which academic knowledge is only one. Other domains might include experience and procedural knowledge acquired in professions like counseling and pastoral care, or experience in understanding and managing people's relationships and goals (e.g., human-resource-related careers). At least at the time of writing, the MSCEIT expert-scoring system fails to take into account these various levels of expertise, relying exclusively on expert judgment from emotions researchers to determine the correctness of responses.

(ii) *Consensus-scoring.* In this form of scoring, a normative sample first completes the test. The proportion of participants choosing each response option subsequently becomes the score that is awarded for that option. For example, if 61% of the normative sample selected a scale point of "1" for rating the presence of happiness in the face of Figure 3.2, a response of "1" would get a score of 0.61 (see also Legree, Psotka, Tremble, & Bourne, 2005; MacCann, Roberts, Matthews, & Zeidner, 2004).

Using consensus to deduce the best answer might be conceptually problematic in some cases, particularly for ratings. As an example, people exceptionally good at facial expression recognition might perceive nuances of expression that the ordinary person would miss, and rate faces as showing some slight level of emotion where most people see no emotion at all. (This is presumably a skill much valued by those working in national security, protecting a country's borders.) These exceptionally sensitive people would receive low scores with consensus-scoring, despite a high level of perceptual skill. In short, consensus-scoring may actually punish the extremely gifted or talented, or certainly fail to differentiate between these "superior" and "normal" individuals.

Another concern with these scoring rubrics is that consensus and expert scores should be strongly related if they represent valid scoring methods. Currently, MSCEIT consensus scores are indeed strongly related to MSCEIT expert scores (correlations exceed 0.90; Mayer et al., 2001). However, this convergence of scoring was not true of earlier versions, particularly for Emotion Perception measures, where some correlations were near zero (Roberts et al., 2001). This discrepancy might have occurred because an earlier version of the MSCEIT used only two experts to derive the scoring key, who were both of the same ethnicity and gender, and close in age and socio-economic status. In any event, the composition of both the expert and consensual group needs to be carefully monitored. And, in principle, since we do not yet know how it influences the actual scoring rubrics, attempts should be made to ensure a representative sampling of both experts and novices across gender, ethnicity, socio-economic status, and age. Thus far, it does not appear that careful enough attention has been given to these issues in approaches to measurement adopted by exponents of the MSCEIT.

2. *Some questionable empirical findings with the MSCEIT.* While researchers report high reliability coefficients (i.e., 0.90 or above) for higher-order constructs such as general EI, Experiential EI, and the like, several subtests (e.g., Blends) and branches (e.g., Facilitation) of the MSCEIT have marginal (i.e., less than 0.60) reliabilities (see e.g., Barchard & Hakstian, 2004; Bastian et al., 2005). Strategies for improving the reliability of EI tests, such as increasing the number of test items, have so far not been tried out systematically. The addition of items is likely necessary if subscale scores, in particular, are going to be used to make high-stakes decisions (e.g., selecting an applicant to college or using the information to design a clinical intervention). There are also relatively few studies of the test-retest reliability of the MSCEIT. In sum, while the reliability of the MSCEIT appears adequate for global constructs, the jury is out on whether subscales, and sometimes even measures designed to assess very specific subcomponents of EI, have

high enough reliability for use in applied settings (Zeidner et al., 2009).

Another problematic feature of the MSCEIT concerns researchers' inability to recover all four branches of EI using the previously described technique of factor analysis. Although some studies suggest that the MSCEIT has four factors (Mayer, Salovey, Caruso, & Sitarenios, 2003), this has proven difficult to replicate. The problem appears largely with Emotional Facilitation (i.e., using emotions to facilitate thought) (see e.g., Roberts et al., 2006), which often fails to emerge as an independent construct. Missing from this program of research too, are tests for factorial invariance in EI across different age, gender, social, and ethnic groups. (Factorial invariance allows one to determine if the same test items define the same constructs regardless of what group is being analyzed and compared.) Indeed, in the absence of this information, purported group differences often found in the literature should be treated with a certain degree of caution.

Finally, while there are some compelling relations between ability-based EI and a range of criteria, including well-being, school grades, and job performance (see above), some studies fail to provide strong support for criterion validity. For example, the MSCEIT fails to predict job ratings when suitable statistical controls are put into place (e.g., Rode et al., 2008; Rode, Arthaud-Day, Mooney, Near, & Baldwin, 2008). This result also appears to hold true for leadership (Harms & Credé, 2010). Absence of supportive data has not deterred a cottage industry of trade texts linking EI to leadership (see e.g., Goleman et al., 2002). Related to this set of findings, another concern is that studies that do report positive results often fail to control for the overlap between cognitive ability and ability EI, and to a lesser degree, between personality and ability EI. Brackett and Mayer (2003) found that only one out of six correlations between the MSCEIT and social-emotional criteria remained significant with personality and ability controlled.

ASSESSING EI USING MAXIMUM PERFORMANCE APPROACHES: THE SECOND WAVE

In addition to the problems noted above for the MSCEIT, research needs to be conducted with different task paradigms (Roberts et al., 2008). When all research is conducted with the MSCEIT, there is effectively a single task paradigm (ratings of stimuli scored by consensus or expertise) always used to measure one construct (emotional abilities). With such biases, the disentanglement of method and construct effects through the use of multivariate designs and analyses cannot be undertaken (Shadish, Cook, & Campbell, 2002). An analogy from the intelligence research described above reveals the extent of this problem. Imagine if we only had one instrument that defined this important construct. It is unlikely knowledge concerning the aging of cognitive abilities or the valued outcomes intelligence predicts would be well understood, if at all. For example, we could not separate the differing effects of aging on fluid and crystallized intelligence. Indeed, methodological issues in EI measurement limit the number and types of claims that can be made about EI and its relationships with other constructs and criteria.

In the passages that follow, we describe three different research traditions that might be brought to bear on the assessment of EI. The first tradition is those set of paradigms that have frequently appeared in the experimental literature on emotions. These have seldom been examined in terms of individual differences or educational, clinical, or workplace applications. The second research tradition acknowledges the importance of information processing tasks in the three-stratum model and the fact that similar measures could be constructed to reflect the speed of emotional processing. The third research tradition is a fledgling: Promising new approaches to directly measure EI, which have appeared in the recent peer-reviewed literature. In these passages we provide a brief theoretical overview, a selection of findings, and a number of advantages that these measures hold over current EI assessments.

Emotion Recognition Tasks as Measures of EI

The study of emotions in facial expressions is a far older field of research than is the study of EI. Scientific research on facial expressions dates back more than a century, to Charles Darwin's seminal work, *The Expression of the Emotions in Man and Animals* (1872). In psychology, Paul Ekman and Carroll Izard's contributions to this field date back to the 1950s. Ekman's corpus of work includes the specification of lawful rules linking muscular changes to facial expressions in the form of the Facial Action Coding System (FACS; Ekman & Friesen, 1978; Ekman & Rosenberg, 1997). The FACS has been used as the basis for several research tools assessing the recognition of facial expressions (and, on a side note, has been explored by animation companies such as Pixar). We briefly describe a variety of recognition of facial expression tests in Table 3.6.

The vast research corpus in this domain should be applied to research on emotional abilities, especially given the prominence of these constructs to the Branch-1 factor. However, early research focused on these tasks as experimental paradigms or alternatively measures of group processes rather than individual differences; only in the last few years have some researchers begun to use these as EI indicators (see e.g., Austin, 2005; Roberts et al., 2006). An important feature of this group of tasks is that they have all been developed to have an answer key with one correct response (i.e., a veridical score). Obviously this is highly desirable when compared with the problems already noted for scoring the MSCEIT.

In addition to tests from this family of tasks that use faces as stimuli, there are currently assessments of emotion recognition ability for tone-of-voice, such as the Vocal Expression Recognition Index (Vocal-I). The DANVA "suite" of assessments also includes tests that assess the recognition of emotions from

TABLE 3.6 SAMPLE MEASURES OF EMOTION RECOGNITION ABILITY (ADAPTED FROM ROBERTS ET AL., 2010)

Test	Source	Description
Facial Recognition		
Japanese and Caucasian Brief Affect Recognition Test (JACBART)	Matsumoto et al. (2000)	Stimuli consist of briefly presented Japanese or Caucasian faces portraying one of seven emotions: happiness, contempt, disgust, sadness, anger, surprise, and fear.
Diagnostic Analysis of Nonverbal Accuracy in Adult Facial Expressions (DANVA2-AF)	Nowicki and Carton (1993)	Stimuli are happy, sad, angry, and fearful facial expressions, balanced by gender. The participants' task is to indicate which of the four emotions is present. A youth form is also available (as are forms with different ethnic groups).
Vocal Recognition		
Diagnostic Analysis of Nonverbal Accuracy in Adult Prosody (DANVA2-AP)	Baum and Nowicki (1998)	The stimuli are audio files where two professional actors (one male, the other female) say a neutral sentence in one of four emotional states (happy, sad, angry, or fearful). The participants' task is to indicate which of the four emotions is present in the voices. A youth form is also available.
Vocal Expression Recognition Index (Vocal-I)	Scherer (2007)	This task requires participants to make judgments about the emotion heard in a voice spoken in a foreign language. The phrases are uttered by actors so as to portray joy, sadness, fear, anger, and neutral.

Postural Recognition		
Diagnostic Analysis of Nonverbal Accuracy in Posture (DANVA2-POS)	Pitterman and Nowicki (2004)	The stimuli are 2 men and 2 women portrayed standing and sitting, representing happiness, sadness, anger, and fear. The participant is required to identify emotion in human standing and sitting postures.
Multiple Channels		
Multimodal Emotion Recognition Test (MERT)	Banziger et al. (2009)	An instrument that measures emotion recognition ability on the basis of actor portrayals of dynamic expressions of emotions, operationalized as recognition accuracy in four presentation modes (i.e., audio/video, audio only, video only, still picture) combining the visual and auditory sense modalities.
Communication of Affect Receiving Ability Test (CARAT)	Buck (1984)	Items are videotaped sequences showing spontaneous, naturally occurring facial expressions and gestures of college student "senders" to emotionally loaded slides. Participants are required to make judgments about what kind of slide elicited the affect and how pleasant or unpleasant the sender's subjective response was.

postures or gestures. Recently, extending on these collection of ideas, Banziger, Grandjean, and Scherer (2009) have developed an assessment model that combines all of these features (i.e., face, voice, and body) in a single test, known as the Multimodal Emotion Recognition Test (MERT).

These assessments appear to correlate highly with each other when in the same modality, providing some evidence of convergent validity. For example, the DANVA2-AF and the JACBART correlate very highly, at $r = 0.80$ (Mayer et al., 2008). However, Roberts et al. (2006) found that measures from different modalities (i.e., vocal and facial tests) were only weakly correlated. Specifically, the JACBART and Vocal-I correlated very weakly, at $r = 0.17$. In addition, evidence for the relationship between these measures and the MSCEIT Emotion Perception is quite poor. For example, Roberts et al. (2006) reported a correlation approaching zero between MSCEIT Faces and the JACBART. These two findings may be accounted for by carefully considering the nature of emotion recognition tasks. Firstly, the ability to perceive emotions correctly may not be a single unitary primary mental ability, but may be specific to different modalities (a finding that is actually supported by Banziger et al.'s [2009] research using the MERT). Secondly, the MSCEIT method of rating a still photo of a face seems to capture a different skill from multiple-choice assessment of facial expression presented for only a fraction of a second (as in the JACBART).

A recent meta-analysis summarizing 215 independent studies provides predictive validity evidence for scores derived from emotional recognition assessments (Hall, Andrzejewski, & Yopchick, 2009). Hall et al. found that a range of emotional recognition assessments (including all those given in Table 3.6) were positively related to empathy, tolerance, and various social competencies and other indicators of positive adjustment (e.g., salary raises and greater compliance with physician directions). Further, emotional recognition assessments were negatively related to shyness, depression, and miscellaneous indicators of problematic adjustment (e.g., friend-rated rebelliousness).

The variables that were related to emotion recognition were derived from self-, peer-, and supervisor-reports and behavioral assessments. The authors conclude: "There can be no doubt that accuracy in interpersonal perception is connected to healthy psychological functioning that is manifested in both intra-personal and interpersonal domains, including work settings" (Hall et al., 2009, p. 165).

Information Processing Tasks as Measures of EI

In Carroll's (1993) three-stratum model, there is a form of cognitive ability that is explicitly concerned with the rapid processing of very simple stimuli: Broad Decision Speed (Gp). There is nothing inherently special about the four-branch model, which is currently thought to comprise EI: The four constructs were ostensibly derived from the armchair by its developers via a systematic review of the literature. By contrast, all of the primary mental abilities currently comprising cognitive ability derive their meaning (and substance) from systematic empirical inquiry. As such, one might provide alternatives to each of the four-branch constructs. On the basis of what is known about cognitive abilities, one such factor might be the ability to rapidly process very simple emotional stimuli. Information processing tasks are common in emotions research, and below we discuss two such paradigms that might be examined in an attempt to more fully chart the subcomponents of EI.

Implicit Association Tests. Recently, researchers have focused on methods for investigating individual differences in unconscious processing of emotive stimuli; for example, some people have racial prejudices of which they are unaware. The use of Implicit Association Tests (IATs) in detecting subtle biases is well documented—at the time of writing, Greenwald, McGhee, and Schwartz's (1998) article introducing the IAT method has been cited nearly 1000 times in the peer-reviewed literature. In essence, the IAT paradigm assesses the relative strength of positive and negative associations that test-takers have for two opposing ideas (e.g., the strength of positive and negative associations for obese people versus slim people might indicate an implicit evaluative bias in favor of slim people). Mauss, Evers, Wilhelm, and Gross (2006) demonstrate that the IAT may be used to assess the implicit biases towards emotional expression and disclosure (e.g., the words "emotional" and "disclose") as compared to emotional regulation and control (e.g., the words "controlled" and "suppress"). Based on the premise that the people who regulate their emotions have implicit positive evaluations of emotion regulation, Mauss et al. (2006) suggest that their IAT (the Emotion Regulation–Implicit Association Test [ER-IAT]) assesses an individual's emotion regulation.

The ER-IAT has been shown to demonstrate reasonable test-retest reliability but is unrelated to trait measures of emotion regulation. However, this study examined only 36 people. Clearly, both the small sample size and failure to provide discriminant validity evidence render this study (and the status of the ER-IAT as providing a new measure of EI) problematic. Indeed, the IAT measurement approach is not without its critics, as there is some disagreement about what the task actually measures (e.g., Fiedler & Blümke, 2005; Mierke & Klauer, 2003). Nevertheless, it is one of the few available approaches that may have some potential to provide objective measures of emotional management. In addition, the approach can easily be adapted to assess other related constructs (e.g., empathy, emotion perception).

EI Inspection Time. Austin (e.g., 2005) conducted studies relating self-reported, trait EI measures to an Inspection Time (IT) task. Here respondents are given a speeded test and asked to discriminate between happy and neutral faces, sad and neutral faces, and two neutral symbols. IT is considered the minimal response time necessary to distinguish between two stimuli, and may be administered in a variety of different ways. Findings using this approach, however, are not especially compelling. For example, IT correlates near zero with scores on various self-report EI measures (e.g., Austin, 2005; Austin & Saklofske, 2005; Stokes & Bors, 2001). What remains to be seen is if this IT task is substantially correlated with maximum performance measures of EI, such as the MSCEIT. In going beyond the simple ability to distinguish between differing emotions, and considering how quickly an individual can accomplish this task, IT holds promise. The potential utility for such an application is rich, although it is necessary to tie this to real-world outcomes.

Promising New Approaches to Measure EI: The Situational Judgment Test

Recently, the situational judgment test (SJT) paradigm has been proposed as an alternative for measuring emotional abilities (Legree et al., 2005; MacCann & Roberts, 2008; Schulze, Wilhelm, & Kyllonen, 2007). SJTs are a type of test where individuals are presented with a scenario and then asked to select either the most appropriate response or their typical response out of a list of possible choices. In the domain of industrial-organizational psychology, meta-analyses have provided evidence for the criterion-related (McDaniel, Morgeson, Finnegan, Campion, & Braverman, 2001) and incremental validity of SJTs, over and above intelligence and personality measures (McDaniel, Hartman, Whetzel, & Grubb, 2006). As the content of the situations represent different domains such as teamwork, integrity, or academic performance, SJTs can be developed to present scenarios with emotion-related problems.

Situational judgment tests measuring EI (or closely related constructs) are described in Table 3.7. To give the reader a flavor for these assessments, we also provide sample items. Note, however, in the interests of space we do not provide all of the response options, although, as should be self-evident, a variety of different permutations (given the scenario) are possible.

The various measures depicted in Table 3.7 point to the application of *emotional situations* as useful stimuli when assessing EI. In the case of the final two measures in Table 3.7, the situations were based on real emotional experiences of an appropriate sample (i.e., they conformed to the classic SJT

TABLE 3.7 SAMPLE MEASURES OF EMOTIONAL UNDERSTANDING AND MANAGEMENT THAT USE THE SJT (OR SCENARIO-BASED) APPROACH (ADAPTED AFTER ROBERTS ET AL., 2010)

Test	Source	Description	Sample Item
Understanding			
Levels of Emotional Awareness Scale (LEAS)	Lane et al. (1990)	Participants describe their anticipated feelings to various scenes. Anger, fear, happiness, and sadness are elicited. Each scene is followed by: "How would you feel?" and "How would the other person feel?" Each person's answer receives two scores for each emotion described: self and other.	You and your best friend are in the same line of work. There is a prize given annually to the best performance of the year. The two of you work hard to win the prize. One night the winner is announced: your friend. How would you feel? How would your friend feel?
Emotional Accuracy Research Scale (EARS)	Geher et al. (2001)	This scale consists of vignettes followed by pairs of mood items (e.g., mad–delighted; stomping feet–happy for another), where test-takers must select one of the pair as representative of the person in the vignettes.	My best friend's father died this weekend. He had diabetes for a long time and as he got older his health grew worse and worse. I went to his funeral on Monday. Many of my friends from high school were also there …
The Test of Emotional Intelligence (TEMINT)	Schmidt-Atzert and Bühner (2002)	Respondents rate feelings (e.g., aversion, anger, fear) experienced by different targets in various situations. The score represents the degree to which participants' responses diverge from the emotions of the target.	A 30-year-old female computer specialist reports: "My cat was ill. I had to take him to the vet. I thought I had poisoned him with insect spray." How did this person feel in this situation?

Situational Test for Emotional Understanding	MacCann and Roberts (2008)	The test requires the participant to identify emotions felt by a target to given emotion-laden situations.	An irritating neighbor of Eve's moves to another state. Eve most likely feels? (a) Regret, (b) hope, (c) relief, (d) sadness, (e) joy.
Management			
Emotional Management Test (EMT)	Freudenthaler and Neubauer (2007)	Respondents are required to choose from multiple-choice options appropriate responses to emotionally charged scenarios.	Your father is very scared of a complicated operation which is absolutely necessary. Option (1 of 4): To calm him down I advise him to talk to the doctor once more.
Situational Judgment Test for Management	MacCann and Roberts (2008)	Respondents are required to choose from multiple-choice options appropriate responses to emotionally charged scenarios.	Dan has been overseas for a long time and returns to visit his family. So much has changed that Dan feels left out. What action would be the most effective for Dan? Option (1 of 4): Nothing, it will sort itself out soon enough.

approach). This approach not only promises greater ecological validity—that is, the test situation more closely mimics reality—but also legal defensibility, should these measures be used in high-stakes testing. Equally important, especially for the impecunious student considering a group project or a possible dissertation, several of these instruments have a growing evidentiary basis and are available in the public domain, free of charge (e.g., http://supp.apa.org/psycarticles/supplemental/emo_8_4_540/emo_8_4_540_supp.html). Indeed, there is an impressive array of validity data accruing from the scores derived from SJTs that cuts across different sub-disciplines. Below are a series of findings, broken down by whether the SJT assesses Emotional Understanding or Management.

Emotional Understanding. A good deal of research on Emotional Understanding has been conducted with the Levels of Emotional Awareness Scale (LEAS), in particular. For example, using Positron Emission Tomography (a brain-imaging technique), LEAS scores have been found to correlate with neurological mechanisms known to be closely associated with emotional processing (Lane et al., 1998). The LEAS also predicts the accuracy of emotion recognition and people's ability to respond to aversive mood states (Lane, 2000). Its correlation with crystallized intelligence is of similar magnitude to that found for MSCEIT Emotional Understanding ($r = 0.38$; see e.g., Lane, Quinlan, Schwartz, Walker, & Zeitlin, 1990). There are, however, some troublesome findings. In an especially comprehensive study, Lumley, Gustavson, Partridge, and Labouvie-Vief (2005) found that the LEAS shared near zero correlations with MSCEIT branches, alexithymia, emotional expression, and trait meta-mood (the one exception was a small positive correlation with Emotional Understanding from the MSCEIT [$r = 0.22$]).

Of the remaining measures of Emotional Understanding, the Test of Emotional Intelligence (TEMINT) has been the source of the most peer-reviewed studies, largely in German-speaking populations. In one such study (Blickle et al., 2009), emotional reasoning skills were related to emotion recognition ability (i.e., as measured by DANVA2-AF), emotional empathy, and three measures of successful social functioning (i.e., social astuteness, interpersonal influence, and apparent sincerity), each of which were assessed by peers to avoid method effects. These relationships held constant after controlling for personality and occupational environment characteristics. In a second study, Blickle et al. (2009) found that the TEMINT explained additional variance in overall job performance ratings beyond general intelligence (g) and personality traits (see, however, Amelang & Steinmayr, 2006, who found somewhat different effects).

Emotional Management. Although the Emotional Management Test (EMT) predates the Situational Test of Emotional Management (STEM), the latter appears to have garnished a more comprehensive research base. For example, MacCann and Roberts (2008) provide data showing moderate correlations between the STEM and other emotions measures (such as measure of alexithymia, where correlations are around $r = 0.40$) and valued outcomes such as marks in a psychology course (where having high EI might confer real advantages, especially for those going on to study clinical psychology; $r = 0.31$, after intelligence is controlled). These findings have been replicated in several studies, including one examining performance in medical school (e.g., Austin, 2010; Libbrecht & Lievens, 2011). The STEM also appears to consistently relate with Agreeableness. Indeed, across three studies, the magnitude of this relationship is remarkably consistent with the meta-analytic findings for Emotional Management found for the MSCEIT (i.e., $r = 0.30$) (Roberts, Mason, & MacCann, 2011). These scientists also found that the relationship between the STEM and broad cognitive abilities mirrored that of MSCEIT Emotional Management, though correlations with that actual branch were rather modest ($r = 0.25$).

In another study, MacCann, Wang, Matthews, and Roberts (2010) developed a youth version of the STEM, along with a parent-ratings form (by replacing the instruction "what would you do in this situation" with "what would your child do in this situation"). Findings were somewhat striking. For example, the correlation between self- and parent-rated emotional management was weak ($r = 0.19$). Both measures incrementally predicted grade point average, over and above intelligence and personality indicators. For all the mothers in the world (the sample of parents was almost exclusively the mother), there was another striking finding: The parent-rated SJT tended to do a better job of predicting criterion variables than did the self-rated SJT. The old adage, "mother knows best," may have some real substance.

Text-based SJTs are not without their problems, however, as the reading load is very high and because they are based on narratives, not a totally compelling simulation of real-life contexts. With these criticisms in mind, Roberts, Betancourt, Burrus, et al. (2011) have recently "brought to life" some of the content evident in text-based SJTs. The procedure involves film scripts, written by professional writers, who developed the storylines on the basis of interviews with a range of subject-matter experts (including counselors, those in pastoral care, and academics who study emotions). Professional actors were then charged to act out the scenarios in front of a professional film crew, with the film then edited to obtain relevant content and programmed in a web environment. Using this process, these researchers arguably have developed content (and ecologically) valid measures that are largely independent from reading load. To give the reader a very rough sense of this paradigm, screenshots from the multimedia SJT are presented in Figure 3.3. (The multimedia SJT is essentially a series of 16 short films, with accompanying response options that are also filmed, which need to be watched in their entirety to fully understand the items.)

So far we have conducted two studies where this assessment was administered to samples of community college and university students across the United States (Roberts, Betancourt, Burrus, et al., 2011). In a first study, we evaluated

Scenario

Response scale

Response justification

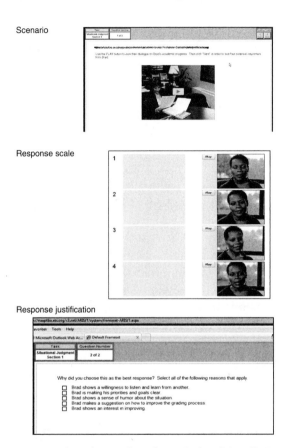

FIGURE 3.3 Figural Representation of a Typical Multimedia SJT Item.

the psychometric properties of this new measure, as well as the relationship the multimedia SJT had with other theoretically meaningful constructs. The measure was found to have acceptable internal consistency reliability, and moderate to high relationships with each of the MSCEIT branches. The SJT also correlated positively with disparate measures of cognitive ability (the highest correlation was with crystallized ability [$r = 0.56$] and the lowest with quantitative ability [$r = 0.27$]). In addition, the multimedia SJT was not too highly correlated with personality, though it did share a moderate correlation with Agreeableness ($r = 0.30$). Finally, regression analyses suggested that cognitive ability, Conscientiousness, and the multimedia assessments consistently added to the prediction of grade point average (GPA). Collectively, these results mirror some of the major findings from the Roberts et al. (2008) meta-analysis of maximum performance measures of EI (cf. the findings just discussed with the results presented in Tables 3.4 and 3.5). These findings also suggest that the multimedia SJT appears to be assessing a construct that encompasses both emotional and intellectual components, and has demonstrable predictive validity evidence.

A second study involved following up a subset of the previous participants to obtain test-retest data, in the process expanding the range of outcomes that the multimedia SJT measure might predict. The test-retest reliability over 6 months was acceptable. In addition, the SJT correlated moderately with indicators of psychological well-being. Of greatest interest, perhaps, is the relationship that the multimedia SJT had with indicators of net positive affect taken over a period of time using the Day Reconstruction Method (DRM; Kahneman, Krueger, Schkade, Schwarz, & Stone, 2004). This DRM essentially has the individual list all of the activities they did over the course of 24 hours and how happy they felt doing these activities. The correlations between the multimedia SJT and reported net positive affect while socializing and working (part-time) exceeded $r = 0.40$. These correlations were lower for other variables (e.g., attending class and surfing the internet), although always positive in sign.

Recently, we have also constructed a short form of this multimedia assessment and administered it to a group of K-12 teachers, currently undergoing their first year of teaching. Although the data are still being collected, the assessment seems to be differentiating between principal ratings of whether these teachers are meeting performance goals. Further data will follow these teachers and assess the extent that their classes are successful in, for example, meeting (or exceeding) state standards. We have also begun collecting data relating the multimedia SJT to measures of leadership, and conducted experimental studies where we induce subjective stress, in order to ascertain whether this measure predicts decision making under stress. We believe the prospects are bright for this paradigm serving as a new form of EI assessment.

What Have We Learnt from Research Using Maximum Performance Measures of EI?

What is the payoff from the burgeoning research on maximum performance measures that we have briefly reviewed? Are scales such as the MSCEIT and STEM little more than repackaged intelligence traits? Or can we use assessments of emotional ability to tell us something about the person's emotional (and cognitive) functioning that we could not ascertain from existing measures of cognitive abilities? As for trait EI, research is still ongoing and hence there are no definitive answers to the questions we have posed. But we can summarize some interim conclusions, as follows:

1. There appears something new about EI if one measures it objectively. This conclusion is relatively robust across different measurement paradigms and theoretical approaches. The literature reviewed throughout this chapter seems to suggest that EI (and related constructs) should be added to the three-stratum model of human cognitive abilities. What appears less clear, despite some early evidence, is whether EI is a broad factor like Gf and Gc, or two to three primary mental abilities that are components of existing factors. In short, we cannot say definitively whether EI is a minor player in the cognitive landscape, or a major star on the horizon. For example, the correlations between Emotional Understanding and crystallized intelligence are of sufficient magnitude to suggest that with more rigorous assessment this could be re-classified as a Stratum I factor comprising

that ability. Similarly, it could be the case that, depending on whether it is assessed through visual or auditory stimuli, Emotion Perception simply constitutes primary mental abilities underlying broad visualization and broad auditory reception, respectively. The jury is out on this issue, simply because the requisite studies (which would involve careful sampling of both emotional and cognitive ability indicators, given to large, representative samples) have not been done.

The problem with assigning a much reduced role to EI in three-stratum theory, however, lay clearly with the Emotional Management factor. This construct relates moderately with intelligence measures (as is demonstrated, for example, in the meta-analysis of Table 3.4) and yet has sufficient distinctiveness from other cognitive ability indicators to suggest that it is something quite apart from existing constructs. This happens to hold true whether assessed by the MSCEIT or different forms of the situational judgment test, which indicates the construct is not ephemeral. Consistent with this argument, Emotional Management also seems to predict a range of outcomes valued by society.

2. *Experiential EI (Emotional Perception and Emotional Facilitation), ironically, needs a strategic overhaul.* In our exposition, we pointed out that there is inadequate evidence for the Facilitation branch of the MSCEIT. For example, factor analytic evidence fails to uncover this construct in all but a few, rather limited, studies. The measures also suffer from what psychologists term poor face validity. Having given this test often, we have frequently observed respondents giggling after being asked to first imagine being joyous, and then indicate on a scale how sweet or hot the individual now feels (and likely not simply because of the double entendre). We can only imagine how job incumbents might be put-off by this test, if ever used in a high-stakes application. And in our review, it is perhaps compelling that not even one study has shown how Facilitation predicts any valued outcome. In short, based on available evidence, its status as a component

of EI is problematic and we would discourage a student or colleague from assessing this dimension if testing time is limited. At the very least, assessment of this construct needs to go back to the drawing board.

Emotion Perception, at least as assessed in the MSCEIT, may be no less problematic. We noted in our review of emotion recognition assessments that a recent meta-analysis points to this family of measures predicting a variety of positive and negative outcomes, something that has not emerged in virtually any studies using the MSCEIT Faces and Pictures test. The difference between these tasks and the MSCEIT, of course, lay in the scoring key. Future test development of the MSCEIT would do well to construct a veridical key. In addition, because of the nature of consensual scoring, it is currently remarkably easy to coach people on how to do very well on MSCEIT Emotion Perception. Endorsing highly only one emotion in any given block, and then rating all other emotions as not being present in the MSCEIT (recall Figure 3.2), almost guarantees success.

3. Strategic EI (Emotional Understanding and Emotional Management) constructs appear to have promise, both as new constructs and as predictors of valued outcomes. In contrast to findings concerning Facilitation (and to a lesser extent Perception, as measured by the MSCEIT), the data concerning Understanding and Management paint a largely promising picture for future research endeavors. Both of the constructs share positive correlations with other cognitive ability measures, have interpretable correlations with personality, and predict a range of valued outcomes. Importantly, findings for these constructs are not limited to one methodology (or instrument, i.e., the MSCEIT), but appear replicable across different methods, samples, and statistical techniques. While the selection of outcomes that might be examined in the future could be more principled, these do appear as building blocks from which one might enhance the science of EI.

4. The four-branch model has proven a useful soup stone for early developments in EI, but it may be time to move beyond it. There is, in many cultures, a traditional folk story, which tells the tale of a group of hungry strangers who arrive in a village with an empty pot. The villagers refuse to share their food, so the strangers begin boiling a stone with water in the pot. The villagers become curious, and soon begin adding a vegetable here, a spice there, in the hope of getting a taste. Pretty soon a delicious pot of soup is enjoyed by all. (The story has many variants, and for those with a culinary interest, the Portuguese *sopa de pedra* literally translates "stone soup"). The four-branch model appears like that soup stone; in the end we may not really need it. But it has proven invaluable in orientating the field to consider individual differences in emotion and to raise issues of measurement, theory, and application.

What next? Our proposal would be to go back to the history of cognitive ability and take more than a few lessons from this sub-discipline to arrive at a full-blown EI model. Most importantly, primary mental abilities were never baked in stone (the reader should pardon the mixed metaphor); rather, the three-stratum model is a function of a wealth of empirical studies, where data were left to form its central tenets. Studies are needed where a variety of the measures discussed in this chapter are clearly selected, modified, administered to large samples of individuals, and then factor analyzed to resolve the underlying dimensions.

5. *Research on EI needs to fill in the blanks if it is to assume the status of a major, new, intelligence.* In our brief review of cognitive ability research, we noted a number of lines of evidence which attest to the empirical efficacy of the three-stratum model. For example, we argued that cognitive ability constructs are replicable across diverse populations using factor analysis. Research has also shown these cognitive abilities are differentially sensitive to training and other forms

of intervention, and that they share different learning and developmental trajectories. At the present point in time, the evidence concerning these aspects of EI is relatively sparse or nonexistent. Future work is needed to demonstrate that EI measures are invariant across special populations, cultures, ethnic groups, and gender. We also need to ascertain whether these abilities change over the life span (plausibly, Emotional Perception will decline, while Emotional Understanding and Management should continue to improve until old age). Training studies and interventions, which target specific constructs in controlled randomized designs, are required. Longitudinal studies, which allow causal inferences to be drawn, are also sorely needed.

CONCLUSION

Our exposition of assessments (and related studies) that have at their core the delineation and exploration of ability EI constructs, has, of necessity, been brief. However, it is clear from this discussion that, whether we look at information processing tasks or situational judgment measures, EI may constitute a hitherto neglected domain of human cognitive ability. The time appears ripe to correct this omission, especially in light of what many consider the proper frame of reference for methodology in the study of individual differences. Elsewhere, Carroll (1995) argues that the goal of this sub-discipline is to explore "the diversity of intellect in the people of this planet—the many forms of cognitive processes and operations, mental performances, and creations of knowledge and art" (p. 429). To achieve this end, Carroll suggested that there are untapped domains of mental activity that must be discovered and encapsulated within a comprehensive taxonomic model. Furthermore, the demonstration of the meaning of these concepts and their relevance to real-world activities and problems is critical to progress in science. We concur with these sentiments. The various constructs covered in this chapter, all assessed by maximum performance measures, suggest EI might be added to this taxonomic model and, at the same time, have real-world significance. In the chapters that follow, we take up these issues in some detail.

Emotional Intelligence in Everyday Life

D an, a sophomore at the University of Colorado, received an emergency phone call from his father conveying the bad news that his good buddy, Gerry, was hospitalized at the university medical center after a near fatal skiing accident. Without hesitating, Dan hopped into his car and drove to the medical center at full speed. Arriving at the medical center, he learned that Gerry, having suffered multiple bone fractures and a number of serious internal injuries, had been removed from the operation theater and was now in recovery room. Outside the recovery room, Dan encountered Gerry's family and friends who manifested palpable signs of anxiety and concern. Peering through the portal of the recovery room, Dan was quite distressed seeing his best friend connected to an infusion and respirator apparatus, with myriad tubes and wires attached to his body.

A number of emotional competencies facilitated Dan's coping with the stressful situation as it unfolded over time. For one, Dan's ability to express his emotions clearly allowed him to effectively communicate his genuine concern and empathic feelings to Gerry and members of his family. Also, the ability to clearly and accurately identify and understand his own emotions, as well as those of others, provided Dan with important information regarding how he and others appraised Gerry's medical condition. When his buddy became conscious, Dan's emotions also facilitated his thought processes by motivating him to think of ways to cheer up his friend, such as bringing him some new music for his iPod and an assortment of popular magazines. Dan's efficient emotion management strategies helped him to regulate his feelings of sadness and anxiety, as well as communicate his care, compassion, and concern to both Gerry and his family. All these emotional competencies alleviated, in part, the pain, shock, and anxiety of both Gerry and his family members during the recovery process. As evidenced in Dan's case, emotional competencies may play an important role in coping with emotionally laden situations in everyday life. You can probably relate to this scenario and think of situations in your own life where emotional competencies have served you well in negotiating stressful or challenging events.

A major force fueling both popular and scientific interest in emotional intelligence (EI) is its potential contributions to day-to-day functioning, its claimed utility in applied contexts, and its contribution to the well-being of both the individual and the society. Thus, EI has been claimed to play an important role in such diverse domains as social relationships, marriage, health behaviors, educational success, occupational performance, and clinical disorders (see Zeidner, Matthews, & Roberts, 2009). Daniel Goleman (1995), one of the EI's most exuberant advocates, has even gone so far as to claim that EI will confer "an advantage in any domain in life, whether in romance and intimate relationships or picking up the unspoken rules that govern success in organizational politics" (p. 36).

Moreover, the popular press has touted EI as a quick fix panacea for manifest problems in social situations, during the educational process, and at work. Have you a problem communicating with your dorm roommate? Are you having problems in your relationships with members of the opposite (or same) sex? Might you be experiencing difficulties in meeting your academic commitments? Are you stressed out at work or failing to move up the corporate ladder? Are you smoking or drinking excessively? Are you failing to monitor your blood pressure or caloric intake? Low EI may be at play. Training people in EI in schools, workplaces, community centers, and health and psychiatric clinics offers a valuable solution to perceived individual, as well as community, needs.

This chapter discusses how EI is related both to everyday functioning and to performance in applied settings. Our concern is not so much with measurement here, as it was in Chapters 2 and 3, but rather with the conceptual basis for linking EI to the challenges of everyday life, and the evidence that studying EI may payoff at a practical level. The literature has recently provided some promising data in support of EI as a reliable predictor of a wide array of important social, educational, and occupational outcomes. Yet, despite much enthusiasm, some caution and skepticism is needed. As we have previously suggested (Zeidner et al., 2009), EI may be nothing more than a popular fad along the lines of New Age excesses such as crystal healing and feng shui (see Figure 4.1). In the following sections, we will present a case for the utility of EI in daily life, concomitantly attempting to tease apart the scientific facts and empirical findings regarding the utility of EI in daily functioning from common myths, fiction, and unfounded speculations.

We focus on the following important domains of everyday life: social functioning and personal relations; health, coping with stress, and subjective well-being; and applied (educational and occupational) contexts. These domains constitute key areas of life outcomes, which have been widely studied in relation to EI (e.g., Farrelly & Austin, 2007; Zeidner et al., 2009). We begin by discussing the role of EI in the social realm, briefly touching upon social interactions and close personal relationships. We then discuss the role of EI in physical and mental health,

FIGURE 4.1 Is EI a fad along the lines of feng shui or a viable scientific construct?
http://en.wikipedia.org/wiki/File:Taipei.101.fountain.altonthompson.jpg

followed by a discussion of EI's contribution to coping with stress and subjective well-being. We move on to probe the role of EI in two key applied organizational settings: schools and workplace. We detail the claims made about the pivotal role of EI in these contexts and critically survey and discuss the empirical evidence supporting these claims.

SOCIAL BEHAVIORS

It is readily apparent that people need to process emotional information and manage emotional dynamics intelligently to effectively navigate the social world. Presumably, high-EI individuals, compared to their low-EI counterparts, would be more accurate in picking up the intended meaning of the message being communicated, understand the implications of the message, and regulate their emotions more effectively in response to emotionally laden messages, all of which should help achieve adaptive social outcomes. Positive emotion has been linked to sociability (Argyle, 2001), whereas negative affect has been shown to keep others at bay (Furr & Funder, 1998).

Consequently, emotional competencies are expected to be of pivotal importance for social encounters and for achieving adaptive outcomes (Lopes et al., 2004).

Social Interactions

A recent review by Mayer and colleagues (Mayer, Roberts, & Barsade, 2008) suggests that ability EI predicts positive social well-being and adaptive social outcomes in both children and adults. Specifically, self-report measures have consistently been found to be related to social adaptive behaviors in children and youth (Mavroveli, Petrides, Rieffe, & Bakker, 2007; Mavroveli, Petrides, Sangareau, & Furnham, 2009) and college students (Schutte et al., 2001). Similarly, positive correlations between ability-based EI and social outcomes have been reported for both children and adolescents (Márquez, Martín, & Brackett, 2006; Rossen, Kranzler, & Algina 2008, 2009) and for college students (Brackett, Mayer, & Warner, 2004; Lopes et al., 2003, 2004). Positive social outcomes include a more positive sense of well-being, greater empathy, and increased prosocial behaviors. As noted in Chapter 3, Managing Emotions appears to be most consistently predictive of these social criteria; the other three branches mostly share trivial relations with the social variables assessed (Lopes et al., 2003, 2004).

Like higher mean EI predicts more favorable social outcomes, lower mean EI is associated with interpersonal conflict and maladjustment (Mayer et al., 2008). Thus, adolescents who are lower on EI were rated as more aggressive than others and were observed to be more prone to engage in conflictual and antisocial behavior than their higher EI peers (Brackett et al., 2004; Mayer, Perkins, Caruso, & Salovey, 2000).

Close Personal Relations

Intimate interpersonal relationships, such as romantic or marital relations, tend to be both emotion-rich as well as high-conflict social contexts (Fitness, 2001). The very emotional ties and intimacy that link two people in an intimate bond often secures the groundwork for both emotional highs and lows and conflict (Carstensen, Graff, Levenson, & Gottman, 1996). Although conflicts in relationships involve a repetitive cycle of emotions (e.g., anger, fear, and shame) the initial source can be quite trivial (e.g., a snide remark, misinterpreting a neutral message as hostile, forgetting a birthday, and leaving dirty clothes on the bedroom floor). If allowed to escalate, these conflicts can ruin the relationship over time. EI may enter the scene by helping individuals who are high on this dimension maintain positive emotional interactions with their partners. It stands to reason that the way a couple handles emotionally laden situations (including conflicts) have serious implications for the stability of the partnership and perceived satisfaction. In the passages that follow, we theorize how specific EI components might contribute to fostering close personal relationships.

Identification and expression of emotions. Research suggests that people vary in their ability to accurately perceive and communicate emotions. Some people are prone to habitually send ambiguous emotional signals to their partners. Other folks are prone to ignore or misidentify even the most obvious of emotional signals from their partners (e.g., misinterpreting neutral signals as hostile ones). EI might help sustain an intimate personal relationship by enabling the identification and open expression of wants and desires, facilitating candid discussion of sensitive issues, and helping a partner decode nonverbal messages. In fact, both verbal and nonverbal patterns of communication and emotion expression may be pivotal for understanding the successful social functioning of couples.

Emotional understanding. As pointed out by Keltner and Haidt (2001), the accuracy and depth of people's emotional understanding can help in decoding the intentions, attitudes, motivations, and thoughts of others in their social surroundings. Poor understanding of emotions in self and others, however, contributes to the misinterpretation of verbal or nonverbal messages, leading to tension and disruption of intimate personal relationships (Fitness, 2006). Thus, in the context of intimate personal relationships, understanding of emotions in self and in others can help nurture positive relationships.

Emotion regulation. The ability to successfully maintain, change, or modify emotions, both in self and others, is very likely an important factor contributing to relationship stability and happiness (Fitness, 2001). (Note that the terms "emotion regulation" and "emotion management" tend to be used interchangeably in the EI literature, although "emotion regulation" is the term more widely used in the broader field of emotion research: e.g., Gross, 2002.) Research suggests that couples capable of reframing negative interactions in a constructive manner are higher in marital satisfaction, when compared to couples reporting less satisfaction. Nevertheless, both too much and too little expression of negative emotions may be maladaptive in interpersonal relations (Zeidner et al., 2009).

As relationship success is a function of how couples handle negative affect, EI would appear to play an important function. In order for partners to cope successfully with ongoing stresses and emotional fissures, their skill in identifying, understanding, and regulating their own emotions and those of their partners becomes critical. Fitness (2001) puts all of this into perspective in the following way: "The art of knowing when, why, and how to say you are sorry in marriage, and the ability to practice forbearance under even the most trying circumstances, require many sophisticated emotional skills, including empathy, self-control, and a deep understanding of human needs and feelings" (p. 98).

Empirical evidence. Overall, the bulk of studies suggest that couples need high EI and a good working knowledge of emotions in the relationship context to be able to make sense of their own and their partner's emotions. In one of the first empirical studies in this area, Fitness (2001) found that couples higher on emotional clarity reported less difficulty in forgiving a partner-caused offense than lower emotion-clarity people. These individuals were also found to be happier in their relationship.

By contrast, partners characterized by low emotional understanding appear more prone to attack partners and interpret partner hurt and distress as hostility. Thus, rather than expressing guilt and remorse, they may act hatefully in return. Over time, such reactions are likely to exacerbate conflict and diminish relationship quality. Emotional misunderstandings can also lead to "negative affect reciprocity," where spouses (broadly defined) reciprocate the negative emotions they perceive in their partners. Brackett, Warner, and Bosco (2005) showed that couples who both scored low on EI reported a greater degree of unhappiness with their relationship when compared with couples who both scored high on EI.

A recent study by Zeidner and Kaluda (2008) examined the relation of EI to romantic love in 100 newlywed couples. Controlling for verbal intelligence, both self-report and ability-based measures showed significant "actor effects." That is, partners with high levels of EI were more in love and satisfied with their intimate relationships. However, no "partner effects" were found. That is, married persons whose partners are higher on EI are not necessarily more in love with their partners. While a modicum of work has addressed the role of EI directly in personal relationship, this does seem to be a promising area for future research. Clearly, it is difficult to untangle cause and effect here, because unhappiness in a relationship may be just as likely to decrease partner's emotional sensitivity to one another as emotional insensitivity may be to decrease happiness in the relationship.

HEALTH, COPING WITH STRESS, AND WELL-BEING

Health

Researchers have argued that high-EI individuals, who are skilled at expressing, understanding, and managing their emotions (Salovey, 2001), and who efficiently cope with the stressors and hassles of everyday life (Bar-On, 1997), should also be psychologically and physically healthier than individuals with low EI. It has also been claimed that EI may play a pivotal role in emotional disorders and also aid in the assessment of emotional deficits that are fundamental to affective disorders, such as anxiety and depression, and other constructs such as alexithymia and sociopathy. Indeed, current research points to a modest association between EI and health-related behaviors. Zeidner, M., Matthews, G., & Roberts, R. D., & (in press). The emotional intelligence, health, and well-being nexus: What have we learned and what have we missed? *Applied Psychology: Health and Well-being.*

The literature suggests a number of possible mechanisms or pathways linking EI and health-related behaviors (Ciarrochi & Deane, 2001; Johnson, Batey, & Holdsworth, 2009; Saklofske, Austin, Galloway, & Davidson, 2007; Zeidner, Matthews, & Roberts, in press). Figure 4.2 summarizes a number of potential mediating factors in the relationship between EI and health behaviors and outcomes. To begin with, higher EI should lead to successful and efficient self-regulation towards health-related

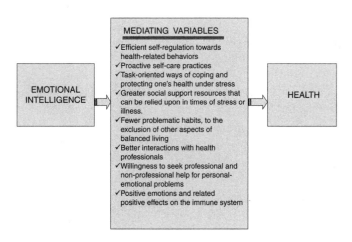

FIGURE 4.2 Some potential mediating factors in the EI–health relationship.

behaviors, thus supporting help seeking and following of medical advice and regimens (taking medications, keeping doctor appointments, avoiding fattening foods, etc.). EI may impact physical health indirectly, through its associations with habitual coping behavior that carry added health benefits. Examples of task-oriented ways of protecting one's health under stress include planned efforts to maintain regular exercise, nutritious diet, proper hygiene, adequate sleep, and supportive social network, all of which have been associated with increased positive mood and better health-related quality of life. EI may act as facilitator of these positive life practices. High-EI individuals are more likely to maintain proactive self-care practices (regular exercise, relaxation, healthy diet) and enjoy greater social support resources that can be relied upon in times of stress or illness.

Also, high-EI individuals are less likely to develop certain problematic habits, like excessive preoccupation with entertainment activities (e.g., gambling, TV, and Internet) to the exclusion of other aspects of balanced living. High capacity for self-insight and self-regulation should prevent involvement in risk behaviors associated with maladaptive coping and instead promote a more positive lifestyle that increases longevity and physical well-being. Furthermore, the interpersonal facet of EI is thought to facilitate interactions with health professionals, with higher-EI persons being more willing to seek professional help for personal-emotional problems, depression, and suicidal ideation (Ciarrochi & Deane, 2001). Finally, the positive emotions associated with EI may have potential positive effects on the immune system, allowing better stress management and lower levels of negative emotions, including psychological stress and depression (Dawda & Hart, 2000; Slaski & Cartwright, 2002).

Empirical evidence. A recent meta-analysis by Martins, Ramalho, and Morin (2010) examined 80 independent studies, 105 effect sizes, and 19,815 participants. This study found that when EI was measured as a trait, it was more strongly associated with health (average $r = 0.34$) than when measured as an ability (average $r = 0.17$). The weighted average association of EI with mental health (average $r = 0.36$) and psychosomatic health (average $r = 0.33$) was higher than the association of EI with physical health (average $r = 0.27$). Gender was found to moderate the EI–health relationship, with the magnitude of observed effects stronger among females than males. Overall, EI appears to be more strongly related to mental than physical health, with the magnitude of relations being measure dependent (see also, Schutte, Malouff, Thorsteinsson, Bhullar, & Rooke, 2007). A limitation of the studies reviewed by Martins et al. (2010) is that they overwhelmingly rely on self-reports of health (often in generally healthy samples), rather than objective medical criteria. An idea familiar from the personality literature (e.g., Watson & Pennebaker, 1989) is that some people may simply find physical symptoms more distressing, even in the absence of an objective medical cause. More work is needed to establish that EI genuinely relates to physical health, as opposed to satisfaction with one's health.

Coping with Psychological Stress

Broadly speaking, stress is the experience of encountering or anticipating adversity or challenges in one's goal-directed efforts (Carver & Conner-Smith, 2010). According to the transactional model, the leading paradigm in stress research, stress exists when people experience situations that tax or exceed their ability to manage or cope with them (Lazarus & Folkman, 1984; Lazarus, 1999). Whenever an individual is hard-pressed to deal with some impediment, obstacle, looming threat, or anticipated harm, the experience is viewed as being stressful.

Recent theorizing and research suggest that EI may be a pivotal factor determining how a person handles stress in daily life and confronts, what Shakespeare so aptly phrased, "the slings and arrows of outrageous fortune." The conceptualization of EI as a set of competencies for handling emotions and coping with stressful and emotionally laden situations is based on a functionalistic perspective that views emotions as a set of responses that guide the individual's behavior and serve as information that may help the person achieve important personal goals (Goldenberg, Matheson, & Mantler, 2006).

EI ought to be related to the coping mechanisms one employs in dealing with daily stressors, life transitions, or even traumatic events (Rode, Arthaud-Day, Mooney, Near, & Baldwin, 2008). Each of the EI branches may be potentially helpful in reducing stress (Gohm, Corser, & Dalsky, 2005).

Empirical evidence. Research has supported the claim that EI is a significant predictor of the impact of stressful events, both in real life (Ciarrochi, Deane, & Anderson, 2002; Mikolajczk, Menil, & Luminet, 2007) and in experimental settings (Mikolajczak, Roy, Luminet, Fille, & de Timary 2007). Thus, under exam conditions, high trait EI was shown to be related to the cognitive appraisal of the situation, with higher trait EI scores associated with less threatening appraisals and higher self-efficacy to pass academic exams (Mikolajczak, Luminet, & Menil, 2006). Also, a recent review by Keefer, Parker, and Saklofske (2009) suggests that higher scores on various self-report measures of EI are significantly related to fewer daily hassles, less subjective fatigue, lower occupational stress, and fewer symptomatic complaints in a wide array of settings.

Keefer et al. (2009) reviewed mood induction experiments addressing the role of EI in handling or recovering from induced stress (e.g., reading passages, writing stories, and viewing short video clips). The results are inconsistent and rather complex. Whereas high-EI individuals did come to the laboratory in a better mood than their low-EI counterparts, high EI did not generally lessen the impact of mood manipulation procedures on mood valence or intensity, and the results have been indeterminate. Yet, despite the variability in mood sensitivity, higher EI predicted more rapid rebound from lab-induced distress and demonstrated greater mood improvement. Emotion management appeared as a moderator in the relationship between stress and mood outcomes.

A recent experimental study by Mikolajczak and Luminet (2008) supports the claim that EI moderates the appraisals of a stressful encounter on self-efficacy. Whereas no differences among high and low EI students were found in neutral conditions, under stressful conditions involving solving math problems under ego-orienting and speeded conditions, students higher on EI appraised the condition as more challenging and less threatening than their low-EI counterparts. High-trait-EI students also exhibit greater self-efficacy to cope with a stressful situation than their low-EI counterparts. This moderating effect of EI on the impacts of stressful encounters has been reported at the neuroendocrine level as well, with high-EI students secreting less glucocorticoids (free flow of cortisol) when being tested than their low-EI counterparts (Mikolajczak, Roy, Luminet, Fillée, & de Timary, 2007). However, some studies have failed to find significant moderating effects (Day, Therrien, & Carroll, 2005).

To better understand the specific cognitive and behavioral strategies that mediate the pathway between EI and successful adaptation to stressful encounters, we next turn to the literature on EI and coping. From a functionalistic perspective, we might expect predictable relations between EI and the use of adaptive coping strategies. The transactional paradigm in stress research, posited by Lazarus and colleagues (e.g., Lazarus & Folkman, 1984), suggests that in order to resolve, tolerate, or escape a stressful encounter, individuals purposefully engage in various coping behaviors designed to manage the demands of a person–environment transaction that is appraised as stressful (e.g., Folkman, 1991). Specifically, when confronted with a potential source of stress (e.g., presenting a seminar paper before the class), the individual directs efforts at regulating emotional stress and/or dealing with the problem at hand, to manage the troubled person–environment transaction (see e.g., Lazarus, 1990). These constantly changing efforts can be cognitive or behavioral, direct and indirect, engaging or disengaging from the stressful situation.

Although a wide array of taxonomies of coping strategies are currently available, researchers have converged on the following three categories:

1. *Problem-focused coping*, where the individual solves the problem by circumventing or removing the source of stress (e.g., carefully planning for a major exam);
2. *Emotion-focused coping*, where the individual regulates, reduces, channels, or eliminates aversive emotions associated with the stressful encounter (e.g., seeking emotional support from friends after performing miserably on a psychology quiz); and
3. *Avoidance coping*, where the individual employs strategies that are designed to circumvent or avoid the stressful situation (e.g., watching TV, reading *Sports Illustrated*, and walking the dog for hours).

It has been frequently claimed that high-EI persons manage stressful encounters better than their low-EI counterparts. Figure 4.3 presents a number of mediating factors that may underlie the claimed lower emotional distress and better coping and functioning of high-EI individuals following a stressful encounter (Catanzaro & Mearns, 1999; Extremera, Durán, & Rey, 2007; Mikolajczak, & Luminet, 2008; Salovey, Stroud, Woolery, & Epel, 2002; Zeidner, Matthews, & Roberts, 2006).

Empirical evidence. Zeidner et al. (2006, 2009) summarized much of the research linking EI and coping, noting that correlations among these constructs range between 0.20 and 0.60. The strength and direction of the relations varies according to the type of coping strategy measured (problem-focused, emotion-focused, or avoidance) and also the way in which EI is operationalized (trait EI versus ability EI). Trait-based measures of EI tend to be positively correlated with adaptive coping styles and negatively correlated with maladaptive coping styles (Bastian,

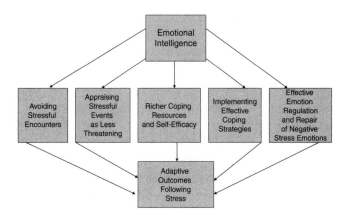

FIGURE 4.3 Mediating mechanisms in the relationship between EI and adaptive outcomes following a stressful encounter.

Burns, & Nettelbeck, 2005; Mikolajczak, Nelis, Hansenne, & Quiodbach, 2008; Saklofske et al., 2007). These relationships may be due, in part, to the strong resemblance between trait-based EI measures and personality-type measures of coping styles. The findings are less clear where ability EI is concerned, largely because there are so few studies. Ability EI appears, however, negatively related to avoidance coping (Matthews, Zeidner, & Roberts, 2006; MacCann, Fogarty, Zeidner, & Roberts, 2011; Peters, Kranzler, & Rossen, 2009), but not to the greater use of coping strategies in general (Bastian et al., 2005). In sum, there are documented links between EI and various means of coping with stressful situations, with these links being stronger when trait-based measures of EI are employed.

Keefer et al. (2009) suggest that poor emotional insight, confusion about one's feelings, and inability to regulate strong emotions can exacerbate the negative impact of stress on health through ineffective and potentially harmful coping behaviors. They also corroborate the evidence that individuals with better emotional and social competencies are more likely to engage in adaptive emotion regulation and mood repair under stress. Overall, however, the specific mechanisms linking EI constructs to coping and stress outcomes remain obscure. For example, studies with the Mayer-Salovey-Caruso Emotional Intelligence Test (MSCEIT) have failed to show that EI moderates stress response as expected (Matthews, Emo, et al., 2006).

Keefer et al. (2009) concluded that "the cumulative findings presented . . . provide compelling support for the notion that adaptive coping might be conceptualized as emotional intelligence in action" (p. 202). Their review suggests that individuals who understand the nature and causes of their feelings and who are proficient in emotion-regulation abilities are generally less likely to collapse under the pressure of experimental or real-life stressors and are more likely to take proactive steps towards restoring their emotional balance and resolving their problems. Conscious use of one's EI resources appears to be instrumental in maximizing the effectiveness of the total coping effort. Adaptive coping acts to reduce the duration for stressful experiences and in so doing lessens the chances of developing health problems associated with chronic hyper-activation of physiological stress-response systems.

Well-Being

Various authors have theorized that EI should be correlated with important life outcomes, including subjective well-being, happiness, and life satisfaction (Law, Wong, & Song, 2004; Palmer, Donaldson, & Stough, 2002; Salovey & Mayer, 1990). A growing body of empirical evidence, reviewed below, suggests that EI in fact correlates with a variety of outcomes that signal social-emotional well-being and success, including greater life satisfaction, more frequent positive affect, higher self-esteem, and social engagement (see Zeidner et al., 2009). However, as shown below and consistent with what we have pointed out now many times, the robustness of this relation seems to be measure dependent.

A number of related mechanisms have been hypothesized to account for the nexus of relationships between EI and social-emotional well-being. First, under the assumption that high-EI individuals are more aware of their emotions and also better able to regulate them, they should experience lower levels of distress and stress-related emotions, and concomitantly, experience higher levels of well-being (Salovey, Bedell, Detweiler, & Mayer, 1999). Second, given the working assumption that high-EI individuals have an advantage in terms of greater social competence, richer social networks, and more effective coping strategies, this should serve to enhance their sense of subjective well-being and personal satisfaction with their social condition (Salovey et al., 1999; Salovey, Bedell, Detweiler, & Mayer, 2000). Third, because emotions provide information about one's relationship to the environment and others, interpreting and responding to that information can direct action and thought in ways that enhance or maintain well-being (Lazarus, 1991; Parrott, 2002). Finally, EI has been found to be associated with a lower propensity to experience negative emotions and a higher propensity to experience positive emotions, thus contributing to a richer sense of well-being (Mikolajczak et al., 2008). Thus, EI may be part of one's affective arsenal and "bag-of-tricks" that one can utilize to manage emotion-laden encounters, thus maintaining a sense of healthy well-being (Lenaghan et al., 2007). These mechanisms mediating the relationship between EI and well-being are graphically summarized in Figure 4.4.

Empirical evidence. There is accumulating evidence in support of the validity of self-report EI measures in predicting well-being and adaptive outcomes (e.g., see Zeidner, Matthews, & Roberts, 2011, for recent review). As discussed above, meta-analysis (Martins et al., 2010) confirms that there are moderate, reliable associations between EI and a range of questionnaire assessments of mental health. To give just a few examples, self-report EI measures have been related to happiness (Chamorro-Premuzic, Bennett, & Furnham, 2007), optimism and mood

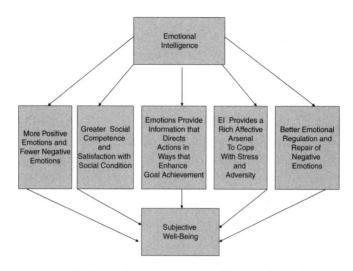

FIGURE 4.4 Mediating factors in the EI–well-being relationship.

(Mikolajczak et al., 2006; Petrides et al., 2007), and affective decision making (Sevdalis, Petrides, & Harvey, 2007). However, as we saw in Chapter 2, much of the predictive validity of self-report EI measures derives from their overlap with standard personality factors such as emotional stability (low neuroticism) and extraversion (Day, 2004).

Overall, ability-based measures of EI have not fared as well as self-report measures in predicting affective indicators of personal adaptation or well-being. Some studies show that EI is related to life satisfaction after controlling for IQ and personality (Ciarrochi, Chan, & Caputi, 2000), but others have yielded weak or non-significant associations between the MSCEIT and indicators of personal adaptation, such as subjective well-being, perceived stress, life satisfaction, satisfaction with social relationships, and depression (e.g., Bastian et al., 2005; Brackett, Rivers, Shiffman, Lerner, & Salovey, 2006; Zeidner & Olnick-Shemesh, 2010). In the Martins et al. (2010) meta-analysis, the association between ability EI and mental heath was found to be a rather unimpressive $r = 0.17$ (11 studies). A recent study by

Rode et al. (2008) reported that when controlling for personality and ability factors, EI did not predict incremental variance in life satisfaction (or GPA) in two samples of undergraduate business school students. However, as we saw in Chapter 3, there appear to be some criteria that may be more robustly predicted by the MSCEIT, including relationship satisfaction, social competencies, and refraining from self-harming behaviors such as substance abuse (see Rivers, Brackett, Salovey, & Mayer, 2007).

The greater validity of questionnaire measures of EI, relative to ability EI, in predicting well-being perhaps reflects their reliance on the person's self-reports of their subjective well-being and adaptive social functioning, which may be biased by self-appraisals. That is, social well-being scales may correlate with questionnaire measures of EI precisely because both types of measure reflect how positive the person's self-opinions are. Of course, confidence in one's social skills may also lead to genuine enhancement of social functioning.

APPLIED CONTEXTS

The debate and controversy surrounding the practical utility of EI in applied settings has made EI one of the most controversial constructs in modern psychology. To many enthusiastic supporters, EI is viewed as a quick fix panacea for manifest problems and difficulties in the classroom and at work. For other, less sanguine supporters, EI is little more than old wine packaged in new and more glittering containers. Furthermore, some rather extravagant claims concerning the practical utility of EI have created considerable excitement about the potential applications of EI in the educational and business communities, as well as for consumption by the general public. Thus, EI has been touted as a major predictor of educational and occupational outcomes and even a stronger predictor than existing measures of ability or personality. Some of the more extravagant claims about the pivotal role of EI in applied settings have been quite deservedly criticized (Salovey, Caruso, & Mayer, 2004), leading to a backlash, often overshadowing and even diminishing the tenability of some of the more careful claims made by more sober EI supporters. We now turn to examine the evidence for the claimed pivotal role of EI in two key applied settings in modern life: schools and workplace.

EI Goes to School

Traditionally, many educators and administrators have embraced a rather narrow and tunneled vision of what successful educational institutions are all about. Accordingly, schools exist to ensure that students master basic skills (especially in reading, writing, and math) and also are provided with a solid background in other important academic areas (e.g., sciences, history, and foreign languages). Recently, however, some experts have advocated a broader and more comprehensive vision of successful schooling—one that enhances students' social and emotional skills, as well as traditional cognitive-based academic skills (Brackett & Katulak, 2007). According to this "new look" in education, to be educated means not only to be cognitively intelligent, knowledgeable, and well versed in the sciences, humanities, and the arts, but also to be emotionally aware of oneself and others, kind, empathetic, compassionate, caring, considerate, responsible, trustworthy, conscientious, honest, pro-social, and in control—emotionally intelligent, in short (Elias, Hunter, & Kress, 2001). This "new look" requires that the traditional focus on cognitive abilities be supplemented by a strong concern with social and emotional training and development. A summary of the potential benefits of raising students' EI is shown in Figure 4.5.

Proponents of EI in the schools have found particularly fertile grounds within the aforementioned "new look" movement in education, latching on in a steadfast manner to the emotional literacy bandwagon. EI advocates have claimed that the

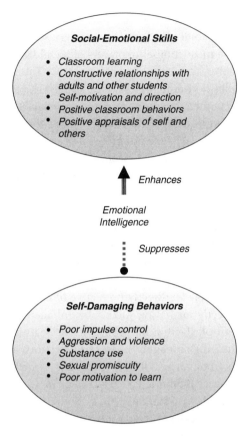

FIGURE 4.5 Potential benefits of EI for the student in enhancing social-emotional skills and suppressing harmful behaviors.

challenges posed by schools can be met by infusing emotional literacy and social and emotional learning programs into the standard curriculum, as well as by creating a school climate that fosters the development and application of social-emotional skills. In fact, social and emotional education has been coined the "missing piece" in school life—that part of a school's mission that, while always close to the thoughts of many teachers, somehow eluded them (Elias et al., 1997). The trend of bringing emotional literacy into schools makes emotions and social life themselves key topics for learning and discussion, rather than treating these most compelling facets of a child's life as irrelevant intrusions.

A number of commentators (e.g., Romasz, Kanotr, & Elias, 2004) have claimed that the acquisition of social and emotional skills are a prerequisite for students before they can benefit from the traditional academic material presented in the classroom (see also Humphrey, Curran, Morris, Farrell, & Woods, 2007; Zins, Payton, Weissberg, & O'Brien, 2007). It is thought that elevating EI will impact both overt academic goals, such as better grades, and the student's broader personal development. EI skills and competencies are commonly believed to be able to help motivate students to reach higher levels of achievement, become more socially and emotionally competent, and to become more responsible and productive members of society. That is, EI may be directly predictive of student success, as well as indirectly mediating success by enhancing motivation and self-control, facilitating constructive learning partnerships, minimizing damaging antisocial behaviors, and protecting students from barriers to learning, such as mental distress, substance abuse, delinquency, teen pregnancy, and violence (Hawkins, Smith, & Catalano, 2004). Some proponents of EI have even claimed that EI can predict success at school as well as, or better than, IQ (Goleman, 1995).

Empirical evidence. There is some evidence to suggest that EI is indeed related, in general terms, to the development of cognitive abilities in children (Denham, 2006; Malecki & Elliot, 2002; Welsh, Park, Widaman, & O'Neil, 2001). However, studies of associations between EI and measures of academic success, such as student grades, are decidedly mixed in their findings (see MacCann et al., 2011; Zeidner, Roberts, & Matthews, 2002). Some of the stronger evidence for beneficial effects of trait EI on academic performance comes from a series of studies of university students conducted in the state of Ontario, Canada, which showed that, even with IQ controlled, EI scores discriminate academic high-flyers from those on academic probation in first year, and predict academic retention (Parker, Summerfeldt et al., 2004; Parker, Hogan, Eastabrook, Oke, & Wood, 2006). Studies of high school students also showed that EI adds to IQ in predicting high grades (Hogan et al., 2010). Unfortunately, although this series of studies is otherwise persuasive, the researchers failed to control for the personality factors that are known to overlap with trait EI. In addition, EI was more modestly predictive of academic performance than IQ, contrary to Goleman's (1995) suggestion. Another recent study (Saklofske et al., 2011) showed small but significant correlations between some facets of trait EI and grades in Scottish undergraduates. In a multivariate analysis, a factor that combined these EI facets with problem-focused coping appeared to predict grades over and above the personality factors of the Big Five. However, this study controlled for personality but not cognitive ability. Amelang and Steinmayr (2006) reported a study that controlled for both potential confounds and found that no associations between EI and school performance remained; intelligence and conscientiousness were more important predictors. As summed up by Amelang and Steinmayr (2006), "The results concerning the incremental validity of both ability and trait EI regarding achievement criteria remains ambiguous and necessitate further research" (p. 460).

Fewer studies have tested the role of ability EI in school achievement. Rivers et al. (2007) reviewed evidence from a small number of MSCEIT studies. They concluded that although the majority of studies found that ability EI correlated with including grades in college students, these correlations tended to disappear once verbal ability was controlled. Burns, Bastian, and Nettelbeck (2007) arrived at a similar conclusion in a study of Australian students. Recent research (MacCann et al., 2011) confirms that the MSCEIT correlated with grades, but has not shown conclusively that the test adds much to IQ as a predictor.

The modest research outcomes we have reviewed contrast markedly with a finding substantiated by meta-analysis that training social-emotional competencies improves grades (Durlak, Weissberg, Dymnicki, Taylor, & Schellinger, 2011). One possibility is that the various psychometric tests for EI, including both questionnaires and ability measures, do not pick up the specific social-emotional qualities that may enhance student learning (although MacCann et al. (2011) argue that the MSCEIT may assess relevant coping abilities). Indeed, training programs often focus on specific, context-bound skills, such as how to say "no" to drugs, as opposed to trying to effect some more general personality change. We can imagine a variety of qualities linked to EI that would plausibly improve grades, including task-directed coping, greater active participation in learning, and keeping out of various kinds of trouble. The available research provides some tantalizing clues that various scales for EI assess some of these qualities better than standard personality and ability measures—but a greater focus on the specific skills involved may be necessary to take the research and its educational implications further.

El Goes to Work

As recently pointed out by Joseph and Newman (2010), the purported relationship between EI and organizational performance has stimulated interest among organizational psychologists and practitioners in EI as a possible tool for personnel selection and training purposes. EI has also become an integral part of the discussion surrounding effective organizational recruitment, placement, and training; functioning and performance on the job; job satisfaction and well-being; organizational citizenship; and organizational leadership (Zeidner et al., 2009). EI has also been touted as a panacea for modern business, organizational functioning, and an essential, but often neglected, ingredient of diverse professions—teaching, nursing, legal, political, medical, and engineering practices (see Zeidner, Matthews, & Roberts, 2001). In fact, the practical importance and potential utility attributed to EI in applied settings is a plausible account of much of the interest generated by EI since its popularization two decades ago, as well as the widespread acclaim this concept continues to enjoy at present in academia, applied settings, the media, and in popular writings (Matthews, Zeidner, & Roberts, 2002).

As pointed out by Cherniss (2010), this is not to say that technical skills and cognitive abilities are unimportant. Managers, executives, and professionals require certain levels of these threshold competencies just to get in the door. Once an individual becomes an executive or manager, what putatively distinguishes that person's performance from another's is self-confidence, self-control, and the ability to motivate others.

Job performance. Various components of EI have been claimed to contribute to success and productivity in the workplace for a number of reasons. First, EI has been claimed to predict occupational success because it influences one's ability to succeed in coping with environmental demands and pressures at the worksite (Bar-On, 1997). Second, workers endowed with high EI are also claimed to be particularly adept at designing projects that involve infusing products with feelings and aesthetics (Mayer & Salovey, 1997). Third, more emotionally intelligent individuals are said to succeed at communicating in interesting and assertive ways, thus making others feel understood and appreciated in the occupational environment (Goleman, 1998). Finally, it has been claimed that EI is useful for group development since a large part of effective and smooth team work is knowing each other's strengths and weaknesses, and leveraging strengths whenever possible (Bar-On, 1997).

EI has been claimed to work through a wide array of specific competencies to impact on work behaviors and success, as illustrated in Figure 4.6. Within this general framework, a large number of competencies have been claimed to be critical for success in occupational settings (see e.g., Boyatzis et al., 2000; Cooper & Sawaf, 1997; Weisinger, 1998). These include accurate emotional perception and self-awareness, emotional management, adaptability and stress management; empathy, service orientation, and organizational awareness; and conflict

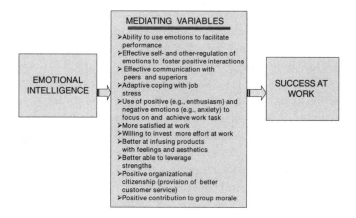

FIGURE 4.6 Mediating factors in the relationship between EI and success on the job.

management, teamwork and collaboration, and leadership (Boyatzis & Sala, 2004). Goleman (1998), for example, lists 25 different competencies necessary for effective performance in various occupational contexts. While trust and empathy appear vital for psychotherapists, social workers, pastors, and marriage counselors, confidentiality is touted as important for loan officers, attorneys, and priests. It is of note that of the 180 competence models identified by Goleman (1998), over two thirds of the abilities deemed essential for effective performance were identified as emotional competencies.

Empirical evidence. What empirical evidence is there for the criterion validity of EI as a predictor of job performance? A meta-analysis conducted by Van Rooy and Viswesvaran (2004) pointed to weak criterion validity for most EI measures, with estimated true correlations close to 0.20. Criterion validity was similarly modest for both objective and questionnaire assessments of EI. When controlling for IQ, EI accounted for only about 2% of the variance in occupational criteria, whereas IQ added 31% to the variance, above and beyond measures of EI. However, EI added to the predictive power of the Big Five personality traits, and even the modest criterion validities that the study demonstrates may be practically useful in certain circumstances. The authors suggest that using EI measures for personnel selection may generate significant savings and improvements for organizations.

Furthermore, Joseph and Newman's (2010) meta-analysis indicates that the incremental validity of the EI measure may vary both by the type of EI measure employed as well as the nature of the job being considered. Thus, whereas ability-based measures of EI show only a modicum of incremental validity over and above cognitive ability and personality in predicting job performance, self-report measures based on *mixed models* of EI show substantial incremental validity over cognitive ability and Big Five personality traits. Why "grab-bag" measures of EI appear to exhibit some incremental validity is not entirely clear, though one intriguing possibility is that the personality assessments are generally brief, and do not sample all of the various facets of personality. Further, as pointed out in Chapter 3, the relationship between ability-based EI measures and job performance appear to be moderated by the emotional requirements of the job. Thus, EI positively predicts performance for high-emotional labor jobs (i.e., jobs that require regulating both feelings and expressions for organizational goals) and negatively predicts performance in low-emotional labor jobs. Joseph and Newman (2010) theorize that occupations in which there is frequent customer–interpersonal interaction (i.e., high-emotional labor) require more emotion regulation; emotion regulation demands can drain resources from task performance unless the employee processes heightened ability to effectively regulate emotion. Given that individuals with high emotion regulation ability are expected to perform especially well in jobs that require high-emotional labor (e.g., sales clerks, insurance agents, workers at Disneyworld, undertakers, and debt collectors) the authors suggest that organizational psychologists should base their decision to use an EI measure on the emotional labor content of the job.

In a recent review of the literature, Cherniss (2010) concludes that EI, measured either by ability or self-report assessments, is rather modestly related to job performance. Cherniss identified 13 studies using self-report measures and 12 studies based on ability-based EI measures that found some relationship between EI and performance. Dependent variables included supervisor and peer ratings, organizational citizenship behavior, and more objective outcomes (e.g., salary increases and negotiation outcomes). Although some of the findings have been rather weak, others were strong, showing some inconsistency in the results.

It is important to note that studies are often weakened by methodological problems, such as lack of a clear rationale for predicting effects of EI, failure to statistically control for the effects of personality and ability factors, over-reliance on subjective ratings, small samples, poor documentation of samples and jobs. Perhaps in consequence, the field is over-reliant on unpublished studies that have not been subjected to the rigors of peer review (Van Rooy & Viswesvaran, 2004).

Job Satisfaction. High-EI individuals have been claimed to experience greater levels of job satisfaction and subjective well-being at the workplace for a number of reasons. First, high-EI persons may utilize their ability to appraise and manage emotions in others, thus enabling them to foster interactions that help boost their morale and that of the group. This, in turn, helps contribute positively to well-being and job satisfaction for all. Furthermore, when compared to their low-EI counterparts, high-EI individuals may be better at regulating their emotions to reduce job stress. Moreover, supervisors who are emotionally intelligent are more adept at helping workers manage their emotions, buffering them from negative events that diminish job satisfaction. Finally, emotionally intelligent managers tend to foster a positive work environment that enhances job satisfaction (Sy, Tram, & O'Hara, 2006). These managers are adept at nurturing more positive interactions between employees, which fosters cooperation, coordination, and organizational citizenship behaviors contributing both to enhanced performance and job satisfaction.

Empirical evidence. Indeed, research suggests that emotionally intelligent individuals report greater satisfaction at work (e.g., Brackett, Palomera, Mojsa-Kaja, Reyes, & Salovey, 2010; Kafetsios & Zampetakis, 2008; Slaski, 2001; Sy et al., 2006; Vigoda-Gadot & Meisler, 2010). Recent work by Kafetsios et al. (2008) suggests that EI might work through positive and negative emotions to impact job satisfaction. However, one might wonder whether overlap between EI and low neuroticism explains these findings.

Organizational Citizenship. EI is frequently held to be an essential element in what it takes to become a productive and contented organizational citizen. Indeed, many companies are now committed to the idea of "corporate social responsibility." Indeed, EI may be construed as one of the components of corporate social responsibility. These companies (e.g., Toyota) are now scouting for people who are compassionate, conscientious, reliable on the job, team workers that can work in harmony, and also care both about their job as well as their coworkers (i.e., emotionally intelligent individuals). In fact, how well we understand and handle our own emotions and those of others has become emblematic of a new rationality and a new working skills "toolkit."

A spate of publications has conceptually linked EI to positive organizational citizenship (i.e., attitudes and actions in the workplace that benefit working relationships and contribute to a positive working climate). Thus, it has been contended (Abraham, 2005) that EI would both augment organizational citizenship behaviors and enhance organizational commitment. Moreover, Jordan & Troth (2002) argue that high-EI individuals are more likely to generate high affective commitment—even during times of stress and instability. Unfortunately, these theoretical models have not yet been put to the empirical test and their validity remains to be established.

Empirical evidence. Empirical studies provide evidence in support of the link between EI and affective outcomes that might be subsumed under the heading of "positive organizational citizenship." These include job dedication (Law et al., 2004); customer orientation (Rozell, Pettijohn, & Parker, 2004); interpersonal sensitivity and pro-social tendencies (Lopes, Salovey, Côté, &. Beers, 2005); altruistic behavior, career commitment, and affective commitment to the organization (Carmeli, 2003); altruism and compliance (Carmeli & Josman, 2006), satisfaction with other group members and with the communication within their group (Lopes et al., 2005); affective tone in negotiations (Foo, Elfenbein, Tan, & Aik, 2004); willingness to change (Vakola, Tsaousis, & Nikolaou, 2004); and conflict resolution styles (Jordan & Troth, 2002). However, these findings need to be replicated across different occupations and in large representative samples of organizational members.

EI and Transformational Leadership. Over the past two decades or so, social and emotional competencies have become integral to any discussion of effective leadership (Goleman, 1998). Leadership is frequently viewed as an emotion-laden process, both from the perspective of leader and follower. As argued by Goleman, Boyatzis, & McKee (2002), the primal job of leadership is *emotional*. In fact, great leaders move us emotionally and ignite our passions and inspire the best in us. Thus, at its roots, the fundamental task of leaders is to prime good feelings in followers. Emotional competencies, it has been argued, can be important at every stage of the process linking effective leadership and work group outcomes (Ashkanazy & Tse, 2000).

EI research on organizational management and leadership has focused on a set of leadership qualities subsumed under the umbrella term of a transformational style of leadership (Bass, 2002). Transformational leadership is characterized by charisma and articulation of a vision of the future, provision of intellectual stimulation to followers, and individualized consideration. The leader transmits a sense of mission that is effectively articulated, instilling pride, faith, and respect in followers (Yammarino & Bass, 1990). EI is viewed as a prerequisite for successful transformational leadership for a number of reasons (Barling, Slater, & Kelloway, 2000). First, EI has been claimed to be a foundational element of charisma, vision, and careful attention to the personal needs and qualities of the individual follower (Prati, Douglas, Ferris, Ammeter, & Buckley, 2003). Transformational leaders, it is claimed, will use charismatic authority and transformational influence and induce collective motivation in team members to improve team performance. Further, transformational leaders are said to be in touch with their own and their follower's feelings and "lead from the heart" (Ashkanasy & Tse, 2000).

Empirical evidence. Some studies have established a relationship between EI and key facets of transformational leadership (Bass, 2002; Barling et al., 2000; Skinner & Spurgeon, 2005). However the data are not entirely consistent, with some studies reporting contrary findings (Palmer, Walls, Burgess, & Stough, 2001). A recent meta-analysis by Harms and Credé (2010), based on 62 independent samples, indicated a validity estimate of .59 when ratings of both EI and leadership behaviors were provided by the same source (self, subordinates, peers, or superiors). However, when ratings of the constructs were derived from different sources, the validity estimate was 0.12. Lower validity estimates were found for transactional and laissez-faire leadership behaviors than for transformational leadership measures. Also, trait measures tended to show higher validities than ability-based measures of EI. Agreement across ratings sources for the same construct was low for both transformational leadership (0.14) and EI (0.16). Based on these findings, future research would benefit from a number of improvements, such as using practicing leaders (rather than students); gathering data on leadership in more objective ways; exploring further measures of EI; and controlling statistically for personality and IQ.

Overall, the current state of EI is somewhat paradoxical; although EI is a popular tool in organizations, currently being used for a wide array of applied purposes, industrial psychology has yet to answer many theoretical, measurement, and validity questions surrounding the construct. Some caustic critics have cast a shadow over employing EI at the workplace (Antonakis et al., 2009) and have claimed that given the sparse empirical support for EI measures, it may be unethical and unconscionable to use these measures in applied settings (hiring, promotion, and retention). As argued by Van Rooy, Whitman, Viswesvaran, & Pluta (2010), before using EI measures in high-stakes testing, like personnel selection and promotion or salary decisions, a number of issues relating to bias, equity in selection, and consequential validity of use of EI measures need to be investigated and settled. Furthermore, as we discussed in Chapter 2, questionnaire (though not ability) EI scales are easy to "fake" (Day & Carroll, 2008), which makes them quite unsuitable for any high-stakes use, such as selecting job applicants.

SUMMARY AND CONCLUSIONS

Various authors have theorized that EI plays a pivotal role in everyday life, with particular focus on applied settings. This chapter reviewed the theory and empirical evidence in support of the role of EI in shaping a number of salient outcomes in everyday life. As discussed, a growing body of empirical evidence suggests that EI, in fact, correlates significantly with a variety of outcomes that signal social-emotional well-being and success in applied settings, including educational and occupational contexts.

With respect to the social domain, it has been claimed that EI is adaptive for handling social encounters, with high-EI persons benefiting from empathic understanding of others and adaptive skills in constructive communication of context-appropriate emotions. Our review suggests that overall high-EI persons tend to perceive themselves as more socially competent and as having a better quality of personal relationships, and are also viewed by others as more interpersonally sensitive than those lower in EI. EI also appears to be related to happiness and satisfaction with marital relations, although partner effects have yet to be demonstrated.

With respect to the health domain, a modest to moderate relationship has been found between EI and both physical and mental health, although the effect size is conditional upon the type of measure used as well as the health criterion assessed. Specifically, meta-analytic data suggest that the association of EI with mental health is significantly higher than the association between EI and physical health. Also, the reported associations between EI and health are higher, on average, for self-report than ability measures. Background variables, such as gender, may moderate the EI–health relationship.

A sizable body of recent research has shed light on the role of EI in coping with stress. The available literature suggests that EI is only weakly related to coping strategies. This research, however, points to a positive relationship between EI and action-oriented coping strategies and a negative relationship between EI and use of palliative and avoidance strategies. EI also appears to be a more robust predictor of general coping styles than measures of actual coping in a specific context. However, the findings appear to be measure-dependent, in part, with self-report measures showing more robust relationships with coping and adaptive outcomes than ability-based measures. Finally, the association between EI and measures of well-being and satisfaction with life has been reported for both trait and ability measures of EI, although the correlations are more robust for self-report measures.

Although it has been commonly claimed that EI is the missing piece in education and a prerequisite for learning and academic achievement, our review of the available literature suggests that EI appears to be modestly related to the development of relevant cognitive abilities as well as to academic success in adolescents and college adults. However, when statistically controlling for cognitive ability and personality factors, there is conflicting evidence on whether or not EI adds a practically relevant quantity of incremental variance to the prediction of school grades or performance. Evidence suggesting that social-emotional learning programs can be quite effective in enhancing students' skills and learning (Durlak et al., 2011) may perhaps suggest that current EI assessments are missing some important facets of real-life emotional competencies.

EI may matter in occupational settings, particularly with respect to job satisfaction and leadership development, but EI accounts for only a relatively modest percentage of outcome variance. Thus, as is the case for educational outcomes, we need to temper our expectations regarding the practical utility of EI in occupational settings (Cherniss, 2010). Although a number of studies clearly support the predictive validity of both self-report and ability-based EI in occupational settings, even when statistically controlling for individual difference variables (personality, intelligence, and both personality and intelligence), the data with respect to performance have been mixed and inconsistent. Focusing on occupations where emotion regulation is especially important, such as customer service, may be needed to substantiate the occupational relevance of EI. A final issue is that some of the studies suffer from poor ecological validity, being based on student samples and using dubious criterion measures (e.g., supervisor's ratings).

For some years now, intelligence researchers have come to the realization that IQ tests may not predict the lion's share of variance in important occupational and educational settings. IQ measures tend to reach a ceiling in predicting criterion measures—accounting for about 25% of criterion score variance, at best. By the same token, EI researchers need to tone down their overly exuberant expectations of the practical value of EI in everyday life and applied settings. Furthermore, it is important to realize that in partitioning variance accounted for by person (EI), situation, and the person by situation interaction, it is the latter two components that may account for the lion's share of the variance in performance in applied settings. As we recently stressed (Zeidner et al., 2009), given the mixed reports in the archival literature, there is an urgent need for the practical value of EI to be consistently demonstrated across diverse areas of everyday life.

5

Training Emotional Intelligence in Applied Settings

im, a sophomore at UCLA, was quite popular among his friends on campus, having the reputation of being very smart, resourceful, and highly emotionally intelligent. During his first day on a part-time job he landed at a major food chain in West LA, he was approached by an elderly gentleman, who looked quite agitated. He wanted to buy half a lettuce, but the cashier at the counter refused to sell him partial produce, claiming it was against company policy. Jim agreed to sell the half a lettuce and then told his boss about the painful customer who wanted to buy only half a lettuce. Jim did not realize the old guy was behind him the whole time. Once realizing that, he spun around, seeing him, and saying "and this is the gentleman who bought the other half."

The manager, who happened to observe the entire scenario, invited Jim into his office for a chat. The manager lauded Jim for his emotionally intelligent and resourceful handling of the emotionally laden situation earlier on. "I can see you have great social and emotional skills," said the manger, and "if you keep up the good work, you certainly will go places within our store chain, young man." "Incidentally, where are you originally from?" asked the manager. "I am from a small town way up in Northern Alaska, called Groundhog Rise, which is not even on the map," Jim replied. "What brought you to California?" inquired the manager. "Well, to tell you the truth, there is not very much going on in Groundhog Rise. Basically, the town folk are either hockey players or hookers." The manager's face turned crimson red and after squirming uncomfortably in his chair for a minute, he blurted out: "It so happens, young man, that my wife was born and bred in Groundhog Rise!" Without batting an eyelid, Jim replied: "Way too cool…which hockey team did she play for?"

Clearly, not everyone has the emotional savvy, wherewithal, and resourcefulness evidenced by Jim in the above awkward and potentially volatile situations. Yet, emotional competencies may play an important role in achieving successful adaptation to emotionally laden encounters in applied settings and are essential for efficiently negotiating such situations. In fact, over the years, emotional intelligence (EI) has inspired numerous intervention programs designed to train EI competencies, such as those manifested above by Jim, along with many others, and these programs have mushroomed in educational and occupational settings across the globe.

This chapter focuses on the ways and means of training EI in the two applied contexts that have received the lion's share of attention in the literature—educational and occupational settings. We begin by discussing EI-inspired educational programs and curricular developments aimed at cultivating students' emotional competencies. We then move on to review current approaches to training EI in the workplace.

TRAINING EI IN SCHOOLS

Educational psychologists (e.g., Elias, Kress, & Hunter, 2006) have speculated that the current crisis plaguing the US school system (which includes underachievement, increasing high school dropout rates, peer violence, alcohol and drug abuse, and teenage pregnancy) may stem, in part, from the failure of educators and administrators to recognize that schools need to address the whole child, including cognitive, motivational, and affective aspects of their personality (Humphrey, Curran, Morris, Farrell, & Woods, 2007). Accordingly, one possible remedy toward solving some of the noted problems in the school system is to thoroughly revamp the school curriculum, balancing the focus on school achievement with a focus on students' social and emotional learning outcomes (e.g., Zins, Payton, Weissberg, & O'Brien, 2007).

As students across the school years are not systematically educated in affective competencies, basic values, social skills, and moral reasoning, they are not given the crucial foundations and skills for becoming caring, empathic, responsible, and compassionate adults. Thus, what is needed, experts maintain, is the direct training of social and emotional competencies in the classroom. These competencies relate to the ability to understand, manage, and express the social and emotional aspects of life in ways that enable one to successfully manage life tasks, such as learning, solving problems, forming relationships, and adapting to the complex demands of growth and development. As Elias and his co-workers (2006) have so aptly put it, "academic knowledge that is not tempered by social-emotional intelligence and ethical guidance can be a danger to society, not a boon" (p. 167).

EI interventions have generally been discussed under the broader rubric of social and emotional learning (SEL) programs. Zins, Weissberg, Wang, and Walberg (2004) define SEL as the process "through which we learn to recognize and manage emotions, care about others, make good decisions, behave ethically and responsibly, develop positive relationships, and avoid negative behaviors" (p. 4). The idea that students' emotional and social problems can be addressed through school-based programs became popular among educational reformers during the 1990s. The delivery of preventive interventions through schools is reasonable given the amount of time that children and youth spend in these settings, the important socializing influence that these institutions exert, and the co-morbidity of learning and mental disorders. There is increasing evidence that social-emotional skills have the potential to promote engagement in learning and long-term academic success and to ameliorate behavioral risk factors that might undermine this process (Durlak, Weissberg, Quintana, & Perez, 2004).

Hundreds of SEL programs are currently implemented in US schools, across K-12. In the UK, a program for Social and Learning Emotional Skills (SEAL) is now underway in the majority of schools (Department for Children, Schools and Families, 2007). However, it is more of a loose enabling framework than a specific set of instructional tools. Perhaps for this reason, an initial evaluation of the UK research effort accompanying SEAL concludes that thus far the program has failed to have an overall positive impact, despite some anecdotal successes (Humphrey, Lensdrum & Wigelsworth, 2010); indeed, significant reductions in pupils' trust and respect for teachers were found. Returning to the more prescriptive—but also more successful—US initiatives, a broad spectrum of EI intervention programs, designed to teach emotional competencies in the school, is now available. These include social skills training, cognitive-behavioral modification, self-management, and multi-modal programs (Topping, Holmes, & Bremner, 2000). Based on reports disseminated by the Collaborative for Academic, Social, and Emotional Learning (CASEL) at the University of Illinois, scores of different emotional literacy programs are currently being used by hundreds of American schools and students at all grade levels are now learning about their feelings quite explicitly.

SEL provides a common framework for programs with a wide array of specified outcomes. Curricular-based SEL programs seek to educate children about the value of emotional and social competencies in social relations as well as to foster the development of specific skills in these areas (e.g., recognition of emotions in self and others, empathy, conflict resolution; see reviews by Cohen, 1999a, 1999b, 1999c; Zins et al., 2004). Such programs seek to teach children to communicate more effectively, cooperate, resolve conflicts creatively and adaptively, reflect on self and interpersonal experience, control impulsivity, and make more thoughtful and collaborative social decisions. A wide array of skills and competencies are addressed, including self-control of behaviors and emotions, self-efficacy, effective coping strategies, perspective taking, empathy, interpersonal problem solving, creative conflict resolution, decision making, and positive connections to school family and other adult role models. Five basic skills are typically targeted in social-emotional intelligence interventions (Elias et al., 2006). We reproduce these basic skills, along with the processes thought to underlie each skill, in Table 5.1.

Working Assumptions of EI Programs

The development and implementation of EI-focused educational programs in the classroom rests on a number of basic working assumptions. To begin with, schools are considered to be key social settings, with learning viewed as a social and highly interpersonal process. Students are therefore believed to learn best in collaboration with their teachers, in the company of peers, and supported by parents, community, and school staff. As social and emotional factors play such an important role, schools must attend to this aspect for the benefit of students.

It is further assumed that emotional competencies, by contrast with fluid intelligence (see Chapter 3), are highly malleable and modifiable attributes, which can be meaningfully trained

TABLE 5.1 FIVE BASIC SKILLS TARGETED BY SOCIAL-EMOTIONAL INTELLIGENCE INTERVENTIONS

Skills	Basic Components
1. Self-awareness	Identifying and recognizing emotions Accurate self-perception Self-efficacy Recognizing strengths and needs and values
2. Social awareness	Perspective taking Empathy Respect for others (including appreciating diversity)
3. Responsible decision making	Problem identification and analysis Problem solving Evaluation and reflection
4. Self-management	Impulse control and stress management Self-motivation and discipline Goal setting and organizational skills
5. Relationship management	Communication Building relationships Working cooperatively Negotiation and conflict management Help seeking and providing help to others

and improved through educational programs throughout the school years (Elias, M. J., Hunter, L., & Kress, 2001). Whereas the components of EI appear being capable of being learned both inside and outside the home, the classroom, as a more formal arena than the family setting, may be a particularly useful source of generalized EI skills that may be applied to other structured environments (e.g., the workplace). As discussed in Chapter 4, EI is also thought to be positively related to academic achievement and productive experience in the world (Elias et al., 1997). This is one of the presumed reasons for the keen interest in the construct in educational circles. Finally, affect and cognition are assumed to work synergistically, so that schools will be most successful in their educational mission if they make a systematic attempt at integrating efforts to promote manifold facets of a child's personality through cognitive, social, and emotional learning.

Guidelines for SEL Programs

A number of guidelines have been proffered in the literature for the development and implementation of SEL programs (e.g., Elias et al., 2006; Zins et al., 2007). These are discussed briefly below.

1. *Curricular materials need to target the whole person.* Effective instruction requires using methods that take the whole person into consideration and seamlessly address students' cognitive, emotional, and social skills, rather than focus on one-categorical outcome. Curricular content also needs to target student attitudes and values about themselves and others, their perceptions of social norms, and their understanding of information about targeted social and health domains. SEL programs need to directly instruct students in strategies by which affect can be appropriately recognized, mediated, and modulated.

2. *SEL skills should be taught in the context of school activities and integrated with the rest of the curriculum.* SEL activities need to be integrated into whatever instructional unit is currently being taught in the classroom. Also, SEL skills should be context-relevant and not divorced from other aspects of the children's lives. For instance, students can learn how to harness emotions like anger and fear in physical education class. Or they might learn how to handle frustration in the context of a math or foreign language assignment, or analyze and understand the emotions of characters in the stories they read in English literature or in History and Civics. They might even learn something about complex emotions (e.g., envy or pride) when their exams or graded essays are returned to them. In short, this form of affective learning proceeds throughout the educational system, and these competencies can be developed in vivo (i.e., as part of

instruction in the sciences, humanities, sports, dance class, arts, or other social activities).

3. *Programs should provide developmentally and culturally appropriate instruction.* Current EI intervention programs should be based on developmentally and culturally appropriate instructional materials. Preschool to high school classroom instruction should attempt to create a caring and engaging learning environment and teach children to apply social and emotional skills, both in and out of school. At the same time, these programs should carefully take into consideration the child's developmental stage and sociocultural background. SEL should also strive to enhance school performance by addressing the cognitive, emotional, and social dimensions of learning.

4. *Arrangements need to be made for training of teachers, administrators, and students.* Programs need to include training on social and emotional skills for administrators, teachers, and students and encourage family, school, and community partnerships. Interventions should receive backing from both teachers and students and should have backing from all levels of the school district and ultimately state and federal agencies.

5. *Systematic program evaluation should be conducted.* SEL programs also need to be grounded in solid psychological theory and systematically field tested. Thus, programs need to be accompanied by systematic program evaluation, including a theory-driven intervention model, intervention hypotheses, solid experimental or quasi-experimental designs, implementation checks, and valid and reliable outcome measures, administered at various points throughout the program.

An Example of an SEL Program: Promoting Alternative Thinking Strategies (PATHS)

It is beyond the scope of this chapter to extensively survey all EI intervention programs or emotion-based curricular materials available on the market today (for a survey of several prevalent programs, see Cohen, 1999a, 1999b, 1999c; Matthews, Zeidner, & Roberts, 2002; Zeidner, Matthews, & Roberts, 2009; Zins et al., 2007). In the section to follow, we briefly describe the PATHS, the most widely known and rigorously researched among the various intervention programs designed specifically to promote emotional competencies (Greenberg, Kusché, & Riggs, 2004; Kelly, Longbottom, Potts, & Williamson, 2004). PATHS is a universal, teacher-taught social-emotional learning curriculum for students in Grades pre-K–5. PATHS is designed to improve preschool and elementary school children's social-emotional skills in four domains: emotional understanding and emotional expression skills; self-control/emotion regulation; pro-social friendship skills; and problem-solving skills (interpersonal negotiation, conflict resolution skills, and so forth).

The program is based on the Affective-Behavioral-Cognitive-Dynamic model of development (Greenberg & Kusché, 2006), which places primary importance on the developmental integration of emotion, language, behavior, and cognitive understanding as they relate to social and emotional competence. PATHS focuses direction on a wide range of processes, including developing and utilizing a larger emotions vocabulary; increasing the students' ability to discuss emotions; and developing understanding of the meta-cognitive aspects of emotions (e.g., awareness of cues for recognizing emotion; understanding display rules; simultaneity of emotional experiences; strategies for changing emotional states; negotiating an problem-solving skills).

Five major conceptual domains are covered in each didactic unit: emotional understanding; self-control; building self-esteem; relationships; and interpersonal problem-solving skills. At each grade level, the curriculum includes a set of lessons that are delivered twice a week for 20–30 min, depending on the age of the students. Each unit of study is integrated and builds on the learning preceding it. Lessons are sequenced according to increasing developmental difficulty and include dialoguing, role playing, storytelling, modeling for teachers and peers, social and self-reinforcement, attribution training, and verbal mediation.

Learning is promoted in a multi-method manner through the combined use of visual, verbal, and kinesthetic cues. Emotion lessons focus on teaching specific feeling words and skills related to emotional processes, including emotion recognition, communication regarding emotions, and emotion regulation. Original stories and activities are included to encourage motivation and skills in reading. In addition, friendship lessons focus on skills related to the increase of positive social behavior (e.g. social participation, pro-social behavior, and communication skills) and the skills needed to make and sustain friendship (e.g. good manner, negotiation, and effective communication). Development of self-control, affective awareness, communication, and beginning problem-solving skills are integrated with the use of various techniques.

Extensive generalization techniques are included to assist teachers in applying and transferring skills to other aspects of the school day. Thus, in addition to formal lessons, PATHS includes strategies that can be used throughout the day by teachers and other school staff to generalize the core concepts and promote a climate that fosters SEL. These strategies include classroom-wide problem-solving discussions and teacher–student dialoguing to facilitate self-control and social problem-solving in real situations. A critical focus includes facilitating the dynamic relationship between cognitive/affective understanding and real-life situations.

Evaluation of Program Effects

PATHS meets some of the more rigorous requirements for emotional intervention programs (Kelly et al., 2004). Thus, PATHS is grounded in a coherent and complex model of emotional development and was developed with reference to developmental models of competencies. PATHS has also been extensively researched in school contexts and has been found to have a positive impact on emotional understanding and interpersonal skills and behavior. Research among school children has shown that the use of PATHS is associated with significantly improved social cognitions and more socially competent behaviors, in both regular and special education students (Riggs, Greenberg, Kusché, & Pentz, 2006). Findings indicated significant reductions in both internalizing and externalizing behavior at 1 year post-intervention (Kam, Greenberg, & Kusché, 2004; Riggs et al., 2006).

Further evidence of the efficacy of PATHS comes from a large multi-site trial, which included 198 intervention and 180 comparison classrooms from schools within high-risk neighborhoods (Conduct Problems Prevention Research Group [CPPRG], 1999a, 1999b). In the intervention schools, first grade teachers delivered a 57-lesson version of PATHS, which focused on improving self-control, emotional awareness, peer relations, and problem-solving. At the end of Grade 1, PATHS classrooms had lower aggressive behavior scores than did the control classrooms. A significant intervention effect was also observed on hyperactive/disruptive behavior. Longitudinal analyses comparing students who had received 3 years of the PATHS curriculum with students in control schools demonstrated significantly lower rates of aggressive behavior, inattention, and poor academic behavior and higher rates of pro-social behavior. In addition, peer sociometric reports indicated significantly lower rates of peer-rated aggression and hyperactive/disruptive behaviors for boys and higher rates of pro-social behavior for both boys and girls. In fact, the PATHS curriculum is cited among the most effective social competence programs by CASEL.

OTHER SEL PROGRAMS: EVALUATION, RECOMMENDATIONS, AND NEXT STEPS

Overall, current SEL programs being implemented in the school system vary considerably on key parameters, particularly with respect to their evidential base. Some SEL programs have been rigorously evaluated (e.g., PATHS, Seattle Social Development Project and Resolving Conflicts Creatively Program [RCCP]) and the results appear to be promising (Weissberg & Greenberg, 1998). Other programs, by contrast (e.g., Yale-New Haven Social Competence Promotion Program), have enjoyed few systematic evaluations. Some evaluation studies may be construed as "one-shot," while others have conducted follow-ups after 5 years or more (Elias & Clabby, 1992).

A recently published, landmark study (Durlak, Weissberg, Dymnicki, Taylor, & Schellinger, 2011) involved a meta-analysis of 213 school-based SEL programs involving 270,034 kindergarten through high school students. The meta-analysis explored interventions for the entire student body ("universal interventions") rather than programs for indicated populations (e.g., those students already presenting with adjustment problems). The findings indicated that, compared to controls, SEL participants demonstrated significantly improved social and emotional skills, attitudes, and positive social behavior. The mean intervention effect for social and emotional skills (over half a standard deviation) was higher than that found for attitudes, positive social behaviors, conduct problems, emotional distress, and academic performance (ranging from 0.22 to 0.27 standard deviation units). Overall, this meta-analysis documented that universal SEL programs yield significant positive effects on targeted social-emotional competencies and attitudes about self, others, and school; adjustment in the form of increased pro-social behavior; and improved academic performance.

In a sensible evaluation of current SEL programs, Zins et al. (2004) concluded that "a number of analyses of school-based prevention programs conducted in recent years provide general agreement that some of these programs are effective in reducing maladaptive behaviors, including those related to school success" (p. 5). Zins et al. (2007) also showed that students who participate in high-quality SEL programs have improved attitudes toward school, enhanced self-efficacy, a better sense of community, and greater trust and respect for teachers. These students were also found to have positive school behaviors such as being more pro-social, actively participating in the classroom and extracurricular activities (e.g., sports), fewer absences and suspensions, and less classroom disruptions and incidences of interpersonal violence. In addition, their school performance appears enhanced in terms of improved learning-to-learn skills, and improved skills in math, language, arts, and social studies.

However, not all reviewers have reached such optimistic conclusions about the effectiveness of implementing SEL programs in the school system. Kristjánnson (2006), for example, questions whether SEL programs might be setting over-ambitious goals that cannot be attained in practice. He also speculates that EI programs may simply promote self-serving manipulation of others, as opposed to supporting moral or responsible pro-social development. Furthermore, Humphrey et al. (2007) concluded that key limitations of current SEL program evaluations seriously limit the extent to which firm conclusions can be drawn about the malleability of EI. In the following section, we survey a number of the conceptual and methodological limitations alluded to in the above, which appear to limit current EI intervention programs. Concomitantly, we earmark some desired features and principles for future EI programs.

1. *Minimal EI-relevant content.* The specific emotional content varies widely from program to program, but typically includes such curricular contents as problem-solving or conflict resolution skills (Elias & Clabby, 1999), which are only tangentially related to EI. Aside from a handful of interventions, hardly any of the other myriad programs labeled as EI training or emotional intervention programs systematically target all major facets (or branches) of EI. Indeed, in most cases, only one or two facets are actually addressed, at best.
2. *Few theoretically grounded intervention programs are designed to gauge EI skills on an a priori basis.* A related problem in

assessing the effectiveness of EI interventions is that few programs were initially designed to promote, develop, or foster EI skills. Most of the programs cited by Goleman (1995) as supporting the effectiveness of EI interventions, for example, were not, in fact, designed for this purpose. Instead, these programs were designed for other purposes (e.g., promoting conflict resolution skills, enhancing problem-solving skills, reducing drug use, and preventing school violence or teenage pregnancy). Given that the specific EI content is quite meager, there is very little to be evaluated in program evaluation studies. This begs the question of what is in fact taught in such programs and the relationship of this content to those program outcomes assessed.

3. *Protean nature of some SEL programs.* In Greek mythology, Proteus was a Greek God, who could take on many forms (see Figure 5.1). Current EI intervention programs are like Proteus, highly diverse with respect to curricular content and activities. Programs are also protean in scope and objectives, targeting an unusually wide array of objectives, including improving social, communication, and life skills (problem-solving strategies, assertiveness training); modifying emotional regulation and coping techniques; effective peer-relation training; fostering conflict resolution and responsible decision-making skills; promoting health; preventing alcohol, tobacco, and drug use; reducing violence; developing self-esteem; and enriching linguistic experiences (see Zins et al., 2007). Many of these programs are highly fragmented, with separate activities to promote psychological health, enhance school bonding, teach problem-solving skills, reduce bullying and teenage violence, prevent dropping out, and so forth.

In fact, schools in the US are nationally implementing a median of 14 practices to prevent problem behaviors and to promote safe environments (Zins et al., 2004). Thus, practically everything "under the sun is" encompassed under the SEL umbrella, with programs lumping together character development, moral

FIGURE 5.1 Artist's rendering of Proteus, a sea god, who can foretell the future, but changes his shape to avoid having to. We have to wonder whether current SEL programs are similarly slippery and assume too many forms.
http://en.wikipedia.org/wiki/File:Proteus-Alciato.gif

reasoning and behavior, decision making, antisocial and pro-social behavior, as well as highly divergent issues comprising school discipline, drug abuse, pregnancy, ethical and moral behavior, pro-social relationships, alienation, dropping out, and school failure. It is not that there is necessarily anything wrong in so doing, though it becomes difficult for the scientist or practitioner to isolate which features of a program are responsible for impacting desired outcomes (see below).

4. *Difficulties in teasing out effects of multi-component, multi-year programs that are targeting diverse outcomes.* Given the protean nature of SEL programs, it is quite difficult to compare the effectiveness of different EI intervention programs because these programs often have targeted different facets of EI in different or developmental age groups. Thus, EI programs

for younger children tend to focus on building a "feelings vocabulary" and recognizing facial expressions of emotions. EI programs for middle-school students, by contrast, often address impulse control and emotion regulation. Finally, programs targeting high school students generally focus on the role of emotions in helping students resist peer pressure to engage in risky behaviors (e.g., sexual behavior, drug or alcohol use, aggression, and violence). Additional research is needed showing which content of SEL programs is most developmentally appropriate and useful for various sub-populations, including those based on gender and ethnicity.

5. *Incomplete understanding of how SEL programs work.* A still further problem in the evaluation of EI programs is that we really do not know how they work (Salovey, Bedell, Detweiler, & Mayer, 1999). Even though evidence for the efficacy of programs is accumulating (Durlak et al., 2011), the psychosocial mechanisms that mediate positive change is uncertain. Remember that in Chapter 4 (see Figures 4.2–4.6) we saw that there are many plausible but unsubstantiated mechanisms that may be responsible for benefits of EI in everyday life. Presumably, effective training targets some of these mechanisms, but research has yet to identify those that are critical in education. Identifying mediating factors is critical for winnowing out successful from failing programs, and for enhancing further those that seem to work in practice.

6. *Small effect sizes and/or lack of rigorous methodology proving efficacy.* As discussed above, the Durlak et al. (2011) meta-analysis establishes that, overall, effect sizes are large enough to be practically significant. However, effect sizes for some individual SEL programs may be rather small, so the clinical significance of the changes in the dependent measure is often uncertain. For example, in assessing the effects of the RCCP program, small and inconsistent effects were found (Aber, Jones, Brown, Chaudry, & Samples, 1998). The authors claim that this result is not surprising since children's developmental trajectories toward aggression and

violence are multiply determined (and RCCP targets only some causal factors). In addition, program evaluations frequently rely on self-reports of students, teachers, or parents, rather than observational or behavioral data (e.g., Lantieri & Patti, 1996), with the outcomes poorly defined.

7. *Ineffective program implementation.* Programs may fall short of their true potential because they are not completely or effectively implemented. A number of problems seem to obstruct the efficient implementation of the program (see Weist, Stiegler, Stephan, Cox, & Vaughan, 2010), which we present in Table 5.2. As implementation checks are infrequently conducted for EI interventions in the schools, it is difficult to gauge the extent of this problem. Humphrey et al. (2010) attribute the limited accomplishments of the British SEAL program to implementation issues such as lack of structure and consistency in program delivery, insufficient monitoring and lack of teacher motivation (in some cases).

8. *Transferability of social and emotional skills.* A final concern is that students may not be able to readily transfer the skills taught in an EI course to real-life. Thus, one can teach

TABLE 5.2 **FACTORS THOUGHT TO OBSTRUCT THE EFFICIENT IMPLEMENTATION OF SEL PROGRAMS**

Source	Examples
Student-related factors	Significant student emotional and behavioral problems, making implementation difficult
Teacher-related factors	Low teacher turnout in training programs Difficulty of teachers in juggling between teaching curricular content and allocating time and resources to program
School-level factors	Poor staff involvement in the training of teachers Competing teaching and school demands
Program-level factors	Failure to implement essential program elements Leaving classrooms without trained teachers to implement program

students knowledge of specific skills (e.g., like knowing the ingredients for baking apple pie or raisin challah bread, akin to declarative knowledge) without students being able to use them effectively in social situations (e.g., being able to bake raisin challah bread, akin to procedural knowledge). Clearly, the practical use of social-emotional skills extends beyond abstract knowledge to motivation and situation-dependent knowledge needed to use the skill "in the heat of the moment." Indeed, this proposition resonates with much of our previous criticism of current assessments of EI; the procedural aspects of this construct are rarely taken into account (see Roberts, Schulze, Zeidner, & Matthews, 2005). Even so, transfer is also a major problem for intervention programs targeted at cognitive skills (e.g., Kyllonen, Roberts, & Stankov, 2008), so this criticism should be accordingly tempered.

TRAINING EI IN THE WORKPLACE

Organizational and occupational settings appear to be in the midst of an "affective revolution," marked by a significant positive shift in attitudes toward emotion and emotional competencies in the workplace (Hughes, 2005). Whereas emotions were traditionally viewed as something to be avoided when making organizational decisions, recent thinking underscores the importance of cultivating emotions in the workplace, in concert with cognitive abilities and expertise, in the decision-making process (Emmerling & Cherniss, 2003). Furthermore, current thinking suggests that the combination and integration of explicit cognitive knowledge and tacit emotional knowledge may help one see what pure logic overlooks and thereby help one steer the best, safest course to success on the job.

As most adults in today's world spend more of their waking hours at work than any other place—with the number of hours spent at work steadily on the rise—the workplace may be one of the best settings for reaching adults and fostering their social and emotional competencies. As evidence of this, a September 2008 count showed at least 57 consulting firms devoted principally to EI; 90 organizations that specialize in training or assessment of EI; 30 EI certification programs; and 5 EI "universities" (see http://www.eiconsortium.org/). The EI framework has provided organizational settings with a basis for implementing competencies that identify skills that enable employees to deal with emotions in the workplace (Jordan, Murray, & Lawrence, 2009). The workplace is the area in which the greatest growth in EI popularity has occurred. At the same time, considerable controversy still rages regarding a number of salient issues, including the effectiveness of EI training at the workplace and the practical utility of EI for decision making, selection, and performance assessment (Jordan et al., 2009).

Overview

As the modern business world continues to evolve, organizational personnel need cognitive abilities, technical skills and expertise, along with a broad arsenal of emotional and social skills, to succeed at work. Much of the interest surrounding EI in organizational settings is based on the working assumption that by investing in the training of emotional competencies, organizations can play a key role in making the workplace a more productive, profitable, and enjoyable place. Furthermore, in today's competitive business world, organizations are likely to seek ways to increase performance and productivity—the key outcomes of human resource development practices (Muyia & Kacirek, 2009). Socio-emotional competencies demanded in the modern workforce include, for example, passion for working effectively toward achieving organizational goals, effective communication, negotiation, and leadership skills.

Decades of research on the effects of psychotherapy, self-help programs, cognitive-behavioral therapy, and a myriad of training programs have shown that people can change their behavior, moods, and self-image (Boyatzis, 2007). By the same token, based on the working assumption that EI is malleable and can be trained, there is a growing impetus toward the provision of personal and workplace interventions that purport to increase EI or strengthen emotional competencies at work (Zeidner, 2005). In fact, many organizations invest vast amounts of resources into skill development for individuals in leadership positions. Thus, in the US alone, organizations spend billions each year on training "soft skills" related to social and emotional competencies (Cherniss, 2000)—although we suspect economic recession may have taken its toll on such programs. Consequently, it is hardly surprising that the workplace has become the most popular context for applications of EI.

For a number of reasons, the workplace appears to be a most appropriate setting for systematic efforts to improve EI competencies. First, emotional competences are claimed to be critical for maintaining effective performance on the job. In fact, it has been claimed that about two thirds of the competencies linked to superior performance are emotional or social qualities, such as self-confidence, empathy, and the ability to get along with others (Boyatzis, 1982). Second, many workers enter the workforce without the necessary emotional competencies and social skills that will enable them to cope with the demands, challenges, and sources of stress and adversity on the job. Third, compared to other potential sites for implementing interventions, the workplace often has available means for providing necessary training experiences.

Various organizations and commercial ventures offer a wide range of EI training and development packages. In fact, the American industry spent about 50 million dollars each year on competencies training, with much of these programs' focus on social and emotional abilities during the late 1990s and early 2000s (see Cherniss, 2000). Whether this figure is still so high in a post-recession world is yet to be determined, but the point is still valid: Organizations consider training of these skills important. Empirical evidence of the effectiveness of these programs is still required. Police departments have adopted training designed to help officers better regulate their own emotional reactions, particularly anger, and also help law enforcement officers manage those of others in conflict. Similarly, physicians have been given training on how to be more empathetic toward their patients and to their families (Cherniss, Goleman, Emmerling, Cowan, & Adler, 1998). These programs have been in place prior to the advent of EI.

Best Practice Guidelines for Training EI at the Worksite

As noted elsewhere (Roberts, Zeidner, & Matthews, 2007), a number of preconditions are required to develop efficacious assessments and interventions of EI in applied setting. Table 5.3 lists these processes, aligned with what we see as important strategic directions that a company would need to be convinced these are targetted in order for such programs to be implemented.

These suggested preconditions reflect the need to assure a close partnership between theory, assessment, and application in EI practice. Currently, it could be argued that both theory and measurement of EI have not especially "helped the cause" of successfully advancing applications of EI so that they become valuable tools in the practitioner's arsenal.

Furthermore, proponents of EI programs at the workplace have claimed that the development and training of emotional competencies requires deep changes and the re-tooling of ingrained habits of thought, feeling, and behavior (see e.g., Cherniss et al., 1998; Goleman, 1998). Any successful effort to improve EI in an organization must be active and experiential, not just verbal and cognitive. Accordingly, there are strong response habits that must be altered in emotional learning and existing neural pathways must be weakened and eventually extinguished before new ones can be established. What this means in practice is that the learning process requires repeated

TABLE 5.3   PRECONDITIONS THAT ARE REQUIRED TO
DEVELOP EFFICACIOUS ASSESSMENTS AND
INTERVENTIONS OF EI IN WORKPLACE SETTINGS

Strategic Domain	Recommendation
Framework	Derivation of a context-specific and relevant theoretical framework
	Clear definitional framework for the universe of discourse surrounding EI
	Identification of key facets and components relevant to different applied settings
Assessment	Developing sound context-relevant assessment, scoring, and analytic procedures
Training	Developing sound training techniques tailored to specific contexts
	Adapting EI applications congenial to the affordances and constraints of the specific occupational, cultural, and social context
	Consideration of developmental age, social background, and cultural norms and values of the target users

practice over a much longer time. Thus, learners must enter the process with a high degree of motivation, and there must be considerable guidance and support to help them maintain motivation until a new way of thinking becomes second nature (Cherniss et al., 1998). Otherwise, following a short-term training and development program, participants will simply get a short-term buzz of energy that lasts no more than a few days or weeks, after which they fall back into whatever their habitual mode was before. (The astute reader will note here a correspondence with the transfer problem discussed earlier for SEL programs.)

To maximize the effectiveness of EI training programs, Cherniss (2000) and Cherniss and Goleman (2001) have offered some "best-practice" guidelines for implementing EI training programs at work. These guidelines, presented below, are based on a synthesis of theory and research on organizational behavior, training, and development.

1. *Phase 1: Preparation for Change.* Before change can take place, efforts should be made to assure the motivation, commitment, and self-efficacy of members of the organization. The training begins with a set of guidelines for introducing SEL into an organization and securing organizational "buy in." Training programs will be more effective if they include activities designed to help learners develop positive expectations for the training and greater self-efficacy. Thus, individuals are more likely to be motivated to improve emotional competencies if they are convinced that such a change will lead to desirable consequences. Operationally, efforts to improve emotional competencies should begin with an assessment of the competencies most critical for organizational and individual effectiveness. If employees are ready, motivation and commitment can be strengthened by helping them to set specific meaningful and realistic goals. Competencies required by the organization are identified and a careful diagnosis is made of the specific skills in which the client is lacking, to help bridge the gap between demanded skills and present skills. The program trainers need to make an effort to help the clients appreciate the benefits of mastering those competencies as well as socializing them to the process of acquiring them through cognitive and behavioral changes.

2. *Phase 2: Training and Development.* Phase 2 involves the actual training and development of members of the organization. This includes the change process itself and processes that previous research suggest are important to help people change. Training involves experiential learning rather than lecture and discussion, with ample opportunity for the learners to practice the new skills in as many domains as possible. Furthermore, emotional and social change needs to occur in a safe and supportive setting, and the relationship between trainers and learners becomes crucial in defining how safe

and supportive the learning environment is for the participants being trained.

Operationally, about a dozen sessions are needed, with clients receiving feedback on practice. Training materials encourage the learners to anticipate what barriers and problems they might encounter when they begin to apply what they have learned in their day-to-day lives. Then they need to learn how these might affect them emotionally and what they might do to deal with these problems. Clients are trained to improve their ability to identify their own emotions and to distinguish them from the emotions of others. Clients are also taught to improve their ability to use multiple and increasingly subtle cues to identify emotions in their co-workers. Learning skills of emotion perception, understanding, and regulation requires that EI training be experiential, based on repeated practice and use of role playing techniques. In addition, clients are also encouraged to form social support groups with similarly minded people for the purpose of practicing their newly acquired EI skills and providing mutual reinforcement. Live models are employed that demonstrate the skills and competencies to be mastered, which are believed to be more effective than simply focusing on declarative knowledge.

3. *Phase 3: Outcome evaluation.* The last phase of the training protocol involves systematic assessment of the outcomes (cognitive, social, emotional, and behavioral) of the intervention. Training efforts should be evaluated to determine whether people feel good about them and also whether they produce meaningful changes in on-the-job behavior. This is especially important for EI promotion efforts, given the considerable skepticism about whether such training is useful. Evaluation research should be used to help program managers see why and how a training effort works and ways in which it can be improved in the future.

AN EXAMPLE OF A WORK TRAINING PROGRAM: EMOTIONAL COMPETENCE TRAINING

One example of an experiential training program is the *Emotional Competence Training* program, developed at American Express Financial Advisors in 1992. It has since been used by managers in that company and several others in the US (Cherniss & Adler, 2000; Goleman, 1998). There are several versions of the program, but the one that is claimed to be most effective involves about 40 h of training, divided into two group sessions of 2 or 3 days each, which are separated by a month or two. Carefully selected, doctoral-level psychologists who understand the special challenges involved in implementing such a program in work organizations deliver the program. Although there are some didactic segments of the program, much of it involves highly experiential activity, such as role playing, simulations, and the like. The program covers a number of topics, including the role of emotion in the workplace, different ways of expressing how we are feeling, the impact of "self-talk" on feelings and behavior, active listening, and norms for the expression of emotion at work. A series of EI activities and games that can be utilized in training EI have been published over the years (e.g., Lynn, 2007).

Techniques such as keeping a "feeling journal," examining the rationality of appraisals individuals at work make in relation to their emotional reactions, identifying their patterns for dealing with negative emotions such as anxiety, as well as providing clients with tools for more systematically reflecting on their current and past emotional experiences, may all be helpful in effective decision making at work. Techniques that serve to focus the client on the physiological manifestations of various emotions (e.g., racing heart) may also help clients to recognize and label their emotional experiences. Incorporating others' perspectives (e.g. through the use of 360-degree feed-back techniques) may also help those with limited emotional self-awareness to gain insight into their emotional lives.

Introducing a framework of EI into the counseling relation-ship can be useful, as it can help identify clients who may have difficulty perceiving and working with emotions. Interventions can help clients at work better understand and regulate their emotions and appreciate how emotions may affect their social interactions and effectiveness at work. Emotions are clearly related to issues such as dependency, authority, identity for-mation, and chronic indecision. The client may be helped by working through their emotional reactions, which can facilitate various aspects of interactions in the organization.

Evaluation of EI Training Programs

The evidence for the effects of EI training on EI skills and adap-tive outcomes at work is mixed. On the one hand, a number of researchers have reported non-significant effects in overall EI scores of participants after training (Dulewicz & Higgs, 2004; Muyia & Kacirek, 2009). On the other hand, a number of studies have reported statistically significant differences in the EI scores of participants after training (Boyatzis, 2001; Grant, 2007; Groves, McEnrue, & Shen, 2008; Slaski & Cartwright, 2002, 2003). For example, research conducted by Murray, Jordan, and Ashkanasy (2006) in a large public organizational setting in Australia demonstrates that EI can be increased through train-ing. Using a quasi-experimental design, these researchers allo-cated participants to (a) a control group, (b) an interpersonal skills training group, or (c) an EI intervention group, based on the Mayer and Salovey ability model of EI. The results demon-strated a significant pre- to post-test increase in EI for the EI training group, but no significant change in EI for the con-trol group or the group receiving interpersonal skills training. Similarly, Boyatzis (2007) reports that a series of longitudinal studies underway at Case Western Reserve University suggest that students can change on EI and cognitive competencies. The improvements are reported to last for over 2 years.

Based on their survey of the intervention literature in the domain of management training programs, Cherniss and Goleman (2001) conclude that interventions targeted at EI-based competencies are indeed effective and tend to enhance such desired outcomes as self-awareness and rapport. In addition, self-motivation training (e.g., lecture and discussion) can help in fostering creativity and harnessing stronger achievement drive and business performance. Thus, they conclude "Taken together, all these interventions demonstrate that it is possible for adults to develop EI competencies" (p. 214).

CRITICAL ASSESSMENT OF EI TRAINING AND NEEDED RESEARCH

Programs for helping managers and would-be leaders, as well as students, to become more emotionally intelligent and socially effective have mushroomed. Although many of these programs seem promising, a number of problems make it difficult to assess the overall effectiveness of these training programs at the worksite. To begin with, the bulk of programs lack a clear theoretical and methodological rationale and employ a miscellany of techniques, whose psychological bases are not always clear (Zeidner, Roberts, & Matthews, 2002). Second, few programs actually test the EI training programs they implement (Caruso & Wolfe, 2004; cf. Landy, 2005, 2006). Cherniss et al. (1998) report the results of a survey of companies conducted by the American Society for Training and Development. Of the 27 companies claiming to have tried to promote emotional competencies through training and development, more than two thirds did not attempt to evaluate the effect of these efforts.

Furthermore, training programs are generally not based on appropriate experimental designs (e.g., randomized trials) and have typically lacked repeated assessments and systematic tracking of outcomes over time to gauge delayed or prolonged effects. Many training programs (Boyatzis, 2007) may show a "honeymoon effect," starting with marked improvement in outcome variables immediately following program implementation, but possibly showing a precipitous drop in outcome measures within months. Furthermore, current designs do not tell us whether EI training directly affects performance, performance affects EI, or both variables are influenced by some third factor. Tracking changes in EI and performance across time, post-intervention, is necessary to address issues of causality.

Finally, reviews of EI programs at work are often based on managerial training programs and the like, which have existed for many years prior to the emergence of contemporary EI training protocols (e.g., sensitivity training). The success of these commonplace and longstanding programs is inappropriately taken as evidence for the effectiveness of EI programs.

Future Directions

Although there is a growing literature suggesting that EI may matter in the workplace (Cherniss, 2010), the jury is still out regarding the effectiveness of many EI training programs and interventions. Future theory and research need to address a number of issues to allow more valid assessments of EI training effects. The quality of existing applied research varies enormously. There are examples of excellent practice together with poor-quality work that fails to meet even minimal standards for scientific investigation, including lack of conceptual frameworks, implementation analyses and checks, and sound evaluation designs. Thus, systematic evaluations of theory-driven programs specifically targeting key EI competencies are sorely needed.

It is also presently unsettled whether training in EI should be more geared to benefiting the worker or the organization. On the one hand, the intent may be to train self-aware, emotionally literate employees, who can make decisions that best serve their own interests. On the other hand, the intent may be to enhance social-emotional competencies and produce happy and satisfied workers to enhance productivity and inculcate loyalty to the organization. To be sure, personal and organizational interests do not necessarily coincide. Sometimes the emotionally intelligent choice may be to put personal needs first, in managing work–life conflicts, for example.

It also remains unclear which of the components of EI are most malleable and responsive to training or which type of interventions are effective to use for low vs. average EI clients. EI training work may be unnecessary for those high on EI, whereas for true bred emotional dunces, EI training may be ineffective and a perfect waste of time and resources (cf. Emmerling & Cherniss, 2003). Equally, more light needs to be shed on a number of important EI training parameters, including specific EI intervention goals; the most effective interventions to use for different age levels; and the minimal level of EI that a client needs to benefit from intervention.

In addition to developing standards for program implementation, there is also a need for assessing the return for costs associated with delivering EI programs. Future research definitely needs to demonstrate that training EI offers something new, above and beyond existing training programs, and that it adds to and augments current practice and practical interventions already in place at the worksite.

SUMMARY AND CONCLUSIONS

EI training programs designed to help students, workers, managers, and would-be leaders to become more emotionally intelligent and socially effective have mushroomed. The effectiveness of educational programs is supported by a recent meta-analysis (Durlak et al., 2011), showing that SEL training enhances social and emotional skills, as well as social behaviors and academic performance. Evaluations of occupational programs are less systematic, and, where available, rather mixed in outcome, although some encouraging findings are starting to emerge (Cherniss, Grimm, & Liautaud, 2010). Although many interventions are promising, the bulk of programs have not been systematically based upon EI theory and research. Intervention programs that have sought to cultivate EI both in occupational and educational settings often lack a clear theoretical and methodological rationale, and employ a miscellany of techniques, whose psychological bases are not always clear. Furthermore, EI and the competencies linked to it are based on temperament, learning experiences, and reflective goal-oriented experiences. One-day seminars or workshops can be valuable in educating people and raising awareness, but they may not by themselves lead to the deeper reprogramming of personality and competencies that is required for significant improvement.

As we noted in our recent review of the literature (Zeidner et al., 2009), it would appear rash at present to dismiss the potential value and importance of attempts to train EI in various applied settings, despite some of the failings of current work. The practical value of training programs is better supported in the educational than in the occupational domain. Following on from the Durlak et al. (2011) review, the tasks for educators are to identify which of the many social-emotional skills and processes of interest are most amenable to training, and how to improve the real but often limited benefits accomplished by existing programs. Studies in the workplace still have more of the basic groundwork to do, in terms of delivering systematic program planning and evaluation studies to substantiate the effectiveness of training. In any case, the fact that there are domains of education and work where the handling of emotional encounters is pivotal renders EI, even if only found to be a theoretical soup-stone, potentially highly influential.

6

Emotional Disorders: Pathology of Emotional Intelligence?

A fool with a heart and no sense is just as unhappy as a fool with sense and no heart.

Fyodor Dostoevsky, *The Idiot*

A rich vein of emotional pathology runs through the various clinical disorders. Sometimes, the issue is an excess of emotion. Many individuals with anxiety and mood disorders are emotionally over-reactive, becoming upset or depressed in response to seemingly minor issues. Bipolar individuals may also show an excess of positive emotion, associated with poor judgment and grandiose schemes. Patients with eating disorders may eat as a strategy for regulating negative emotions, where other means of coping would be more adaptive. Sometimes, emotions flare up inappropriately, as in people with anger control problems. In other patients, the problem is too little emotion, not too much. Schizophrenics often show a lack of emotion, along with an impoverished experience of living. Sometimes too, the problem is in using emotions to connect with others. Autistic children fail to respond with positive emotions to family members.

The emotional responses seen in clinical patients often seem less than intelligent. Excessive anxiety is likely to be counterproductive in dealing with threat. Indeed, some displays of emotion, such as an angry outburst, may well turn others against the person, making the underlying issue even harder to deal with. But does the concept of emotional intelligence (EI) give us anything more than a convenient way of labeling maladaptive behaviors? Could it be that impairments in EI play a causal role in mental disorders? Should therapy be directly concerned with raising EI? We will address these and other issues related to psychopathology in this chapter.

OVERVIEW OF EI AND PATHOLOGY

We begin with a quick introduction to clinical psychology. This applied field of psychology typically follows a "medical model" of disorder, in which mental illness can be diagnosed in relation to a fixed set of conditions, such as generalized anxiety, much as a medical doctor might diagnose measles or chickenpox. The available diagnoses are currently codified in the *Diagnostic and Statistical Manual* (*DSM-IV-TR-IV*: see First, Frances, & Pincus, 2004) of the American Psychiatric Association. There are numerous disorders. The psychiatrist or clinical psychologist must work through what is, in effect, a checklist of symptoms for each one in making a diagnosis. If the clinical interviews and diagnostics given to a patient reveal a sufficient set of symptoms, the person "has" the disorder; otherwise, not. Making a diagnosis within *DSM-IV* is seen as essential for deciding on what therapy to recommend to the patient. A new version of the *DSM*—*DSM V*—will be published in 2013, changing some of the diagnostic categories, and placing more emphasis on dimensional, continuous assessments of psychopathology.

DSM-IV formalizes a distinction between the classic mental disorders such as depression and schizophrenia ("Axis 1" disorders) and abnormal personality types such as antisocial and borderline personality ("Axis 2"). Abnormal personality refers to underlying dispositions that do not in themselves constitute a mental disorder, but may cause various problems in living, and increase the person's vulnerability to an Axis 1 disorder (often in conjunction with some precipitating event). Thus, we might look for low EI as being an attribute of abnormal personality.

Recent years have seen a transformation of thinking about abnormal personality. It is now widely recognized that, like normal personality, abnormal personality is best defined by dimensional traits, rather than separate categories (Widiger & Mullins-Sweatt, 2009). Thus, antisocial personality is not an all-or-nothing condition; instead, there is a spectrum of antisocial tendencies.

Indeed, some dimensional models of abnormality converge with the Five Factor Model (FFM) of normal personality that we discussed in Chapter 2. Abnormal traits such as social avoidance and anxiety may correspond to extreme neuroticism, and antisocial traits may be a counterpart to very low agreeableness (Schroeder, Wormsworth, & Livesley, 1992). Whether abnormal personality is nothing more than extremes of normal trait dimensions is an open question. For example, some of the more bizarre schizophrenia-like symptoms of schizotypal personality, such as hallucinations and delusions, may not correspond closely to any normal personality trait.

It is simple enough to obtain data linking psychopathology to low scores on tests for EI. We have already seen that questionnaire scales for EI correlate with a variety of other questionnaires that assess pathological traits such as anxiety and depression, in normal, non-clinical groups (Bar-On, 2000; Summerfeldt, Kloosterman, Antony, & Parker, 2006). Comparable findings may be obtained from studies of clinical patients, diagnosed with mental disorders according to *DSM-IV*. Downey et al. (2008) administered a typical EI questionnaire, the Swinburne University Emotional Intelligence Test, to 62 patients diagnosed with major depression. They found that the patient group was lower in EI than matched controls. Subscales for emotion recognition and expression, emotion management and emotion control all showed significant effects of depression. Other lines of evidence also suggest that depressives have difficulties with these aspects of emotional functioning.

In Chapter 3, we noted evidence that ability tests for EI may predict lower levels of psychopathology, upon which we will now elaborate. Hertel, Schütz, and Lammers (2009) gave the Mayer-Salovey-Caruso Emotional Intelligence Test (MSCEIT) to three patient groups, representing different types of emotional problem: depression, borderline personality disorder (BPD), and substance abuse disorder (SAD). BPD may be seen as a disorder of emotion regulation, characterized by impulsivity, mood swings, and difficulties in maintaining interpersonal relationships. The SAD group in this study consisted of mostly alcohol abusers.

All three groups showed lower EI on the MSCEIT than controls (the substance abusers had the lowest scores of all). There were also some differences between the patient groups on the four branches of the MSCEIT (see Chapter 3). For example, as might be expected, the BPD and SAD groups were particularly low in emotion regulation (i.e., the management of emotions). By contrast with Downey et al.'s (2008) findings, depressed patients were not significantly lower in emotion regulation than controls, and none of the patient groups showed a deficit in emotion perception. EI research seems to send rather mixed signals on the exact nature of emotional deficits in this disorder.

CLINICAL PERSPECTIVES ON EI: KEY ISSUES

Findings such as those that we have discussed are only a starting point. They show that patient groups may differ in EI test scores from control groups free of emotional disorder. Many questions remain unanswered. We will focus on the following:

1. *Is low EI a cause or effect of mental disorder?* According to the standard psychiatric model, very low EI might be a vulnerability factor for a range of disorders. When some external stressor comes along that turns the person's life upside down, the individual low in EI may not be able to fathom their emotions or cope effectively with stress (see Chapter 4), contributing to emotional disorder. The emotionally intelligent person may be better able to make sense of negative emotions, and to figure out a realistic strategy for coping with events. However, cause and effect might work in the opposite direction. Emotional disorders typically disrupt the person's ability to understand and manage events, not least because attention becomes fixated on personal issues as the person ruminates on or worries about their difficulties (Wells & Matthews, 1994). Thus, low EI might be a symptom or consequence of mental disorder, rather than a causal factor.

2. *Does mental disorder reflect some general deficit in EI?* In looking at EI in normal individuals, we have already picked up on a tension between treating EI as some overarching personal quality, like IQ, versus identifying numerous, distinct

emotional competencies and skills that may be only loosely related, if at all. If we look at mental illness, the majority of the separate conditions defined by *DSM-IV* involve some degree of emotional dysfunction. But does the emotional abnormality seen in conditions as various as anxiety, schizophrenia, and autism really have some common source in low EI? Or (following current clinical practice) should we define multiple emotional pathologies that generate different disorders?

3. *What are the mechanisms for emotional pathology?* As previously discussed, much research on EI is rather descriptive in nature, failing to probe the underlying neural or cognitive mechanisms that produce variation in EI. Similar concerns attach to EI in the clinical context. Clinical psychology theory recognizes a wide variety of abnormal processing mechanisms that produce pathology. For example, sources of anxiety may include excessive sensitivity of brain systems for threat, selective attention processes that "lock onto" threat, dysfunctional coping strategies that lead to prolonged worry, and learned beliefs that one is vulnerable and defenseless (Wells & Matthews, 1994). Thinking in terms of EI is only liable to be clinically useful if EI can be linked to specific processes that promote mental illness.

4. *How do we treat low EI?* Current clinical psychology is practically useful precisely because it specifies underlying mechanisms as well as descriptive accounts of symptoms. A physician or psychiatrist can, ideally, find a drug to treat an abnormal brain process, or a training program to correct self-defeating coping strategies. Although there is growing interest in therapies that directly address emotional dysfunction (Greenberg, 2006), as opposed to their neural or cognitive antecedents, the study of EI has not yet led to any major innovations in therapy (Vachon & Bagby, 2007). The hope is that better understanding of the underlying mechanisms

for deficiencies in the core competencies that define EI will improve psychotherapy, but such advances lie in the future.

We have to acknowledge at this point that clinical studies of EI are at the stage of promising research directions, but little immediate practical payoff for the therapist. Thus, in the remainder of this chapter we will focus on illustrating what the potential of this research is for better understanding of a range of emotional disorders. After returning to the causality issue, we will answer our second question above, on the generality of EI, by suggesting that we can discriminate at least three rather separate forms of low EI, relating to emotion dysregulation, social-emotion disconnection and impulse control, respectively. We will then highlight some illustrative research directions.

EI AND PATHOLOGY: CAUSE AND EFFECT

We noted the chicken-and-egg problem for EI and clinical disorders above: Is low EI a cause or consequence of disorder? We could plausibly see low EI as a causal influence on the development of a range of mental disorders, in conjunction with other causal factors such as environmental stressors. For example, Todd may have muddled through life for a number of years despite his difficulties in relating emotionally to others. Then, his father dies, provoking a strong grief reaction, which Todd cannot make sense of or manage. Todd's response is to stop going to work and hide in his apartment, eventually developing symptoms of clinical depression. In this case, Todd's low EI (inability to cope with grief) is a causal factor, along with the life event that precipitated the emotional crisis.

However, another scenario is possible. Tina has typical emotional competencies. She enjoys spending much of her time with her parents, with whom she is close. Her father dies suddenly, and she experiences an overwhelming grief like nothing she has experienced before. She spends much of her time feeling depressed and brooding on why her father should be taken from her. Her preoccupation with his death interferes with her ability to process the emotions of others, and cuts her off from more positive emotional experiences. She fails to register or understand her mother's reactions to their loss, and gets into arguments with her. Now Tina is experiencing diminished EI, but in this case, it is a *consequence* not a *cause* of emotional disorder.

Which view is correct? Is low EI a lurking vulnerability just waiting for adverse circumstances to flower into pathology? Or is low EI just one of the various symptoms of emotional disorder, which will disappear following treatment? Issues of causality have long been a concern for researchers on standard personality traits. Barnett and Gotlib (1988) noted that, although patients with emotional disorder often show elevated neuroticism, this personality trait tends to return to normal levels following therapy, suggesting that emotional instability is a symptom rather than a stable vulnerability factor. However, more recent longitudinal studies have shown that elevated neuroticism predicts future disorder (Matthews, Deary, & Whiteman, 2009), confirming a causal role. It is likely that there is some reciprocal process where both causal directions operate (i.e., from personality to pathology, and pathology back to adverse personality change).

Answering causal questions of this kind requires fairly substantial longitudinal studies that can determine whether abnormality in personality precedes the development of clinical symptoms, or vice versa. Such studies have not yet been systematically conducted in relation to the role of EI. Given the high overlap between trait EI and low neuroticism (see Chapter 2), we might expect that low EI would operate as a vulnerability factor for various clinical disorders simply because those low in EI are high in neuroticism.

One of the few studies to provide direct evidence was conducted by Hansenne and Bianchi (2009) in a sample of

54 depressive inpatients in a Belgian psychiatric unit. Some time later, 20 of the patients were retested following successful treatment, and remission of the disorder. The Schutte Self Report Inventory (SSRI) was used to assess trait EI. As expected, the sample of depressed individuals was initially lower in EI than matched controls, especially in regard to mood regulation and appraisal of emotions. However, remitted depressives were no different in EI than the mentally healthy controls, although it is known that depressives in remission remain vulnerable to further episodes of clinical disorder. Hansenne and Bianchi (2009) concluded that lower EI appears to be more of a consequence of being severely depressed rather than a stable vulnerability factor for future depression. By contrast, some standard personality traits linked to depression, such as harm avoidance and (low) self-directedness, remained elevated in the remitted sample. We should remember that this is only a single study, with a modest sample size. Nonetheless, the suggestion is that standard personality scales may do a better job of isolating risk factors for depression than trait EI, at least as measured by the SSRI.

In sum, researchers on EI still have to accomplish the basic task of demonstrating that low EI is a true vulnerability factor. Even if low EI does prove to be more of a symptom than a consequence, the concept may still be important for understanding pathology and patients' difficulties in emotion regulation and interpersonal functioning. It is also the case that low EI may serve to perpetuate and maintain pathology, even if it is not a precipitating factor. For now, given the lack of research, we will give proponents of EI the benefit of the doubt and further explore the possible clinical expressions of low EI, in a variety of guises.

VARIETIES OF EMOTIONAL PATHOLOGY

Clinical psychology provides a striking variety of expressions of dysfunctional emotions. Pathology in anxiety and depression often seems inwardly focused, as the person broods on their problems, arriving at disproportionately negative assessments of their worth and prospects. The fundamental disorder seems to be one of the self: faulty self-beliefs and counterproductive strategies for handling emotional distress (Beck, Emery, & Greenberg, 1985). By contrast, in disorders associated with emotional aggression and impulse control, there seems to be too little self rather than too much. The person may lash out, steal, or dive off a high cliff for fun (known in Britain as "tombstoning") without reflecting on the personal consequences of the action.

A third type of disorder is social in nature, reflected by a lack of emotional regulation of interpersonal interactions. Most of us easily, and partly unconsciously, "read" the emotions of those we converse with from their facial expressions, body language, and speech content. (The reader will note these are all important components of emotion perception, as outlined in Chapter 3.) We also express our own emotions in response to our reading of others. This rather hidden emotional dialogue regulates interactions and may even be a basic function of emotions (Oatley & Johnson-Laird, 1995). Individuals with autism seem to be deficient in these capabilities and hence they fail to "get" the emotions of another, fail to express their own feelings, and hence exhibit socially inappropriate behaviors such as headbanging or repetitive actions. Schizophrenia—although quite distinct from autism—is also associated with difficulties in social functioning.

THE CLASSIC EMOTIONAL DISORDERS

Table 6.1 expresses these three loose clusters of disorder in terms of the *DSM-IV* axes for mental disorder (Axis 1) and underlying abnormal personality traits (Axis 2). We might see the traits as representing predispositions or vulnerabilities to the disorders, although we have already discussed the challenges of differentiating cause and effect. The first cluster is characterized by excessive negative emotion, often experienced as strong, persistent anxiety or depression. These conditions have been described as conditions of "over-regulation" of emotion (Mullin & Hinshaw, 2007). The person seems oversensitive to minor events and, indeed, to their own emotional and bodily discomfort, leading to irrational fears and worries. By contrast, the second cluster refers to disorders of under-regulation. The person is unable to control various unwise impulses, including those toward reckless risk-taking and angry, aggressive responses to provocation. The third cluster is concerned with regulation of social encounters. Individuals with schizotypal personality find it difficult to connect emotionally with others, and may drift through life without establishing close relationships with others. Schizotypy may be a precursor to schizophrenia, a psychosis in which, typically, social dysfunction co-exists with bizarre disruptions of conscious experience, such as hallucinations and delusions. Autism is a separate condition in which the individual seems unable to understand the intentions and emotions of others, including those most dear to them, often leading to severe behavioral problems.

The first category in Table 6.1 describes traits and disorders associated with excessive vulnerability to negative emotions, including anxiety and depression. We do not have space here to discuss these various conditions in detail (see Antony & Barlow, 2010), but they include both conditions in which negative emotion is pervasive and "free-floating" (e.g., generalized anxiety), as well as phobias to specific sources of threat (e.g., open spaces), panic, post-traumatic stress, and obsessive-compulsive disorder. Symptoms include not only excessive negative emotion, but also cognitive symptoms such as unrealistic negative beliefs, physical sensations of anxiety (in panic disorder), and behaviors such as compulsions.

TABLE 6.1   THREE LOOSE CLUSTERS OF DISORDERS OF "LOW EI"

Category	DSM Axis-I	DSM Axis-II
Emotional disorders	Mood disorders Anxiety disorders	"Neurotic" personality disorders: e.g., Dependent Borderline Obsessive compulsive
Externalizing disorders	Impulse Control Disorders not elsewhere classified (e.g. kleptomania, pyromania)	Antisocial personality disorder
	Disruptive Behavior Disorders (e.g., Conduct Disorder (CD))	Antisocial personality disorder (also psychopathy)
Social disconnection	Schizophrenia	Schizoid and schizotypal personality disorder
		Autism, Asperger syndrome

Processes for Excessive Negative Emotion

These disorders may in part result from abnormalities in the functioning of brain neurotransmitters, such as serotonin. Here, we will focus on psychological cognitive and affective processes that may be associated with excessive anxiety and/or depression. There are several distinct processes of this kind, including the following:

1. *Unrealistic negative self-appraisals.* Patients typically exaggerate their weaknesses and inability to cope. In Beck et al.'s (1985) schema theory, negative self-beliefs reflect an underlying self-schema that encodes unrealistic beliefs and expectations.

2. *Dysfunctional coping.* Patients often employ coping strategies that make their emotional symptoms worse, not better, such as blaming themselves for issues beyond their control. Social phobics may cope by avoiding the company of others, which reinforces their sense of social isolation.

3. *Attention and meta-cognition.* Patients are often preoccupied with their inner world of emotion and worry, believing that is important to maintain this interior focus (Wells, 2000). This self-focus of attention tends to cause excessive rumination and worry, which may actually accentuate emotional symptoms—another type of dysfunctional coping strategy.

4. *Integration of cognition and emotion.* Patients may have trouble in cognitive understanding of emotions. For example, those with post-traumatic stress appear to have difficulty assimilating the extreme emotions following a trauma, such as rape, into the cognitive structures used to make sense of everyday life (Cahill & Foa, 2007). A common (though not universal) condition in emotional disorder is *alexithymia* (Taylor, Bagby, & Parker, 1997), referring to difficulties in identifying and verbalizing emotions.

These psychological sources of emotional disorder are quite well understood, and support a range of therapeutic strategies for correcting dysfunctional cognitive-emotional functioning. We can say that abnormalities in functioning are "emotionally unintelligent" in a loose sense, in that they interfere with the person's capacity to manage emotive encounters, but is there any more precise sense in which those with emotional disorders are lacking in EI?

A basic problem is that current accounts of EI are largely 'structural' in nature. That is, they focus on stable features of the individual's personality or abilities, as defined by a factor model (e.g., the four-branch model discussed in Chapter 3). By contrast, contemporary clinical psychology has found far more value in "process" models that specify the changes in neural, cognitive, and social functioning when the person is confronted by some challenging event.

For example, Mayer, Salovey, Caruso, and Sitarenios (2003) describe emotion management as a structural component of EI. Data showing that anxious or depressed individuals obtain low scores on psychometric scales for emotion management (Downey et al., 2008) make an empirical contribution, but tell us little more. It is trite to attribute depression to poor emotional management. We need to know more about which *processes* for emotion regulation operate differently in normal and depressed individuals, and how these processes shape emotional and other symptoms. As our brief list above shows, there are a variety of different possibilities, and different emotional disorders may be associated with different abnormalities in emotion regulation. Current models of EI are too neglectful of processing to give us much clue as to the most promising research directions.

The failure of much work on EI to connect with process models limits its clinical relevance, although future research may bridge this gap. We will finish our look at emotional disorders by describing one of the more productive research areas of relevance, on alexithymia. As noted above, this condition refers to difficulties in integrating cognition and emotion.

Alexithymia and Negative Emotion

Clinical psychologists typically encourage their clients to talk about their problems, for example, describing their feelings in some challenging situation, or what thoughts and images are evoked by a distressing memory. Sometimes, the client has obvious difficulties opening up about her inner world. She may be unable to express and elaborate on emotional states, preferring instead to talk only about concrete, external events. Such individuals are said to be high in "alexithymia," derived from Greek words meaning "lacking words for feelings" (Sifneos, 1973). Alexithymia is more than just a barrier for the clinical psychologist. It may be that deficits in recognizing and under-standing one's inner emotional states increase the person's vulnerability to a range of emotional disorders (Taylor et al., 1997).

Lumley, Neely, and Burger (2007) have provided an accessible review of the clinical significance of alexithymia. They point out that alexithymia was initially apparent in patients with psychosomatic disorders, perhaps because alexithymics tend to confuse emotions with physical symptoms. Since then, research has shown elevated alexithymia in medical patients with conditions ranging from cardiac disease and breast cancer to chronic itching. There is even some evidence that alexi-thymia is associated with poorer immune system functioning (Temoshok et al., 2008). In psychiatry, alexithymia tends to be elevated not just in emotional disorders, but also in a range of other conditions, including pathological gambling and schizo-phrenia (e.g., Seghers, McCleery, & Docherty, 2011). Recent work has also identified interpersonal deficits that may be asso-ciated with alexithymia, such as lack of empathy (Grynberg, Luminet, Corneille, Grèzes, & Berthoz, 2010).

As we have noted, in the therapeutic context, alexithymia is often a nuisance. Patients with this characteristic may have difficulties in communicating their feelings, gaining insight into their emotions, and connecting emotionally with the ther-apist (Lumley et al., 2007). However, understanding the condi-tion can help the therapist in choosing an appropriate therapy. Alexithymics do not do well with classic insight-oriented psy-chotherapies, but more structured cognitive-behavioral treat-ments (e.g., exercises to improve communication skills) work better for them (Lumley et al., 2007). Indeed, these patients may welcome the chance to follow an explicit behavior-train-ing program, without the need to open up on the impenetrable mysteries of feelings.

Some fairly sophisticated psychometric analyses have shown that alexithymia is a true dimensional trait, rather than a cate-gorical, all-or-none condition (Parker, Keefer, Taylor, & Bagby,

2008). The most popular measuring instrument is the Toronto Alexithymia Scale (TAS-20: Parker, Taylor, & Bagby, 2003), which is made up of three subscales:

1. *Difficulty identifying feelings* and distinguishing between feelings and the bodily sensations of emotional arousal;
2. *Difficulty describing feelings;*
3. *Externally orientated thinking,* a preference for concrete details of everyday life over imagination, fantasy, and inner experience.

Scores on the TAS-20 correlate with neuroticism, and, to a lesser degree, with lower extraversion and openness (Luminet, Bagby, Wagner, Taylor, & Parker, 1999). As several authors have pointed out (e.g., Lumley et al., 2007), in clinical research it is often difficult to differentiate the roles of alexithymia and the negative emotionality with which it overlaps. Given that alexithymia is substantially correlated with neuroticism, it comes as no surprise that various questionnaire measures of alexithymia correlated with low trait EI (e.g., Mikolajczak, Luminet, Leroy, & Roy, 2007). Small but significant negative correlations are found between the TAS-20 and the MSCEIT (Lumley, Gustavson, Partridge, & Labouvie-Vief, 2005), with MacCann & Roberts (2008) also replicating this finding with situational judgment tests of emotional management and understanding. However, we cannot reduce trait EI solely to alexithymia: Mikolajczak et al. (2007) reported that trait EI predicts emotional reactivity even with alexithymia controlled.

In sum, there is no doubt of the theoretical and practical relevance of the alexithymia construct for the clinical psychology of the emotional disorders, and other psychiatric and medical conditions. Difficulties in emotional understanding and expression seem quite common in patients, and should inform treatment (Lumley et al., 2007; Parker, 2005). There is no doubt too that there is some overlap between questionnaire

scales for alexithymia, trait EI, and standard personality traits. However, the clinical implications of this overlap remain unclear, in the absence of research connecting EI to specific emotion-regulation processes. As Vachon and Bagby (2007, p. 351) conclude "alexithymia may be a more useful construct than EI precisely because it is a narrowly constructed, theory-based, well-researched condition that clinicians can recognize, measure, and treat."

EXTERNALIZING DISORDERS: IMPULSIVITY AND ANTISOCIAL BEHAVIOR

A concept from clinical child psychology is useful for understanding our second category of disorders. The term "externalizing disorders" refers to disorders in which the child seems to be acting out his issues through behaviors such as aggression, delinquency, and other conduct problems (Mullin & Hinshaw, 2007; Zeidner & Matthews, in press). In *DSM-IV*, these disorders include the following:

- Oppositional Defiant Disorder (ODD). Key symptoms include excessive anger, temper tantrums, and willful opposition to authority figures such as parents and teachers. This disorder can be especially disruptive to families.
- Conduct Disorder (CD). Like ODD, this disorder may be expressed through aggressive behaviors. However, it involves a wider range of severe behavioral problems including stealing, lying, bullying, harming animals, or destroying property leading, in adolescence, to various forms of criminality.
- Attention-Deficit/Hyperactivity Disorder (ADHD). This is the most common psychiatric disorder in children. There are two categories of symptoms. Symptoms of *inattention*

include distractibility, boredom-proneness, and difficulties in completing tasks. *Hyperactive-impulsive* symptoms include running around, talking and engaging in other activities without pausing, as well as impulsive behaviors. The two types of symptoms may occur alone or in combination with one another. In either case, ADHD is especially challenging in the classroom, where the child must sit still and pay attention.

Externalizing disorders are especially salient in childhood, accounting for over half of referrals for mental health services by children in the United States (Kazdin, 1995), and are more common in boys than in girls. (Anxiety and depression are only weakly associated with conduct problems in children, and are examples of "internalizing disorders.")

There is increasing recognition that externalizing disorders, such as ADHD, may persist into adulthood. However, externalizing issues are more commonly apparent in adulthood in the form of abnormal personality (DSM Axis 2), rather than Axis 1 disorders. The most salient trait is antisocial personality, which is often associated with criminality and even psychopathy. Modern dimensional models of abnormality (Egan, 2009; Livesley & Larstone, 2008) recognize a broad trait of antisocial tendencies, associated with rejection and suspicion of others, which overlaps with low agreeableness in the FFM.

It is not unusual for externalizing disorders to be accompanied by emotional symptoms. Indeed, poor emotional regulation may play a central role in them (Mullin & Hinshaw, 2007). Children with CD may have a short emotional fuse, so that they are easily incited to retaliate in anger against classmates who tease them, for example. In some cases, emotional symptoms may be secondary to other forms of pathology. For example, children with ADHD may become frustrated with their difficulties in paying attention in class, so that negative emotion follows from their cognitive-attentional deficits. In other cases, emotional dysfunction, such as excessive anger responses, may play a more direct role in creating pathology, although, as in other areas of clinical psychology, it is often difficult to determine the causal role of emotional processes.

Self-Control as a Facet of EI

In descriptive accounts of EI, self-control is often cited as a key competency (e.g., Goleman, 1995), although it is not an explicit part of the Mayer-Salovey model. Plausibly, there are advantages in life in being able to inhibit angry, aggressive responses, in thinking through actions that may be risky, and in making short-term sacrifices for eventual long-term gain. Some but not all questionnaires for trait EI include self-control scales. For example, self-control appears as one of four higher-order factors of the Trait EI Questionnaire (TEIQue), defined by emotion regulation, stress management, and low impulsiveness (see Chapter 2). Vernon, Villani, Schermer, and Petrides (2008) found a correlation of –0.74 between self-control and neuroticism, as well as correlations of 0.48 and 0.35 with conscientiousness and agreeableness, respectively. On this questionnaire, at least, self-control seems poorly differentiated from the Big Five. By contrast, self-control does not seem to be central to the Mayer, Salovey, and Caruso (2000) ability model of EI; presumably, it is subsumed under the broader category of emotion management/regulation.

In spite of the conceptual links between EI and self-control, and psychometric discrimination of relevant facets of EI, there has been rather little research on EI, self-control, and impulsive response. Various studies using the MSCEIT have shown relatively low test scores in a variety of deviant groups (Rivers, Brackett, Salovey, & Mayer, 2007), but research of this kind has rarely probed further to identify emotional processes associated with low EI that may produce pathology. Thus, much of what we will have to say about impulsivity is concerned more with directions for future research than with solid empirical findings on EI.

Emotional Deficits and Mechanisms in Externalizing Disorders

We can identify three somewhat different types of emotional deficit that may contribute to externalizing disorders (although these deficits may be inter-related to some extent). These deficits are lack of effortful control, distorted appraisals of others, and lack of empathy. Next we sketch out the potential relevance of each of these character flaws for EI.

Lack of Effortful Control. Research on child development has identified effortful control as a major dimension of temperament (Rothbart, Sheese, & Conradt, 2009). As the brain areas that allow for self-control start to develop in the second and third years of life, the child becomes able to resist impulses that will provide immediate reward but later punishment, such as stealing from the cookie jar in the kitchen. In research, a classic example is the "marshmallow test" for delaying self-gratification to obtain a larger subsequent reward (see Mischel & Ebbesen, 1970; Mischel, Shoda, & Rodriguez, 1989). Some 4-year-old children are able to delay eating a marshmallow placed in front of them to obtain two marshmallows if they wait 15 min. Others just can't resist the lure of the succulent treat placed in front of them. Various YouTube videos demonstrating the phenomena exist (see http://www.youtube.com/watch?v=6EjJsPylEOY), Sesame Street has produced a video aimed at training delay of gratification (http://www.sesamestreet.org/parents/save/), and the political satirist Stephen Colbert parodies the test in a 2011 episode (see http://www.colbertnation.com/the-colbert-report-videos/389614/june-14–2011/close-sesame).

Remarkably, delaying the pleasures of marshmallow heaven predicts later adjustment. As adolescents, preschoolers able to resist temptation are more attentive, more tolerant of frustration and are perceived as more interpersonally competent by parents and peers (Mischel, 1996). Similarly, Rothbart et al. (2009) cite studies showing that lack of control is a risk factor for later persistent antisocial behavior, and for some of the symptoms of ADHD (Nigg, 2006). Effortful control appears to be a precursor to adult conscientiousness (Rothbart et al., 2009).

We should at this point emphasize that correlations between childhood temperament and adult personality and psychopathology are typically modest in magnitude (Lewis, 2001). Although we can find statistical associations between measures taken at different stages of personality development, we cannot predict the destiny of individual children. The child that grabs the marshmallow at the first opportunity is not necessarily doomed to a life of underachievement or crime.

Effortful control may be viewed in a purely cognitive light; indeed, Rothbart et al. (2009) link it to an attention network supporting a range of executive control functions, especially the inhibition of stimuli irrelevant to the current task. However, one of its several functions may be the suppression of emotionally driven impulsive responses. Mischel (1996) sees delay of gratification as reflecting the ability of a "cool" cognitive control system (located in the prefrontal cortex) to override a more primitive, stimulus-driven emotional processing system. He suggests that it depends on the use of emotion-regulation strategies to divert attention away from the tempting treat, such as focusing attention onto other mental activities.

Thus, we could reasonably see poor effortful control as a form of low EI, contributing to externalizing disorders. It is important, though, that studies of effortful control differentiate it rather sharply from other influences on emotion regulation, such as the worry-based strategies typical of the emotional disorders (see Rothbart et al., 2009).

Distorted Appraisals of Others. In externalizing disorders such as CD, aggressive behaviors are common. We may distinguish "reactive aggression," where the perpetrator lashes out in anger and frustration, from "proactive aggression," in which the aggressive act is rather more cool and calculated

(Caprara, Barbaranelli, & Zimbardo, 1996). A combination of high negative emotionality, coupled with poor effortful control, may promote reactive aggression (Frick & Morris, 2004). Consider the child who is mildly teased at school. If prone to reactive aggression, he interprets the teasing as driven by deliberate malice, rapidly becomes angry, and chooses violent actions as an effective coping strategy (Coie & Dodge, 1998). The aggressive behavior reflects systematic distortions in appraising others, and in evaluating the utility of possible coping strategies.

Misperceptions of others as more hostile than they actually are might be seen as an instance of lower EI. Indeed, low scores on questionnaire measures of EI related to more frequent externalizing behaviors in 10-year olds (Santesso, Reker, Schmidt, & Segalowitz, 2006). Similarly, Petrides, Sangareau, Furnham, and Frederickson (2006) found that children in this age group low in EI were more likely to be rated by both their teachers and their peers as being disruptive and aggressive. (Note that neither of these studies tested whether effects of EI were dependent on FFM traits linked to aggression such as low agreeableness and high neuroticism.) The next step for EI research in this field seems to be an investigation of whether the relationship between low EI and aggression is mediated by distorted others-appraisals. By contrast, there is extensive evidence showing that low agreeableness is related to a variety of cognitive biases that promote antisocial behaviors (Jensen-Campbell, Knack, & Rex-Lear, 2009).

Lack of Empathy. Some of the most striking and disturbing instances of violent behavior are seen in psychopaths. The term suggests the serial killers of numerous movies and TV shows, and, indeed, real serial killers, such as Jack the Ripper, Dennis Rader, and Jeffrey Dahmer, are examples of psychopaths. Research, however, suggests that, like other abnormal personality characteristics, psychopathy represents a continuous trait (see Hare & Neumann, 2009, for a review). Almost everyone possesses the central psychopathic traits of lack of empathy, manipulativeness, impulsivity, and antisocial tendencies to at least some minor degree. Relatively few people, though, show these traits to the extent that they lead to actual violence or criminal behavior. Cooke and Michie (2001) identified three rather distinct facets of psychopathic personality, which are illustrated in Table 6.2. Psychopathy is not a disorder recognized in *DSM-IV*, although it does overlap with antisocial personality disorder.

Impulsivity and antisocial tendencies are common to a variety of externalizing disorders, but lack of empathy is especially pronounced in psychopathy. The criminal psychopath shows an unusual and callous indifference to the suffering of his victims. Broadly, empathy refers to the recognition and sharing of others' feelings, but it is often broken down into two components: emotional sensitivity to others and cognitive understanding of others' perspectives.

Although aspects of empathy may be impaired in a variety of conditions, including alexithymia (Grynberg et al., 2010) and autism (see next section), psychopaths show a particular pattern of impairment. Jones, Happ, Gilbert, Burnett, and Viding (2010) compared a sample of boys (aged 9–16 years) meeting

TABLE 6.2 **THREE FACETS OF PSYCHOPATHY**

Arrogant and deceitful interpersonal style	Superficial charm Grandiose sense of self-worth Pathological lying Manipulative
Deficient affective experience	Lack of remorse and guilt Shallow emotion Lack of empathy Callousness
Impulsive and irresponsible behavioral style	Need for stimulation Parasitic lifestyle Lack of realistic goals Impulsivity Irresponsibility

clinical criteria for pronounced psychopathic tendencies with other groups of boys. They were presented with short descriptions of various aggressive encounters, and asked to rate how much they cared about various outcomes, such as their feelings of guilt and fear of punishment. Compared to normal controls, the psychopathic boys reported feeling less concern about the feelings of others, less concern about their own feelings, and less fear. They appeared to be deficient in emotional empathy, but not in the cognitive ability to understand the perspectives of others. As Jones et al. (2010) suggest, other research demonstrates that psychopaths have difficulty in recognizing distress in others.

Scales for empathy are a staple of EI questionnaires (e.g., the Bar-On EQ-i has items measuring this component). We would also expect empathy to correlate with trait EI on the basis that empathy is a central attribute of agreeableness in the FFM. Rather little research has directly examined the role of EI in empathic response, however. An exception is provided in a recent study (Ali, Amorim & Chamorro-Premuzic, 2009), in which participants rated their feelings after viewing images of happy, sad, and neutral individuals. Psychopathy was correlated with more positive emotions following exposure to a sad image, corresponding perhaps to the tendency of psychopaths to enjoy the suffering of others. However, trait EI was unrelated to response to emotional images; instead, trait EI was associated with more positive emotions following presentation of neutral images. In addition, trait EI was unrelated to "primary" psychopathy (core symptoms of the trait), but correlated significantly negatively with "secondary" psychopathic symptoms (e.g., impulsivity and antisocial behavior). This study seems to point toward the callous-unempathic elements of psychopathy as being rather distinct from low EI. It is possible, though, that questionnaire assessments of EI, whose limitations we discussed in Chapter 2, do not pick up the empathic deficiencies of psychopathy.

We should also briefly mention two further twists to the issue. First, clinical studies suggest that some psychopaths, at least, show signs of elevated emotional competencies. These individuals may be charismatic and capable of manipulating others to their own ends. For example, a Casanova is able to charm others into entirely selfish sexual compliance. Such tendencies may be assessed using scales for "Machiavellianism," referring to Niccolò Machiavelli, the devious political philosopher of Renaissance Italy. In fact, trait EI is negatively related to Machiavellianism (Ali et al., 2009; Austin, Farrelly, Black, & Moore, 2007). However, as Austin et al. point out, Machiavellianism scales measure approval of emotionally manipulative behavior, rather than actual competence. Indeed, Machiavellianism seems to be negatively associated with social and emotional understanding (Barlow, Qualter, & Stylianou, 2010). Thus, it remains unknown whether EI relates to true manipulative abilities, and there may be a "dark side" to EI that is untapped by current scales for the construct. For example, the real serial killer Ted Bundy, as well as the fictional Hannibal Lecter in "The Silence of the Lambs," were psychopathic but able to sway other people through personal charisma.

The second twist is that there may be a downside to emotional empathy. We typically think of empathy as beneficial—only a psychopath wants to be a psychopath—but Ferguson (in press) draws attention to the phenomenon of "empathic distress." A capacity for empathy may be a source of negative emotions derived from sharing the pain of others. Indeed, one study links empathy to higher depression (Youngmee, Schulz, & Carver, 2007). Too much empathy may thus be a disadvantage for those in the caring professions who must deal with human suffering on a daily basis. In this context, at least, EI may require a degree of tough-mindedness and emotional distancing. (The notoriously callous humor of medical students may derive from a similar need.)

To summarize, we can find several distinct respects in which individuals with poor impulse control may be said to be emotionally unintelligent—including poor self-control, distorted interpersonal perceptions, and deficient empathic emotion. These qualities may be picked up by psychometric tests for EI, although we noted the complexities of empathy. However, research has still to identify a distinctive contribution for the concept of EI. While the various impulse control disorders have some common elements, therapy requires a focus on the differences between the various conditions (Mullin & Hinshaw, 2007). Indeed, ADHD and CD may themselves be broken down into subtypes that require different treatment approaches. To the extent that a focus on EI blurs rather than highlights the key differences in conditions, it may hinder rather than assist therapy.

DISORDERS OF SOCIAL DISCONNECTION

There are several clinical conditions in which patients have difficulties in connecting socially with others. Given that a primary function of emotion is to facilitate communication and social interaction (Oatley & Johnson-Laird, 1996), we might wonder whether the severe social impairments seen in autism and schizophrenia relate to deficits in emotional competencies.

Autism and Emotional Functioning

Autism refers to a spectrum of impairments in social interaction (including nonverbal behaviors), language use, and producing socially appropriate behavior. At the lower end, the child may be severely cognitively impaired, with no prospects for independent living. However, in cases of Asperger syndrome, intellectual ability may be normal or even elevated. (In *DSM-IV*, Asperger syndrome is a separate disorder to autism; *DSM-V*, somewhat controversially, proposes to abolish the distinction).

High-functioning Asperger individuals suggest a kind of clinical model for low EI. Although seemingly cognitively normal, such individuals find it hard to fathom the intentions of others, and to figure out how they are supposed to behave in a social encounter. Intellectually distinguished people with Asperger syndrome include Temple Grandin, Ph.D., who has made important contributions to livestock management, and has written extensively about her experience of being autistic. (Her story was made into a fascinating biopic starring Claire Danes that screened on HBO in 2010; of note, her early academic career involved majoring in psychology.) In an autobiographical account (Grandin, 1996), she states that she typically thinks visually, "in pictures." Both verbal and social thinking were a struggle for her, learnt somewhat intellectually, like foreign languages.

Thus far, it may seem that we are dealing with social intelligence rather than EI. However, emotional difficulties are not uncommon in autism, including alexithymia (Fitzgerald & Bellgrove, 2006) and lack of empathy (Montgomery, McCrimmon, Schwean, & Saklofske, 2010). In the study described above, Jones et al. (2010) found that autistic children seemed to show more of a deficit in the cognitive elements of empathy (taking the perspective of others) than in emotional empathy. By contrast, psychopaths showed a deficit in emotion but not in cognitive perspective-taking.

Losh and Capps (2006) point out that autistic individuals were once thought to lack the capacity to express or experience emotion. Modern research reveals a much more nuanced picture: High-functioning individuals are often motivated to engage in social-emotional interaction and possess emotional knowledge. According to Losh and Capps (2006), autism does not preclude recognition and expression of basic emotions, but even high-functioning persons may struggle with more complex or self-conscious emotions such as embarrassment and pride.

The need to understand self-conscious emotions in a social context is a source of difficulty, and, potentially, a facet of EI. (It is perhaps ironic that empirical studies of EI have focused much more on basic emotions than on socially embedded emotions.) Montgomery et al. (2010) showed that autistic young adults obtained considerably lower scores than controls on a Bar-On's EQ-i. Unfortunately, given that the Bar-On measure largely assesses FFM traits (see Chapter 2), they did not test for personality differences. They found the largest differences between normal and autistic groups on the Bar-On General Mood scale, suggesting that their autistic sample may have been high in neuroticism. Curiously, they found no effect of autism on the MSCEIT; indeed, the autistic individuals obtained higher scores than controls on the Understanding Emotions branch. Montgomery et al. suggest that abstract knowledge of emotion may be normal in high-functioning autistic individuals, but they may have difficulty in applying this knowledge to real-life encounters. In addition, Montgomery et al. (2010) found that trait but not ability EI was associated with parent-rated social skills in the sample.

Social-Emotional Deficits in Schizophrenia

Turning to schizophrenia (a disorder quite distinct from autism), social deficits are again prominent as symptoms, along with the well-known hallucinations and delusions that contribute to psychosis. For example, Mancuso, Horan, Kern, and Green (2011) empirically identified three clusters of deficits: A hostile attributional style, lower-level social cue detection, and higher-level inferential and regulatory processing. All three types of deficit have some emotional content. We have discussed hostility in perceptions of others already; recall that in Mancuso et al.'s sample of schizophrenics, it was related to negative emotion. Lower-level social cue detection included identification of emotion in faces, as well as other aspects of decoding nonverbal behavior. Higher-level social processing referred to both rather subtle elements of social cognition (detection of sarcasm), as well as emotion management (measured in their study by the MSCEIT). Social deficits are also a feature of schizotypy, an abnormal personality trait associated with lack of interest in social relationships and restricted emotional experience (Claridge, 2009).

Several studies have confirmed that individuals with schizophrenia typically obtain lower scores on the MSCEIT, as well as performing poorly on a variety of tasks requiring emotional processing (Kee et al., 2009). College students high in schizotypal personality also obtain lower MSCEIT scores (Aguirre, Sergi, & Levy, 2008). An exception to the general trend was obtained by Holmen, Juuhl-Langseth, Thormodsen, Melle, and Rund (2010), who found no deficit on the MSCEIT in a sample of adolescents with early-onset schizophrenia. They suggest that the contexts for social cognition (e.g., workplace events) described in the MSCEIT items are unsuitable for this age group. Overall, the MSCEIT has sufficient credibility for schizophrenia research to be included in a standard test battery intended to measure the effectiveness of cognitive treatment effects in clinical trials of patients with schizophrenia (Keefe et al., 2011).

Both Kee et al. (2009) and Aguirre et al. (2009) found some evidence that the MSCEIT was predictive of measures of social dysfunction in their samples. Another study of schizophrenic patients (Eack et al., 2010) obtained rather mixed findings. The MSCEIT (total score and/or selected branch scores) was associated with scores on several of the clinician's own rating scales for symptom severity. Overall psychiatric symptoms were associated with poorer emotion perception and understanding on the MSCEIT. The total score on the MSCEIT related to a scale for social functioning (but not to overall social adjustment). The authors also used a measure of social-cognitive behaviors called the Social Cognition Profile (Hogarty et al., 2004), which requires the clinician to rate the patients behavioral functioning in four domains, relating to tolerance, perception, supportiveness, and self-confidence. Neither overall MSCEIT score nor branch scores correlated with social-cognitive functioning, according to this measure. As Eack et al. (2010) point out, it may be necessary to investigate which specific social-cognitive deficits are related to MSCEIT scores.

Mechanisms for Social-Emotional Dysfunction

Research has also started to identify some possible mechanisms that underpin these various conceptual and empirical linkages between clinical disorders and low EI. Two examples follow:

Theory of mind. A leading theory of autism (Baron-Cohen, 2001) identifies the condition with a deficit in "theory of mind." The autistic individual has difficulty in attributing beliefs, intentions, and emotions to others, and so cannot understand their behavior. Evidence also shows deficiencies in theory of mind in schizophrenics (Mancuso et al., 2011), and schizotypal personality appears to be more strongly related to deficits in theory of mind than to deficits in simple emotion perception (Aguirre, Sergi, & Levy, 2008). Ferguson and Austin (2010) administered two theory of mind tasks to a non-clinical sample, as well as a questionnaire for trait EI and MacCann and Roberts' situational judgment test for emotional understanding (see Chapter 3). EI was unrelated to one of the theory of mind tests, but both trait and ability tests correlated with a social-cognitive theory of mind test, requiring the person to detect instances of socially inappropriate behavior, such as mistaking a customer for a server in a restaurant. Somewhat similar findings linking both trait and ability EI measures to poorer performance on theory of mind tasks were obtained in Barlow et al.'s (2010) study of school-age children.

Emotional experience. Another type of impairment may be in the experiencing of emotion itself. Quite often, schizophrenic individuals seem to be lacking in core human qualities such as interest in social relationships and the capacity to experience pleasure. These are referred to as negative symptoms. Could there be something in the neurocognitive bases of schizophrenia that leads to loss of the ability to experience emotions fully? Kee et al. (2009) showed that MSCEIT scores were negatively correlated with several of these negative symptoms, including anhedonia (lack of pleasure), affective flattening (limited emotional experience), and avolition (apathy and general lack of motivation).

Losh and Capps (2006) raised the question of whether autistic individuals experience emotion differently (or even less) than matched controls. As we discussed, they concluded that autistic persons experience impoverished emotion, especially in relation to more complex, socially-infused emotions. In their study, high-functioning autistic children were asked to talk about instances in which they felt a variety of emotions. Losh and Capps interpreted the results as suggesting that autism relates to a deficit in emotional memory. They state that "the autistic group's emotional accounts conveyed a sense of fleeting, uncontemplated emotional encounters that failed to become fully engraved in autobiographical memory" (p. 816). That is, these children had difficulties in integrating their emotions into some meaningful personal narrative. To the extent that we use emotional memories to make sense of our world, autistic individuals may be lacking an essential tool for doing so.

To summarize, difficulties in social connection are common in clinical disorders, including autism and schizophrenia. Deficits in interpersonal functioning may reflect low EI, suggesting that impairments in emotional competencies may contribute to the clinical conditions. Broadly, the available research tends to confirm that autistic, schizophrenic, and schizotypal individuals score lower on tests for EI, although ability EI seems to be normal or even elevated in high-functioning autistic individuals (Montgomery et al., 2010). A variety of emotional and social-cognitive deficits have been observed in both autistic and schizophrenic individuals, although more research is needed to determine exactly what these deficits are (Zeidner, Matthews, & Roberts, 2009). Research has also made progress in exploring some of the mechanisms that may contribute to relevant deficits in EI, including (in autism) the social-cognitive processing needed for building a theory of mind (Ferguson & Austin, 2010) and the emotional memory representations that may shape emotional experience (Losh & Capps, 2006). As ever, too little attention has been paid to the role of personality and ability confounds of EI in these studies. The causal status of EI also remains unclear. Is a deficiency in "theory of mind" a cause or consequence of low EI?

SUMMARY AND CONCLUSIONS

It is easy, and perhaps too easy, to state that individuals with emotional disorders lack EI. Certainly, emotional dysfunctions of various kinds are prominent in a range of conditions. The more difficult issue is whether studies of EI add anything novel to current theories of abnormal psychology and to strategies for treatment. In this chapter, we posed several questions for clinical conceptions of EI. Some answers are starting to emerge, although much more work is still required.

We asked, first of all, whether EI is a cause or effect of mental disorder. Both causal possibilities are plausible, but evidence is lacking. Associations between EI and childhood temperamental qualities, such as poor effortful control, may substantiate a causal influence of EI. EI may also relate to personality traits such as neuroticism and schizotypy that appear to increase vulnerability to disorder.

We posed the question of whether EI is associated with a general vulnerability to mental illness. In fact, working with a more differentiated conception of multiple emotional competencies seems more promising. Distinctive forms of maladaptive emotion regulation are seen in the classic emotional disorders, such as anxiety and depression, in externalizing disorders and in "social disconnection" disorders. Each of these three classes

TABLE 6.3 THREE CLUSTERS OF DISORDER RELATED TO KEY MECHANISMS

Type of Condition	Salient Disorders and Conditions	Key Mechanisms
Emotional disorder	Major depression Generalized anxiety Other anxiety disorders: e.g., panic, post- traumatic stress disorder (PTSD), phobias, obsessive-compulsive disorder (OCD)	Unrealistic negative self- appraisals Dysfunctional coping Self-focused attention and meta-cognition Poor integration of cognition and emotion: e.g., alexithymia
Externalizing disorder	CD Antisocial personality Psychopathy ADHD	Lack of effortful or executive control Distorted appraisals of others Lack of empathy
Social disconnection	Schizophrenia Schizophrenia High-functioning autism	Lack of theory of mind Deficient representation of emotional experience

of disorder also contains various specific disorders that should also be distinguished from one another.

Similarly, we can answer our question about the mechanisms for pathology by identifying a variety of distinct abnormalities. In Table 6.3, we link the three broad classes of disorder to the various mechanisms discussed in this chapter. These are only broad correspondences—note that (1) different disorders within each class may relate to different mechanisms, and (2) mechanisms including alexithymia, lack of empathy, and poor executive control may contribute to multiple disorders.

We can pick out some more general themes here, grouping together some of the specific mechanisms as follows:

1. *Basic deficits in emotional functioning.* Some patients may lack basic capacities to identify and experience emotion, due in

part to abnormalities in neural functioning. Some neurological evidence—beyond the scope of this chapter—supports this perspective.

2. *Basic deficits in information processing.* Deficiencies in attentional and cognitive control mechanisms may impair processing of emotional stimuli (as well as other types of processing). There may also be deficits in processes specific to emotional processing, such as emotional memory, and processes for integrating cognition and affect.

3. *Deficiencies in self-regulation.* Higher-level cognitive processes regulate the appraisal and evaluation of self and others, and guide choices of strategy for coping and emotion regulation. Deficits of this kind may also reflect faulty beliefs about the self and others. Effective self-regulation also requires the capacity for understanding the self within a specific social context.

4. *Social thinking.* Work on theory of mind points toward the special challenges of understanding other people, which may be critical for social-emotional functioning.

Each of these different approaches to understanding emotional dysfunction suggests promising lines for uncovering specific pathways that may mediate the influence of EI on social-emotional functioning, and we have described some examples of relevant research in this chapter.

Finally, we posed the question of the practical utility of research on EI, in relation to improving psychotherapy. Our closing suggestion is that a focus on specific mechanisms for pathology may be more productive than attempting to remediate low EI in some more generic sense. Each type of mechanism suggests a specific type of intervention (see Zeidner et al., 2009, for a more detailed account). Neurological deficits may require drug treatments, and information-processing deficits may be countered by training relevant skills. Deficiencies in self-regulation may be addressed through cognitive-behavioral therapies that promote more adaptive and realistic thinking about the self. A novel feature of contemporary treatments are techniques for promoting more constructive thinking, specifically about negative emotions such as detached mindfulness (e.g., Ciarrochi & Blackledge, 2006) and supporting adaptive emotional expression (Kennedy-Moore & Watson, 1999). There seems to be no easy way to treat the lack of theory of mind evident in autism, although, as the example of Temple Grandin shows, the social-emotional faculties that most of us acquire intuitively can be learnt as explicit skills.

Conclusions

The emotions aren't always immediately subject to reason,
but they are always immediately subject to action.

William James

In Chapters 1–6, we have presented much of what we currently know about the three pillars of emotional intelligence (EI) research—conceptualization, measurement, and applications in various life domains. We have seen that the various lines of research on EI have achieved some success in showing that the various tests and measures pick up significant personal qualities beyond conventional cognitive ability. Table 7.1 summarizes the outcomes of the various meta-analyses we have referred to in this book, which provide evidence for the criterion validity of ability and self-report scales. (Recall that meta-analysis is a technique for averaging correlations or other statistics across multiple studies.) Generally, studies have substantiated that scales for EI predict various indices of well-being and constructive social interaction (Martins, Ramalho, & Morin, 2010). Evidence for a major impact of EI on

TABLE 7.1 A SUMMARY OF KEY META-ANALYSES RELEVANT TO EI

Study	Research Issue	Conclusions
Van Rooy et al. (2005)	How are EI measures related to one another, and to personality and cognitive ability?	Questionnaire and ability EI are minimally related Questionnaire EI relates to personality more than to ability Ability EI relates to ability more than to personality
Roberts, Schulze, and MacCann (2008)	How do the branches of the MSCEIT relate to cognitive ability and personality?	The MSCEIT is moderately correlated with general crystallized ability, more weakly with fluid ability Emotional Understanding is the branch most strongly associated with ability MSCEIT is weakly associated with FFM; strongest association between agreeableness and Emotion Management
Van Rooy and Viswesvaran (2004)	Does EI relate to job performance?	Questionnaire and ability EI are only modestly related to performance criteria With cognitive ability controlled, EI adds only minimally to the prediction of performance

228

Joseph and Newman (2010)	Does EI relate to performance of jobs differing in emotional labor required?	EI is more predictive of performance on high emotional labor jobs than low emotional labor jobs Questionnaire EI is more predictive than ability EI
Martins et al. (2010)*	Does EI relate to well-being and mental health?	Questionnaire EI is substantially related to questionnaire assessments of mental and physical health Ability EI is a significant but weaker predictor of health
Durlak et al. (2011)	Do SEL programs in schools improve various criteria for social-emotional functioning?	SEL programs improve social and emotional skills, attitudes, and social behaviors Intervention effects were substantial for social and emotional skills, positive but weaker for other criteria

Note. We have selected key findings; listing of outcomes is not comprehensive.

*An earlier meta-analysis (Schutte, Malouff, Thorsteinsson, Bhullar, & Rooke, 2007) reached similar conclusions.

occupational and educational success has been more elusive, although more targeted approaches, focusing on "emotion-critical" jobs, for example, seem to have potential (Joseph & Newman, 2010). The success of training programs for social and emotional learning (SEL) (Durlak, Weissberg, Dymnicki, Taylor, & Schellinger, 2011) also implies the existence of social-emotional competencies and skills that are pivotal in real life.

At the same time, it is fair to say that research on EI has not substantiated the more extreme claims made for its importance in human affairs. There are two broad reasons why excessive enthusiasm should be curbed. First, it is far from clear that there really is any such thing as general "EI". Research has identified a variety of aptitudes, competencies, and skills that may be helpful in challenging or emotive situations. However, it has not been shown that there is a single underlying personal quality that underlies the various characteristics that support social-emotional functioning. For example, meta-analyses show that whatever qualities are measured by the Mayer-Salovey-Caruso Emotional Intelligence Test (MSCEIT) and by questionnaire assessments are really quite distinct from one another (Van Rooy, Viswesvaran, & Pluta, 2005). Certainly, evidence for there being some general EI falls far short of that supporting general cognitive intelligence: IQ stills trumps EQ.

The second reason for caution is that evidence suggests that the validity of tests for EI (in its various guises) is typically modest. Ability tests, notably the MSCEIT, predict a range of relevant criteria related to well-being and social functioning, but the correlation magnitudes are typically small or moderate in size. So, whatever personal quality is measured by the MSCEIT is somewhat helpful in real life. However, ability EI is just one of a range of personality traits and abilities of relevance—not the cornerstone of personal adjustment that some have suggested. By contrast, general intelligence (g) can be pinned more strongly to specific psychological processes such as working memory (Ackerman, Beier, & Boyle, 2005), and to outcomes such as job proficiency (Schmidt & Hunter, 2004).

We have also seen (see Chapter 2) that questionnaire assessments of EI possess seemingly better validities than ability tests as predictors of well-being and other criteria. Trait EI scales are certainly useful for evaluating qualities such as stress tolerance, self-control, and style of emotion regulation. The problem here is that much, though not all, of the predictive power of these questionnaires comes from their overlap with standard personality traits, such as those of the Five Factor Model (FFM) (Burns, Bastian, & Nettelbeck, 2007). With the FFM controlled, validity for trait EI remains (Petrides, Furnham, & Mavroveli, 2007), but it is much reduced. And like IQ, personality predicts a range of important outcomes, including job earnings, retention, and mortality, independent of EI (e.g., Lindqvist & Vestman, 2011; Roberts, Kuncel, Shiner, Caspi, & Goldberg, 2007). Again, we seem to be dealing with a set of personal qualities that will increase our understanding of personality, rather than revolutionize it.

So, we should neither assume that EI is a panacea for all the woes of the individual and of society, nor reject the construct out of hand. The authors' position is that "EI" works better as a label for a broad field of inquiry into individual differences in affective functioning, than as any single well-defined personal quality. In the remainder of this concluding chapter, we will briefly outline the different constructs that may be brought together under the umbrella of EI, summarize their practical significance, and highlight some promising directions for new research.

EI: A SYMPHONY IN FOUR MOVEMENTS

Previously (Matthews, Zeidner, & Roberts, 2005; Roberts, Zeidner, & Matthews, 2007) we have claimed that at least four different types of construct may contribute to EI behavior. The four types are summarized in Table 7.2. A more systematic differentiation of these constructs may replace conceptual cacophony with a more

TABLE 7.2 FOUR DIFFERENT ASPECTS OF "EI"

Construct	Possible Current Measure	Key Processes	Trainability
Temperament	Standard personality measures (e.g., FFM) Many trait EI scales	Neural and cognitive processes controlling arousal, attention, and reinforcement sensitivity	Low—temperament is set by genes and early learning
Information processing	Speeded facial emotion recognition tasks Tasks requiring implicit processing of emotional stimuli	Specific processing modules	Low—except that fixed stimulus-response associations may become automatized through training
Emotion regulation	Selected trait EI scales (e.g., TMMS)	Self-concept and self-regulation	Moderate—temperament has an influence, but specific strategies may be learnt, e.g., via modeling and directed practice
Context-bound emotional knowledge and skills	MSCEIT (declarative skills) SJTs	Multiple acquired procedural and declarative skills	High—learning of specific skills and knowledge

harmonious structuring of ideas in the field. We will briefly out-line each one, and how it may be measured.

Temperament

As we discussed in Chapter 2, people differ in basic tempera-mental qualities such as sociability and vulnerability to negative emotions. Temperament is evident from infancy, and reflects the interaction of genetic influences with culturally shaped social learning. The FFM is a popular (though not universally accepted) account of the main dimensions of temperament sup-porting questionnaires such as the NEO-PI-R.

Long before the first questionnaires for EI, it was clear that the FFM traits are central to individual differences in emotional and social functioning (Matthews, Deary, & Whiteman, 2009). We can link extraversion to social influence, neuroticism to neg-ative emotionality, conscientiousness to self-control, agreeable-ness to caring for others, and openness to artistic expression (e.g., McCrae, 2000). Importantly, there may be downsides to seemingly beneficial traits (Matthews, Zeidner, & Roberts, 2002). For example, extraverts may be prone to impulsive behaviors, agreeable persons may struggle in competitive situ-ations, and the neurotic individual may go to the doctor more often, allowing a potentially fatal disease to be detected in its infancy (cf. Mayne, 1999). Thus, temperamental traits primarily represent styles of adjustment or adaption rather than unequiv-ocally desirable or undesirable qualities.

Questionnaires for EI, such as those reviewed in Chapter 2, likely belong within this sphere of temperament or personal-ity (Petrides et al., 2007). Indeed, they may usefully extend the range of personality traits that can be assessed, although it is hard to see these new traits as being different in kind from those already known. Where trait EI research is most useful is in identifying traits or clusters of traits that are poorly assessed by existing personality scales. For example, the "emotionality" fac-tor identified by Petrides et al. (2007; see also Tett, Fox, & Wang,

2005) is only moderately correlated with the FFM. However, it is clear that trait EI research tells us nothing about ability or intelligence.

Emotional Information Processing

We can get measures that are more plainly part of the ability domain by constructing objective, often speeded tests that require the person to process emotive stimuli. Ability can be assessed from measures of response time and/or accuracy. Standard cognitive psychological paradigms for studying attention, memory, and speeded reaction can be adapted to specify the processes concerned in some detail. For example, Chapter 3 discusses tests based on speeded response to facial emotional stimuli. The use of cognitive neuroscience methods may also allow us to probe the brain systems that control response (e.g., Freudenthaler, Fink, & Neubauer, 2006).

Work on such behavioral tests is certainly worth pursuing. Two issues loom large, however. The first is that there is no evidence for any general "emotional information-processing" factor or factors corresponding to factors for overall speed of response found in intelligence research (e.g., Roberts & Stankov, 1999). Indeed, response speed on some tasks may reflect general ability irrespective of whether or not stimuli are emotional or neutral in nature (Fellner et al., 2007; Roberts et al., 2006). The second issue is the adaptive significance of individual differences. Does recognizing facial emotion a few milliseconds faster than the average really make a difference to a person in real-life situations? Plausibly it might, especially in instances where there is a threat to one's life. But research has yet to address such issues in a systematic manner.

We expect that research will focus on more complex social-emotional processes, such as those underlying unconscious, "implicit" judgments of self and others. In Chapter 3, we briefly discussed the potential relevance of one of the leading measures of this type, the Implicit Association Test (IAT).

As Schnabel, Asendorpf, and Greenwald (2008) discuss, implicit measures have quite a good track record of predicting relevant behaviors, over and above standard personality traits. Perhaps there is some cluster of implicit processing routines that confers a true adaptive advantage in social-emotional settings. Thus far, research provides few clues toward whether such an "implicit EI" exists, and further study is required.

Emotion Regulation

There is something special about the self. It is not just that we feel ourselves to be special and unique (we are☺), but that there may a unique set of processes that regulate our internal representations of who we are (see Boekaerts, Pintrich, & Zeidner, 2000). Emotions provide us with an immediate, integrated signal of the status of the self—e.g., approaching a reward, being in danger, being demeaned, feeling happy, and so forth (see Lazarus, 1999). Regulation of emotions is thus critical for handling the opportunities and threats of life. Individuals who can effectively monitor and modulate their emotions in support of their personal goals may have a general life advantage. Conversely, emotional dysregulation, such as impulsive response to emotion or pointless brooding on problems, may poison our well-being, or even contribute to psychopathology (see Chapter 6).

Self-regulation overlaps in part with temperament and personality. For example, high-neuroticism individuals may hold excessively negative beliefs about themselves or others that on occasion interfere with their pursuit of life goals. Scales, such as Salovey, Mayer, Goldman, Turvey, and Palfai's (1995) Trait Meta-Mood Scale (TMMS), seek to assess broad emotion-regulation traits such as clarity of awareness of emotion and mood repair. Conversely, scales in the abnormal domain, such as the Metacognitions Questionnaire (Wells & Cartwright-Hatton, 2004), pick up dispositions that may drive harmful styles of emotion regulation, such as worrying excessively about being anxious.

CHAPTER 7

However, such personality-like scales are limited in that they assess general traits and tendencies, rather than the actual strategies for regulating emotions that are used in specific encounters. For example, given suitable instructions, people can voluntarily change their regulative style (e.g., from suppressing outward signs of emotion to reappraising the sources of emotion) (Gross, 2002). What makes a difference in real life is being able to regulate emotion effectively in specific contexts—staying cool in congested traffic (hard to do in New York, Los Angeles, or Atlanta), being emotionally supportive to troubled co-workers, tolerating a relative's endless whining about minor issues, and helping a fellow student get over a disappointing grade. New measurement approaches are needed to assess these situationally rooted styles of regulation, whether adaptive or counterproductive.

Emotional Skills

Many of the ways we deal with emotional encounters reflect learned skills for handling them, skills shaped by the social and cultural context. Some of these skills are quite general in nature, such as expressing sympathy to a distressed person, or avoiding confrontational behaviors with someone who is clearly angry. Others are highly specific, such as our knowledge of how to deal with the emotional states of the various people to whom we are very close.

In intelligence theory, the distinction between crystallized and fluid intelligence expresses the difference between acquired intellectual skills (e.g., how to solve a crossword puzzle) and raw aptitude (see Chapter 3). Similarly, there may be a broad crystallized EI representing acquired general knowledge of emotional functioning (Roberts et al., 2011). Indeed, the emotion understanding and emotion management branches of the Mayer-Salovey ability model may represent generic knowledge of this kind.

It is questionable, however, whether the MSCEIT picks up more context-bound knowledge. In addition, as Brody (2004) has pointed out, the MSCEIT assesses knowledge of how to handle emotion in the abstract, rather than practical skills. A psychology student might know the principles of psychotherapy very well, but have no capacity to work with actual clients. The key distinction here is between *declarative* knowledge (verbal expression of principles) and *procedural* knowledge (actual practice of the skill; see Anderson, 1987). The MSCEIT and other tests may be quite effective in probing declarative knowledge, but researchers currently lack good tools for assessment of proceduralized skills, such as expressing emotion so as to influence another beneficially.

It is reasonable to suppose that someone with a cheerful, friendly temperament, who processed emotional information rapidly, who had good control of emotion, and who had extensive declarative and procedural skills would be seen as "emotionally intelligent." Our impressions of the EI of others may thus emerge as an integration of various, somewhat separate qualities. However, in research we need to sharpen the distinctions between these qualities so that we can get more valid, "cleaner" tests for each one, and explore their inter-relationships systematically. (We might also want to add a moral criterion for EI, unless we want to allow for some psychopaths being emotionally intelligent.)

What Is EI Good For?

Only a cynic would respond "absolutely nothing!" A starting point for evaluating the applied utility of research on EI comes from the evidence on the validity of the various measures of EI (see Table 7.1). We have seen in various places in this book, and especially in Chapter 4, that scales for EI are related to criteria for superior social-emotional functioning in a range of real-life contexts. These include personal relationships, the workplace, and education. Low EI is also implicated in a range of mental disorders (Chapter 6). However, there are several reasons for interpreting these findings with caution. In general, (1) EI relates more strongly to subjective than to objective outcome variables, (2) predictive validity partly reflects overlap with existing personality and ability constructs, and (3) the underlying psychological and neurological processes that mediate effects of EI are not well-understood. Nevertheless, it seems that the various measures of EI are indeed indexing personal characteristics (including both abilities and personality traits) that make a difference in real-life.

We have also seen (Chapter 5) that at least some of the qualities that constitute EI can be trained, as evidenced by the Durlak et al. (2011) meta-analysis—acknowledging the uncertainties over what exactly is being trained, and how. Indeed, the multifaceted perspective on EI presented in the previous section may help our understanding of training. *Temperament* is the facet least likely to be trainable, given its basis in brain systems and stable self-beliefs (Matthews et al., 2009), although it may be more plastic in childhood. The message from much cognitive psychological research is that *basic information-processing* routines tend to be trainable to the extent that there is a fixed stimulus-response mapping (Fisk & Schneider, 1983). Thus, it seems that recognition of facial emotion may be trained using video materials (Ekman, 2003). As the Gross (2002) studies show, people display flexibility in using different *emotion-regulation* strategies, implying trainability, although there seems to be limited relevant research. Training effects are best known from psychotherapies geared toward reducing use of dysfunctional strategies (Wells, 2000). Learning is intrinsic to the concept of *emotion knowledge*, which should be readily trainable. However, it may be easier to instruct the person in explicit knowledge, of the kind assessed by the MSCEIT Understanding Emotions branch, than in implicit, procedural skills. We suspect that the training programs reviewed in Chapter 5 may address both types of learning (although it would help if programs specified learning processes more clearly).

Thus, except perhaps in the case of temperament, there appears to be plenty of scope for training people in several facets of EI. In the remainder of this section, we will set out what we see as the most promising strategies for enhancing three of the benefits that may stem from superior social-emotional functioning: greater personal well-being, more constructive social relationships, and superior performance in occupational and educational settings.

Well-Being

Meta-analysis confirms that EI typically relates to criteria for subjective well-being and satisfaction more strongly than to other outcomes (e.g., Martins et al., 2010). As discussed in Chapter 4, EI relates to job satisfaction in the workplace. We have seen also that much of the association between trait EI and well-being is dependent on the overlap between EI and temperamental traits that are linked to emotionality. Traits are hard to change, so what "added value" can a focus on EI add to the starting point that some people are more disposed to enjoy life than others?

One option may be to enhance coping skills. As we saw in Chapter 4, ways of coping with challenging events are intrinsically malleable (Lazarus, 1999). We typically deploy coping strategies flexibly depending on the nature of events. Temperamental qualities may bias use toward one or other means of coping, but, in any given context, experience and learning may be equally or more important than temperament.

The importance of coping is already understood in practical training programs, such as those implemented in schools (see Chapter 5). Three of the core competencies identified by Elias, Kress, and Hunter (2006) relate directly to coping. *Responsible decision making* requires problem- or task-focused coping in the service of making better life choices. *Self-awareness*, such as recognizing one's own emotional state, is important for constructive emotion-focusing. A person cannot regulate their own emotions effectively if they lack this awareness. *Self-management* is also important for supporting effective emotion-focusing—e.g., recognizing and inhibiting reckless emotion-driven impulses, and working systematically on problematic emotional reactions.

As discussed in Chapter 5, the successes of SEL programs suggest that techniques for enhancing coping can be applied beyond the school setting. Indeed, the importance of coping has long been recognized in stress-management programs for the workplace (Quick, Quick, Nelson, & Hurrell, 1997). In the clinical context (see Chapter 6), clients' issues are typically more deep-rooted than use of maladaptive coping strategies alone. However, psychotherapists often work on training skills that will support coping. Such skills may be directed toward internal emotion regulation, such as gaining control over anxieties and worries, or they may be more behavioral in nature, such as social skills.

Applied studies of EI affirm the importance of coping for well-being. EI may prove to be one of several relevant dispositional factors that shape coping efforts (Zeidner, Matthews, & Roberts, 2006), though further work is necessary to determine its exact role. A central issue is that coping is best trained in some specific context, rather than in some broad generic sense. In other words, we need to address emotional skills, including procedural skills, which current conceptualizations of EI have tended to neglect. Accounts of SEL (Elias et al., 2006) do seem to have made progress in bridging abstract notions of coping with specific targets for intervention.

In principle, understanding of EI should especially promote more effective emotion-focused coping. Stress research tends to highlight the more dysfunctional forms of emotion-focused coping such as self-criticism and rumination, as well as avoidance of feared situations. Indeed, those high in EI may shun these coping strategies (Zeidner et al., 2006). However, valuing our emotions should lead us toward more constructive forms of emotion-focused coping, such as positive reappraisal (Lazarus, 1999). We may hope for more insight into emotion-focused coping from EI research in the future.

Social Interactions

We can start with two self-evident truths. First, the quality of our encounters with those around us is critical for both subjective well-being and for enhancement of social status. Thus, enhancing social functioning may contribute to well-being over and above the influence of coping. The list of key competencies relevant to SEL programs drawn up by Elias et al. (2006) includes *social awareness* and *relationship management.* Second, we are vulnerable to the influence of temperament. Prospects are dim for making the low-agreeableness person warm and cuddly or the high-neuroticism individual a model of coolness under pressure. So, what can we take from research on EI that may help people of all temperamental characteristics enjoy more constructive social relationships?—surely an important topic of both scientific and personal interest!

Looking beyond temperamental factors, we saw in Chapter 4 that close relationships, in particular, call for skills in emotion regulation. People to whom we are close are likely to annoy or frustrate us on occasion (some more than others), and managing these emotions is important for maintaining a constructive relationship. Maintaining the positive emotions elicited by social interaction is also likely to be important, such as "keeping the flame alive" in an intimate relationship. However, there is little direct evidence on this issue, other than the evidence that higher EI is associated with greater satisfaction in intimate relationships (Brackett, Warner, & Bosco, 2005; Smith, Ciarrochi, & Heaven, 2008).

Several authors have pointed toward the importance of EI in counseling for those experiencing relationship difficulties (e.g., Cooper & Ng, 2009). A focus on training the components of EI relevant to couples seems feasible. However, there seems to be little research on counseling strategies that is directly based on theoretical accounts of EI, although Smith et al. (2008) point out the importance of communication strategies in relationships. Possibly, success in relationships depends on context-bound declarative and procedural skills, rather than on more general application of emotion-regulation strategies.

Training coping skills (see Chapter 5) may also benefit both intimate and more, dare we call them, "mundane" relationships. Sometimes, difficulties may be open to problem-focused strategies of identifying a source of discord, and developing behavioral methods for resolving the difficulty, such as setting aside time for talking about a relationship difficulty. Again, though, this is not a particularly novel suggestion. Research on EI has yet to identify new trainable coping strategies for enhancing social relationships, although it has highlighted the dangers to relationships of avoidance of issues (Smith et al., 2008).

A final thought on relationships is that research may have neglected the more interpersonal elements of EI. It is telling that two studies (Smith et al., 2008; Zeidner & Kaluda, 2008) have found that a relationship partner with high EI benefits herself (or himself), but there is no benefit to the other person in the relationship. It seems like there should be personal qualities that help the "significant" other to also flourish emotionally—but measures of EI so far field-tested do not seem to pick up on these qualities.

Performance in Occupational and Educational Settings

A theme of this book is that tests for EI tend to be more predictive of subjective criteria, including self-reports of well-being and relationship satisfaction, than they are of objective outcomes. Nevertheless, there has been persistent interest in the potential contribution of high EI to improving academic success and job performance. Indeed, much of the early excitement about EI stemmed from over-blown and unsubstantiated claims that high "EQ" might be more important than IQ to work success (Goleman, 1995). Even if we reject excessive claims, it seems plausible that better management of the emotions will help to maintain attentional focus on tasks in work and classroom settings, and so enhance performance.

Crudely, much of the research suggests that high EI helps you feel better about your life and relationships, but has minimal impact on objective behavior. For example, meta-analysis has failed to substantiate the opinion that high EI is critical for job performance (Van Rooy & Viswesvaran, 2004), although EI might be more important for other valued work behaviors, including organizational citizenship, commitment, teamwork and support of other employees, and constructive negotiation of interpersonal conflict (Jordan, Ashkanasy, & Ascough, 2007). There have also been several studies showing that EI is unrelated to objective indices of academic success, such as grade point average (GPA) (e.g., Amelang & Steinmayr, 2006; Barchard, 2003; Rode, Arthaud-Day, Mooney, Near, & Baldwin, 2008), when ability and personality are controlled. The evidence is somewhat mixed here though. Some studies have shown that EI adds uniquely to the prediction of academic outcomes (e.g., MacCann & Roberts, 2008; Van der Zee, Thijs, & Schakel, 2002), and it seems that SEL interventions can boost grades at school (Durlak et al., 2011).

It may be too optimistic to expect high EI to produce across-the-board improvements in behavior. We may have more luck in identifying specific groups of individuals or performance contexts in which high EI is especially important. Petrides, Fredrickson, and Furnham (2004) investigated predictors of academic performance in 650 high-school age British children. They confirmed that, in general, IQ was a much stronger predictor of performance than trait EI. However, they showed that for English (though not for math or science), trait EI was associated with better performance in those low in IQ, suggesting that EI may help the child to compensate for a lack of intellectual ability.

In the occupational context, as discussed in Chapter 4, Joseph and Newman (2010) found that EI was helpful to performance only when the job required "emotional labor" (i.e., making an effort to be nice to customers, as found in service industries). Similarly, Côté and Miners (2006) found high EI conferred advantages for organizational citizenship as directed toward the organization, but not toward specific individuals. It appears worthwhile identifying further subgroups and contexts in both education and the workplace in which EI is especially important.

WHAT NEXT FOR EI?

In the authors' view, research has failed to establish EI as a major personal characteristic, as important as "IQ." Instead, we believe the contribution of research has been to identify a variety of separate abilities, traits, and skills that feed into individual differences in social-emotional functioning. The four facets of EI outlined at the beginning of this chapter may help to guide further research, but we expect improvements in knowledge to be incremental, not revolutionary. We finish with some brief comments on some promising research directions for developing existing constructs labeled as EI.

Toward Multi-Polar Models

The psychometrics of the field remains sketchy, but it will be fairly straightforward to collect data that will allow different attributes of EI to be inter-related within a structural model. Thus, the various dimensions of trait EI and dispositional mood regulation may be slotted into prevailing personality models, such as the FFM. We doubt if any radical change to such models will result. Similarly, performance-based dimensions of emotional information-processing and factors based on declarative knowledge (notably, branches of the MSCEIT) should find a home within Carroll's three-level model of abilities (see Chapter 3). It remains an open and interesting question what higher-level factors might emerge beyond existing constructs such as fluid and crystallized intelligence. Perhaps "declarative emotion knowledge" will emerge as a mid-level factor.

There may be more to EI than simply constructing outbuildings and extensions to "Personality Towers" and "Chateau

Intelligence." Our sense is that the most novel and exciting elements of EI are not well captured by either conventional personality or ability tests in the field. In particular, what makes a difference in real-life situations may be acquired contextualized skills for handling social-emotive challenges. We have only a limited sense of how to measure proceduralized skills, what the underlying dimensions of individual differences might be, and even whether there are any dimensions beyond very specific skills.

Inter-relating different types of EI dimension is also challenging, assuming we have good models of the various temperamental traits, abilities, skills, and knowledge. As the weakness of associations between trait EI and ability EI tests shows, we have to find ways of characterizing rather subtle relationships between different types of construct. Zeidner, Matthews, Roberts, and MacCann (2003) suggested that developmental models may be most appropriate. Temperament, cognitive ability, and facets of EI may all impose somewhat different constraints on the child's social-emotional development. Social-emotional skills may primarily reflect learning, but also bear the imprints of these various biasing factors.

New Assessment Methods

Both orthodox questionnaires and tests resembling intelligence tests have their limitations. The weaknesses of measuring an "intelligence" through self-report questions are well known (O'Sullivan, 2007). A true intelligence here should be open to valid measurement through use of objective tests with right or wrong answers. The ease with which high EI can be faked is also a barrier to use of questionnaires in high-stakes settings, such as personnel selection. By contrast, the weaknesses of ability tests, such as the MSCEIT, derive from uncertainties over establishing criteria for determining what the correct answers to test items are (see Chapter 3), and assessing procedural skills supporting emotional competency (Brody, 2004). Thus, there is a need for new and imaginative methods for assessment of the different aspects of EI, especially emotional information-processing and skills. In Chapter 3, we discussed some promising new approaches. For example, we can build tests of emotional inspection time and implicit emotional associations to investigate basic aptitudes for processing emotional stimuli. This chapter also covered multimedia situational judgment tests (SJTs). Computer technology may immerse the individual in some realistic emotive setting to gauge their skills for handling the situation more realistically. As technology advances, we can simulate specific types of emotional encounters with increasing fidelity, so that we can assess contextualized skills within a virtual reality.

Another promising area for new assessments is the use of psychophysiological techniques for measuring relevant brain processes. For example, several studies now suggest that individuals high and low in EI differ in their electroencephalographic (EEG) response to emotional stimuli (Jaušovec & Jaušovec, 2010). Killgore and Yurgelun-Todd (2007) used functional magnetic resonance imaging (fMRI) to show associations between EI and brain activations while viewing fearful faces. Such evidence may be used to link EI to the subcortical systems that generate emotion (e.g., amygdala) and to the higher-level executive systems that regulate emotion (e.g., prefrontal cortex). There is a considerable gap between demonstrating correlations between EI and brain responses in group data to developing tests and metrics that will be valid for all individuals. Nevertheless, psychophysiology may provide the means to assess some of the facets of EI, especially those related to basic emotional functioning.

Theory-Driven Training Programs

As we noted in Chapter 5, training programs are often at least somewhat effective, but are also rather ad hoc in nature. Efforts to train specific skills such as self-control and assertiveness predate the invention of EI. To some extent programs have simply adopted "EI" as a convenient label to generate publicity. Similarly, it is unclear what research on EI has to offer existing stress-management programs that enhance coping in the workplace.

Ideally, training would be informed by an explicit theory of EI. Indeed, some of the existing conceptions of EI, notably the Mayer-Salovey four-branch model, lend themselves to more rigorous approaches to training. Emotion perception and emotion understanding seem readily trainable; indeed, software exists for training recognition of brief "microexpressions" of emotion (Ekman, 2003). Emotion management may be more difficult, because of its context-dependence; but some of what is accomplished by the educational programs discussed in Chapter 6 falls under this heading. Quite how assimilation of emotion into thought could be effected is a mystery. Consider the issues raised by training synesthesia, for example, experiencing emotion as a color or bodily sensation. Our conceptual analysis here suggests training might be more explicitly directed toward context-bound skills, including emotion-regulation strategies.

A stronger EI theory might also enhance clinical practice. In concluding Chapter 6, we differentiated four relevant but separate sources of pathology, related to basic emotional functioning, basic information-processing, self-regulation, and social thinking (e.g., theory of mind). Again, the jury is out on what EI research has to add to existing clinical practice. However, it seems to have the potential, at least, to add to training strategies for compensating for basic (and possibly neurological) deficits, and for enhancing the competencies in understanding and managing emotion that are necessary for adaptive self-regulation.

EI and AI

A final research direction is in building emotion into artificial systems (Matthews, 2005). As Picard (2007) discusses, programming computer applications and robots to recognize human emotion and to simulate emotional response to the human being may improve human–computer interaction. Technologies for recognizing human emotion from psychophysiological sensors are improving, as is software for producing emotional responses appropriate to the context. For example, the computer might be able to sense when the human user is frustrated, provide some reassurance, and modify the operation of the interface to reduce frustration. Robots will become increasingly sophisticated, and human-like in their abilities to operate autonomously, without the need for continuous control by a human operator. Emotions evolved, in part, to assist communication between human beings (Oatley & Johnson-Laird, 1996). We may find that we need to learn from evolution in designing effective channels for communicating with intelligent artificial systems also.

CONCLUSION

Research on EI has led to many advances in understanding how individuals differ in their emotional functioning across a range of settings. The various tests we have described provide a systematic means for evaluating a variety of temperamental qualities, aptitudes, competencies, and skills. As such, tests for EI will continue to stimulate significant research. We have found it salutary to exercise some caution and skepticism when evaluating the literature. Some have previously suggested that EI is nothing more than old wine packaged in new and glittering containers, or a passing fad of the type common in business, education, and health domains (Murphy & Sideman, 2006). On the other hand, even if the more grandiose claims made for EI are untrue (and they are), systematic study within the four fields of inquiry that we have identified has good prospects for advancing understanding ability and personality. While the optimist may believe EI is here to stay, the pessimist may believe that EI will burn out before too long. Will EI stay or will it go? Only time will tell.

References

Aber, J. L., Jones, S. M., Brown, J. L., Chaudry, N., & Samples, F. (1998). Resolving conflict creatively: Evaluating the developmental effects of a school-based violence prevention program in neighborhood and classroom context. *Development and Psychopathology, 10*, 187–213.

Abraham, R. (2005). Emotional intelligence in the workplace: A review and synthesis. In R. Schulze & R. D. Roberts (Eds.), *Emotional intelligence: An international handbook* (pp. 255–270). Cambridge, MA: Hogrefe & Huber.

Ackerman, P. L., Beier, M. E., & Boyle, M. O. (2005). Working memory and intelligence: The same or different constructs? *Psychological Bulletin, 131*, 30–60.

Ackerman, P. L., & Heggestad, E. D. (1997). Intelligence, personality, and interests: Evidence for overlapping traits. *Psychological Bulletin, 121*, 219–245.

Aguirre, F., Sergi, M. J., & Levy, C. A. (2008). Emotional intelligence and social functioning in persons with schizotypy. *Schizophrenia Research, 104*, 255–264.

Ali, F., Amorim, I. S., & Chamorro-Premuzic, T. (2009). Empathy deficits and trait emotional intelligence in psychopathy and Machiavellianism. *Personality and Individual Differences, 47*, 758–762.

Amelang, M., & Steinmayr, R. (2006). Is there a validity increment for tests of emotional intelligence in explaining the variance of performance criteria? *Intelligence, 34*, 459–468.

American Educational Research Association, American Psychological Association, National Council on Measurement in Education.

(1999). *Standards for Educational and Psychological Tests*. Washington, DC: American Educational Research Association.

Anderson, J. R. (1987). Skill acquisition: Compilation of weak-method problem situations. *Psychological Review, 94*, 192–210.

Antonakis, J., Ashkanasy, N. M., & Dasborough, M. T. (2009). Does leadership need emotional intelligence? *The Leadership Quarterly, 20*, 247–261.

Antony, M. M., & Barlow, D. H. (Eds.). (2010). *Handbook of assessment and treatment planning for psychological disorders* (2nd ed.). New York, NY: Guilford Press.

Argyle, M. (2001). *The psychology of happiness* (2nd ed.). New York, NY: Routledge.

Ashkanasy, N. M., & Tse, B. (2000). Transformational leadership as management of emotion: A conceptual review. In N. M. Ashkanasy, C. E. Härtel, & W. J. Zerbe (Eds.), *Emotions in the workplace: Research, theory, and practice* (pp. 221–235). Westport, CT: Quorum Books/Greenwood.

Ashton, M. C., Lee, K., & Paunonen, S. V. (2002). What is the central feature of extraversion?: Social attention versus reward sensitivity. *Journal of Personality and Social Psychology, 83*, 245–251.

Ashton, M. C., Lee, K., Vernon, P., & Jang, K. L. (2000). Fluid intelligence, crystallized intelligence, and the openness/intellect factor. *Journal of Research in Personality, 34*, 198–207.

Austin, E. J. (2005). Emotional intelligence and emotional information processing. *Personality and Individual Differences, 39*, 403–414.

Austin, E. J. (2010). Measurement of ability emotional intelligence: Results for two new tests. *British Journal of Psychology, 101*, 563–578.

Austin, E. J., Boyle, G. J., Groth-Marnat, G., Matthews, G., Saklofske, D. H., Schwean, V. L., & Zeidner, M. (2011). Integrating intelligence and personality: Theory, research and implications for clinical assessment. In G. Groth-Marnat (Ed.), *Integrative assessment of adult personality* (3rd ed., pp. 119–151). New York: Guilford Press.

Austin, E. J., Farrelly, D., Black, C., & Moore, H. (2007). Emotional intelligence, Machiavellianism, and emotional manipulation: Does EI have a dark side? *Personality and Individual Differences, 43*, 179–189.

Austin, E. J., & Saklofske, D. H. (2005). Far too many intelligences? On the communalities and differences between social, practical, and emotional intelligences. In R. Schulze & R. D. Roberts (Eds.),

International handbook of emotional intelligence (pp. 107–128). Cambridge, MA: Hogrefe & Huber.

Austin, E. J., Saklofske, D. H., Huang, S. H. S., & McKenney, D. (2004). Measurement of trait emotional intelligence: Testing and cross-validating a modified version of Schutte et al.'s (1998) measure. *Personality and Individual Differences, 36*, 555–562.

Banziger, T., Grandjean, D., & Scherer, K. R. (2009). Emotion recognition from expressions in face, voice, and body: The Multimodal Emotion Recognition Test (MERT). *Emotion, 9*, 691–704.

Barchard, K. A. (2003). Does emotional intelligence assist in the prediction of academic success? *Educational and Psychological Measurement, 63*, 840–858.

Barchard, K. A., & Hakstian, R. A. (2004). The nature of emotional intelligence abilities: Basic dimensions and their relationships with other cognitive-ability and personality variables. *Educational and Psychological Measurement, 64*, 437–462.

Barling, J., Slater, F., & Kelloway, E. K. (2000). Transformational leadership and emotional intelligence: An exploratory study. *Leadership & Organization Development Journal, 21*, 157–161.

Barlow, A., Qualter, P., & Stylianou, M. (2010). Relationships between Machiavellianism, emotional intelligence and theory of mind in children. *Personality and Individual Differences, 48*, 78–82.

Barnett, P. A., & Gotlib, I. H. (1988). Psychosocial functioning and depression: distinguishing among antecedents, concomitants, and consequences. *Psychological Bulletin, 104*, 97–126.

Bar-On, R. (1997). *The Emotional Intelligence Inventory (EQ-i): Technical Manual*. Toronto, ON: Multi-Health Systems.

Bar-On, R. (2000). Emotional and social intelligence: Insights from the Emotional Quotient Inventory. In R. Bar-On & J. D. A. Parker (Eds.), *The handbook of emotional intelligence: Theory, development, assessment, and application at home, school, and in the workplace* (pp. 363–388). San Francisco, CA: Jossey-Bass.

Baron-Cohen, S. (2001). Theory of mind and autism: A review. In L. M. Glidden (Ed.), *International review of research in mental retardation: Autism (vol. 23)* (pp. 169–184). San Diego, CA: Academic Press.

Bartley, C. E., & Roesch, S. C. (2011). Coping with daily stress: The role of conscientiousness. *Personality and Individual Differences, 50*, 79–83.

Bass, B. M. (2002). Cognitive, social, and emotional intelligence of trans-formational leaders. In R. E. Riggio & S. E. Murphy (Eds.), *Multiple intelligences and leadership* (pp.105–118). Hillsdale, NJ: Erlbaum.

Bastian, V. A., Burns, N. R., & Nettelbeck, T. (2005). Emotional intelli-gence predicts life skills, but not as well as personality and cogni-tive abilities. *Personality and Individual Differences, 39*, 1135–1145.

Batey, M., & Furnham, A. (2006). Creativity, intelligence, and person-ality: A critical review of the scattered literature. *Genetic, Social, and General Psychology Monographs, 132*, 355–429.

Baum, K. M., & Nowicki, S. (1998). Perception of emotion: Measuring decoding accuracy of adult prosodic cues varying in intensity. *Journal of Nonverbal Behavior, 22*, 89–108.

Beck, A. T., Emery, G., & Greenberg, R. L. (2005). *Anxiety disorders and phobias: A cognitive perspective.* New York, NY: Basic Books.

Benton, D. (2008). Nutrition and intellectual development. In P. C. Kyllonen, R. D. Roberts, & L. Stankov (Eds.), *Extending intelligence: Enhancement and new constructs.* (pp. 313–330). New York, NY: Taylor & Francis.

Blickle, G., Momm, T. S., Kramer, J., Mierke, J., Liu, J., & Ferris, G. R. (2009). Construct and criterion-related validation of a measure of emotional reasoning skills: A two-study investigation. *International Journal of Selection and Assessment, 17*, 101–118.

Boekaerts, M., Pintrich, P. R., & Zeidner, M. (Eds.) (2000). *Handbook of self-regulation.* San Diego, CA: Academic Press.

Boring, E. G. (1923). Intelligence as the tests test it. *The New Republic, 36*, 35–37.

Boyatzis, R. E. (1982). *The competent manager: A model for effective perfor-mance.* New York, NY: Wiley & Sons.

Boyatzis, R. E. (2001). How and why individuals are able to develop emotional intelligence. In C. Cherniss & D. Goleman (Eds.), *The emotionally intelligent workplace* (pp. 234–253). San-Francisco, CA: Jossey-Bass.

Boyatzis, R. E. (2007). Developing emotional intelligence competen-cies. In J. Ciarrochi & J. D. Mayer (Eds.), *Applying emotional intelli-gence: A practitioner's guide* (pp. 28–52). New York, NY: Psychology Press.

Boyatzis, R. E., Goleman, D., & Rhee, K. (2000). Clustering compe-tence in Emotional Intelligence: Insights from the emotional competence inventory. In R. Bar-On & J. D. A. Parker (Eds.), *The handbook of emotional intelligence* (pp. 343–362). San Francisco, CA: Jossey-Bass.

Boyatzis, R. E., & Sala, F. (2004). The Emotional Competence Inventory (ECI). In G. Geher (Ed.), *Measuring emotional intelligence: Common ground and controversy* (pp. 147–180). Hauppauge, NY: Nova Science.

Brackett, M. A., & Katulak, N. A. (2007). Emotional Intelligence in the classroom: Skill-based training for teachers and students. In J. Ciarrochi & J. D. Mayer (Eds.), *Applying emotional intelligence: A practitioner's guide* (pp. 1–27). New York, NY: Psychology Press.

Brackett, M. A., & Mayer, J. D. (2003). Convergent, discriminant, and incremental validity of competing measures of emotional intelligence. *Personality and Social Psychology Bulletin, 29,* 1147–1158.

Brackett, M. A., Mayer, J. D., &Warner, R. M. (2004). Emotional intelligence and its relation to everyday behavior. *Personality and Individual Differences, 36,* 1387–1402.

Brackett, M. A., Palomera, R., Mojsa-Kaja, J., Reyes, M. R., & Salovey, P. (2010). Emotion-regulation ability, burnout, and job satisfaction among British secondary-school teachers. *Psychology in the School, 47,* 406–417.

Brackett, M. A., Rivers, S. E., Shiffman, S., Lerner, N., & Salovey, P. (2006). Relating emotional abilities to social functioning: A comparison of self-report and performance measures of emotional intelligence. *Journal of Personality and Social Psychology, 91,* 780–795.

Brackett, M. A., Warner, R. M., & Bosco, J. S. (2005). Emotional intelligence and relationship quality among couples. *Personal Relationships, 12,* 197–212.

Brody, N. (2004). What cognitive intelligence is and what emotional intelligence is not. *Psychological Inquiry, 15,* 234–238.

Buck, R. (1984). *The communication of emotion.* New York: Guilford Press.

Burns, N. R., Bastian, V. A., & Nettelbeck, T. (2007). Emotional intelligence: More than personality and cognitive ability? In G. Matthews, M. Zeidner, & R. D. Roberts (Eds.), *The science of emotional intelligence: Knowns and unknowns* (pp. 167–196). New York, NY: Oxford University Press.

Bushman, B. J. (2002). Does venting anger feed or extinguish the flame? Catharsis, rumination, distraction, anger, and aggressive responding. *Personality and Social Psychology Bulletin, 28,* 724–731.

Cacioppo, J. T. (2006). Social neuroscience. *American Journal of Psychology, 119,* 664–668.

Cahill, S. P., & Foa, E. B. (2007). Psychological theories of PTSD. In M. J. Friedman, J. Matthew, T. M. Keane, & P. A. Resick, (Eds.), *Handbook of PTSD: Science and practice* (pp. 55–77). New York, NY: Guilford Press.

Caprara, G. V., Barbaranelli, C., & Zimbardo, P. G. (1996). Understanding the complexity of human aggression: Affective, cognitive, and social dimensions of individual differences in propensity toward aggression. *European Journal of Personality, 10,* 133–155.

Carmeli, A. (2003). The relationship between emotional intelligence and work attitudes, behavior and outcomes: An examination among senior managers. *Journal of Managerial Psychology, 18,* 788–813.

Carmeli, A., & Josman, Z. E. (2006). The relationship among Emotional Intelligence, task performance, and organizational citizenship behaviors. *Human Performance, 19,* 403–419.

Carroll, J. B. (1995). On methodology in the study of cognitive abilities. *Multivariate Behavioral Research, 30,* 429–452.

Carroll, J. B. (1993). *Human cognitive abilities: A survey of factor-analytic studies.* New York, NY: Cambridge University Press.

Carstensen, L. L., Graff, J., Levenson, R. W., & Gottman, M. J. (1996). Affect in intimate relationships: The development course of marriage. In C. Magai & S. H. McFadden (Eds.), *Handbook of emotion, adult development, and aging* (pp. 227–247). San Diego, CA: Academic Press.

Caruso, D. R., & Wolfe, C. J. (2004). Emotional intelligence and leadership development. In D. V. Day, S. J. Zaccaro, & S. M. Halpin (Eds.), *Series in applied psychology. Leader development for transforming organizations: Growing leaders for tomorrow* (pp. 237–263). Mahwah, NJ: Lawrence Erlbaum Associates.

Catanzaro, S. J., & Mearns, J. (1999). Mood-related expectancy, emotional experience, and coping behavior. In I. Kirsch (Ed.), *Expectancy, experience, and behavior* (pp. 67–91). Washington, DC: American Psychological Association.

Cattell, R. B. (1987). *Intelligence: Its structure, growth and action.* Amsterdam, Netherlands: North-Holland.

Cattell, R. B. (1963). Theory of fluid and crystallized intelligence: A critical experiment. *Journal of Educational Psychology, 54,* 1–22.

Chamorro-Premuzic, T., Bennett, E., & Furnham, A. (2007). The happy personality: Mediational role of trait emotional intelligence. *Personality and Individual Differences, 42,* 1633–1639.

Cherniss, C. (2010). Emotional intelligence: Toward clarification of a concept. *Industrial and Organizational Psychology: Perspectives on Science and Practice, 3,* 110–126.

Cherniss, C. (2000). Social and emotional competence in the workplace. In R. Bar-On & J. D. A. Parker (Eds.), *The handbook of emotional intelligence* (pp.433–458). San Francisco, CA: Jossey-Bass.

Cherniss, C., & Adler, M. (2000). *Promoting emotional intelligence in organizations.* Alexandria, VA: American Society for Training and Development.

Cherniss, C., & Goleman, D. (2001). Training for emotional intelligence: A model. In C. Cherniss & D. Goleman (Eds.), *The emotionally intelligent workplace* (pp. 209–233). San Francisco, CA: Jossey-Bass.

Cherniss, C., Goleman, D., Emmerling, R., Cowan, K., & Adler, M. (1998). *Bringing emotional intelligence in organizations.* New Brunswick, NJ: Consortium for Research on Emotional Intelligence in Organizations, Rutgers University.

Cherniss, C., Grimm, L. G., & Liautaud, J. P. (2010). Process-designed training: A new approach for helping leaders develop emotional and social competence. *Journal of Management Development, 29,* 413–431.

Ciarrochi, J. V., & Blackledge, J. T. (2006). Emotional intelligence and interpersonal behavior: A theory and review of the literature. In J. P. Forgas (Ed.), *Affect in social thinking and behavior* (pp. 291–310). New York, NY: Psychology Press.

Ciarrochi, J. V., Chan, A. Y. C., & Caputi, P. (2000). A critical evaluation of the emotional intelligence construct. *Personality and Individual Differences, 28,* 539–561.

Ciarrochi, J. V., & Deane, F. P. (2001). Emotional competence and willingness to seek help from professional and nonprofessional sources. *British Journal of Guidance and Counselling, 29,* 233–246.

Ciarrochi, J. V., Deane, F. P., & Anderson, S. (2002). Emotional intelligence moderates the relationship between stress and mental health. *Personality and Individual Differences, 32,* 197–209.

Claridge, G. (2009). Personality and psychosis. In P. L. Corr & G. Matthews (Eds.), *Cambridge handbook of personality* (pp. 631–648). Cambridge, UK: Cambridge University Press.

Clark, D. A., & Beck, A. T. (2010). *Cognitive therapy of anxiety disorders: Science and practice*. New York, NY: Guilford Press.

Cohen, J. (Ed.). (1999a). *Educating minds and hearts: Social emotional learning and the passage into adolescence*. New York, NY: Teachers College Press.

Cohen, J. (1999b). Learning about social and emotional learning: Current themes and future directions. In J. Cohen (Ed.), *Educating minds and hearts: Social emotional learning and the passage into adolescence* (pp. 184–191). New York, NY: Teachers College Press.

Cohen, J. (1999c). Social and emotional learning: Past and present. In J. Cohen (Ed.), *Educating minds and hearts: Social emotional learning and the passage into adolescence* (pp. 3–23). New York, NY: Teachers College Press.

Coie, J. D., & Dodge, K. A. (1998). Aggression and antisocial behavior. In N. Eisenberg & W. Damon (Eds.), *Handbook of child psychology, Vol. 3: Social, emotional, and personality development* (5th ed., pp. 779–862). New York, NY: Wiley.

Conduct Problems Prevention Research Group (CPPRG) (1999a). Initial impact of the Fast Track prevention trial for conduct problems: II. Classroom effects. *Journal of Consulting and Clinical Psychology, 67*, 648–657.

Conduct Problems Prevention Research Group (CPPRG) (1999b). Initial impact of the Fast Track prevention trial for conduct problems: I. The high risk sample. *Journal of Consulting and Clinical Psychology, 67*, 631–647.

Connor-Smith, J. K., & Flachsbart, C. (2007). Relations between personality and coping: a meta-analysis. *Journal of Personality and Social Psychology, 93*, 1080–1107.

Cooke, D. J., & Michie, C. (2001). Refining the construct of psychopath: Towards a hierarchical model. *Psychological Assessment, 13*, 171–188.

Cooper, J. B., & Ng, K.-M. (2009). Trait emotional intelligence and perceived supervisory working alliance of counseling trainees and their supervisors in agency settings. *International Journal for the Advancement of Counselling, 31*, 145–157.

Cooper, R. K., & Sawaf, A. (1997). *Executive EQ: Emotional intelligence in leaders and organizations*. New York, NY: Grosset/Putnam.

Corr, P. J. (2009). The Reinforcement Sensitivity Theory of personality. In P. L. Corr & G. Matthews (Eds.), *Cambridge handbook of personality* (pp. 347–376). Cambridge, UK: Cambridge University Press.

Costa, P. T., Jr., & McCrae, R. R. (1992). *NEO PI-R Professional Manual*. Odessa, FL: Psychological Assessment Resources.

Côté, S., & Miners, H. (2006). Emotional intelligence, cognitive intelligence, and job performance. *Administrative Science Quarterly, 51*, 1–28.

Coté, S., & Moskowitz, D. S. (1998). On the dynamic covariation between interpersonal behavior and affect: prediction from neuroticism, extraversion, and agreeableness. *Journal of Personality and Social Psychology, 75*, 1032–1046.

Cronbach, L. J., & Meehl, P. E. (1955). Construct validity in psychological tests. *Psychological Bulletin, 52*, 281–302.

Darwin, C. (1872). *The expression of the emotions in man and animals.* Chicago,IL: University of Chicago Press.

Dawda, D., & Hart, S. D. (2000). Assessing emotional intelligence: Reliability and validity of the Bar-On Emotional Quotient Inventory (EQ-i) in university students. *Personality and Individual Differences, 28*, 797–812.

Day, A. L. (2004). The measurement of emotional intelligence: The good, the bad, and the ugly. In G. Geher (Ed.), *Measuring emotional intelligence: Common ground and controversy* (pp. 245–270). New York, NY: Nova Science Publishers.

Day, A. L., & Carroll, S. A. (2008). Faking emotional intelligence (EI): Comparing response distortion on ability and trait-based EI measures. *Journal of Organizational Behavior, 29*, 761–784.

Day, A. L., Therrien, D. L., & Carroll, S. A. (2005). Predicting psychological health: Assessing the incremental validity of emotional intelligence beyond personality, type a behaviour, and daily hassles. *European Journal of Personality, 19*, 519–536.

De Raad, B. (2009). Structural models of personality. In P. L. Corr & G. Matthews (Eds.), *Cambridge handbook of personality* (pp. 127–147). Cambridge, UK: Cambridge University Press.

De Raad, B. (2005). The trait-coverage of emotional intelligence. *Personality and Individual Differences, 38*, 673–687.

Deary, I. J. (2000). *Looking down on human intelligence: From psychometrics to the brain.* Oxford, UK: Oxford University Press.

Denham, S. A. (2006). Emotional Competence: Implications for Social Functioning. In J. L. Luby (Ed.), *Handbook of preschool mental health: Development, disorders, and treatment* (pp. 23–44). New York: Guilford Press.

Department for Children, Schools and Families (2007). *Social and emotional aspects of learning for secondary schools.* Nottingham: DCSF Publications.

Downey, L. A., Johnston, P. J., Hansen, K., Schembri, R., Stough, C., Tuckwell, V., & Schweitzer, I. (2008). The relationship between emotional intelligence and depression in a clinical sample. *European Journal of Psychiatry, 22,* 93–98.

Dulewicz, V., & Higgs, M. (2004). Can emotional intelligence be developed? *The International Journal of Human Resource Management, 15,* 95–111.

Dunning, D., Heath, C., & Suls, J. M. (2004). Flawed self-assessment: Implications for health, education, and the workplace. *Psychological Science in the Public Interest, 5,* 69–106.

Durlak, J. A., Weissberg, R. P., Dymnicki, A. B., Taylor, R. D., & Schellinger, K. B. (2011). The impact of enhancing students' social and emotional learning: A meta-analysis of school-based universal interventions. *Child Development, 82,* 405–432.

Durlak, J. A., Weissberg, R. P., Quintana, E., & Perez, F. (2004). Primary prevention: Involving schools and communities in youth health promotion. In L. A. Jason, C. B. Keys, Y. Suarez-Balcazar, R. R. Taylor, & M. I. Davis (Eds.), *APA decade of behavior Vols. Participatory community research: Theories and methods in action* (pp. 73–86). Washington, DC: American Psychological Association.

Durrell, L. (1960). *Clea.* London: Faber.

Eack, S. M., Greeno, C. G., Pogue-Geile, M. F., Newhill, C. E., Hogarty, G. E., & Keshavan, M. S. (2010). Assessing social-cognitive deficits in schizophrenia with the Mayer-Salovey-Emotional Intelligence Test. *Schizophrenia Bulletin, 36,* 370–380.

Egan, V. (2009). The 'Big Five': Neuroticism, Extraversion, Openness, Agreeableness and Conscientiousness as an organisational scheme for thinking about aggression and violence, In M. McMurran & R. Howard, Eds., *Personality, personality disorder, and risk of violence: An evidence-based approach* (pp. 63–84). Chichester, UK: John Wiley & Sons.

Eilander, A., Gera, T., Sachdev, H. S., Transler, C., van der Knaap, H. C. M., Kok, F. J., & Osendarp, S. J. M. (2010). Multiple micronutrient supplementation for improving cognitive performance in children:

Systematic review of randomized controlled trials. *American Journal of Clinical Nutrition, 91,* 115–130.

Ekman, P. (2003). *METT. Micro Expression Training Tool.* CD-ROM. Paul Ekman.

Ekman, P. (2004). MicroExpression Training Tools (METT) and Subtle Expression Training Tools (SETT). Retrieved from http://www.paulekman.com

Ekman, P., & Friesen, W. V. (1978). *Facial Action Coding System.* Palo Alto, CA: Consulting Psychologists Press.

Ekman, P., & Rosenberg, E., L. (1997). *What the face reveals: Basic and applied studies of spontaneous expression using the Facial Action Coding System (FACS).* New York, NY: Oxford University Press.

Elias, M. J., & Clabby, J. (1992). *Building social problem solving skills: Guidelines from a school-based program.* San Francisco, CA: Jossey-Bass.

Elias, M. J., Hunter, L., & Kress, J. S. (2001). Emotional intelligence and education. In J. V. Ciarrochi, J. P. Forgas, & J. D. Mayer (Eds.), *Emotional intelligence in everyday life* (pp.133–149). Philadelphia, PA: Psychology Press.

Elias, M. J., Kress, J. S., & Hunter, L. (2006). Emotional intelligence and the crisis in the schools. In J. V. Ciarrochi, J. P. Forgas, & J. D. Mayer (Eds.), *Emotional intelligence in everyday life: A scientific inquiry* (2nd ed., pp. 166–186). Philadelphia, PA: Psychology Press.

Elias, M. J., Zins, J. E., Weissberg, R. P., Frey, K. S., Greenberg, M. T., Haynes, N. M., Kessler, R., Schwab-Stone, M. E., & Shriver, T. P. (1997). *Promoting social and emotional learning: Guidelines for educators.* Alexandria, VA: Association for Supervision and Curriculum Development.

Emmerling, R. J., & Cherniss, G. (2003). Emotional intelligence and the career choice process. *Journal of Career Assessment, 11,* 153–167.

Extremera, N., Durán, A., & Rey, L. (2007). Perceived emotional intelligence and dispositional optimism-pessimism: Analyzing their role in predicting psychological adjustment among adolescents. *Personality and Individual Differences, 42,* 1069–1079.

Extremera, N., & Fernández-Berrocal, P. (2005). Perceived emotional intelligence and life satisfaction: Predictive and incremental validity using the Trait Meta-Mood Scale. *Personality and Individual Differences, 39,* 937–948.

Farrelly, D., & Austin, E. J. (2007). Ability EI as an intelligence? Associations of the MSCEIT with performance on emotion processing and social tasks and with cognitive ability. *Cognition and Emotion, 21*, 1043–1063.

Fellner, A., Matthews, G., Funke, G. J., Emo, A. K., Zeidner, M., Pérez-González, J. C., & Roberts, R. D. (2007). The effects of emotional intelligence on visual search of emotional stimuli and emotion identification. *Proceedings of the Human Factors and Ergonomics Society, 51*, 845–849.

Ferguson, E. (in press). Personality is of central concern to understand health: Towards a theoretical model, new hypotheses and directions for health psychology. *Health Psychology Review.*

Ferguson, F. J., & Austin, E. J. (2010). Associations of trait and ability emotional intelligence with performance on Theory of Mind tasks in an adult sample. *Personality and Individual Differences, 49*, 414–418.

First, M. B., Frances, A., & Pincus, H. A. (2004). *DSM-IV-TR Guidebook Edition 1*. Washington, DC: American Psychiatric Publishing.

Fisk, A. D., & Schneider, W. W. (1983). Category and word search: Generalizing search principles to complex processing. *Journal of Experimental Psychology: Learning, Memory, and Cognition, 9*, 177–195.

Fitness, J. (2006). The emotionally intelligent marriage. In J. V. Ciarrochi, J. R. Forgas, & J. D. Mayer (Eds.), *Emotional intelligence in everyday life* (2nd ed., pp. 129–139). Hove, England: Psychology Press.

Fitness, J. (2001). Emotional intelligence and intimate relationships. In J. V. Ciarrochi, J. P. Forgas, & J. D. Mayer (Eds.), *Emotional intelligence in everyday life: A scientific inquiry* (pp. 98–112). New York, NY: Psychology Press.

Fitzgerald, M., & Bellgrove, M. A. (2006). The overlap between alexithymia and Aspergers' syndrome. *Journal of Autism and Developmental Disorders, 36*, 573–576.

Flanagan, D. P., McGrew, K. S., & Ortiz, S. O. (2000). *The Wechsler Intelligence Scales and Gf-Gc theory: A contemporary approach to interpretation*. Needham Heights, MA: Allyn & Bacon.

Foa, E. B., Keane, T. M., Friedman, M. J., & Cohen, J. (Eds.). (2008). *Effective treatments for PTSD: Practice guidelines from the International Society for Traumatic Stress Studies* (2nd ed.). New York, NY: Guilford Press.

Folkman, S. (1991). Coping across the life span: Theoretical issues. In E. M. Cummings, A. L. Greene, & K. H. Karraker (Eds.), *Life-span developmental psychology: Perspectives on stress and coping* (pp. 3–19). Hillsdale, NJ, England: Lawrence Erlbaum Associates.

Foo, M. D., Elfenbein, H. A., Tan, H. H., & Aik, V. C. (2004). Emotional intelligence and negotiation: The tension between creating and claiming value. *International Journal of Conflict Management, 15,* 411–429.

Freudenthaler, H. H., Fink, A., & Neubauer, A. C. (2006). Emotional abilities and cortical activation during emotional information processing. *Personality and Individual Differences, 41,* 685–695.

Freudenthaler, H. H., & Neubauer, A. C. (2007). Measuring emotional management abilities: Further evidence of the importance to distinguish between typical and maximum performance. *Personality and Individual Differences, 42,* 1561–1572.

Freudenthaler, H. H., Neubauer, A. C., Gabler, P., Scherl, W. G., & Rindermann, H. (2008). Testing and validating the Trait Emotional Intelligence Questionnaire (TEIQue) in a German-speaking sample. *Personality and Individual Differences, 45,* 673–678.

Frick, P. J., & Morris, A. S. (2004). Temperament and developmental pathways to conduct problems. *Journal of Clinical Child and Adolescent Psychology, 33,* 54–68.

Friedman, H. S., Kern, M. L., & Reynolds, C. A. (2010). Personality and health, subjective well-being, and longevity. *Journal of Personality, 78,* 179–216.

Furnham, A. (2006). Explaining the popularity of emotional intelligence. In K. R. Murphy (Ed.), *A critique of emotional intelligence: What are the problems and how can they be fixed?* (pp. 141–159). Mahwah, NJ: Lawrence Erlbaum Associates.

Furr, R. M., & Funder, D. C. (1998). A multimodal analysis of personal negativity. *Journal of Personality and Social Psychology, 74,* 1580–1591.

Gardner, H. (1983). *Frames of mind: The theory of multiple intelligences.* New York, NY: Basic Books.

Geher, G., Warner, R. M., & Brown, A. S. (2001). Predictive validity of emotional accuracy research scale. *Intelligence, 29,* 373–388.

Gohm, C. L., Corser, G. C., & Dalsky, D. J. (2005). Emotional intelligence under stress: Useful, unnecessary, or irrelevant? *Personality and Individual Differences, 39,* 1017–1028.

Goldenberg, I., Matheson, K., & Mantler, J. (2006). The assessment of emotional intelligence: A comparison of performance-based and self-report methodologies. *Journal of Personality Assessment, 86,* 33–45.

Goleman, D. (1995). *Emotional intelligence: Why it can matter more than IQ.* New York, NY: Bantam Books, Inc.

Goleman, D. (1998). *Working with emotional intelligence.* New York, NY: Bantam Books.

Goleman, D. (2001). Emotional intelligence: Issues in paradigm building. In C. Cherniss & D. Goleman (Eds.), *The emotionally intelligent workplace* (pp. 13–26). San Francisco, CA: Jossey-Bass.

Goleman, D., Boyatzis, R., & McKee, A. (2002). *Primal leadership: Realizing the power of emotional intelligence.* Boston, MA: Harvard Business School Press.

Grandey, A. A. (2003). When "the show must go on": Surface acting and deep acting as determinants of emotional exhaustion and peer-rated service delivery. *Academy of Management Journal, 46,* 86–96.

Grandin, T. (1996). *Thinking in pictures: And other reports from my life with autism.* Vintage.

Grant, M. A. (2007). Enhancing coaching skills and emotional intelligence through training. *Industrial and Commerical Training, 39,* 257–267.

Greenberg, L. S. (2006). Emotion-focused therapy: A synopsis. *Journal of Contemporary Psychotherapy, 36,* 87–93.

Greenberg, L. S. (2011). *Emotion-focused therapy.* Washington, DC: American Psychological Association.

Greenberg, M. T., & Kusché, C. A. (2006). Building social and emotional competence: The PATHS curriculum. In S. R. Jimerson & M. J. Furlong (Eds.), *Handbook of school violence and school safety: From research to practice* (pp. 395–412). Mahwah, NJ: Erlbaum.

Greenberg, M. T., Kusché, C. A., & Riggs, N. (2004). The PATHS curriculum: Theory and research on neurocognitive development and school success. In J. E. Zins, M. R. Bloodworth, R. P. Weissberg, & H. J. Walberg, H. J. (Eds.), *Building academic success on social and emotional learning: What does the research say?* (pp. 170–188). New York, NY: Teachers College Press.

Greenwald, A. G., McGhee, D. E., & Schwartz, J. L. K. (1998). Measuring individual differences in implicit cognition: The Implicit

Association Test. *Journal of Personality and Social Psychology, 74,* 1464–1480.

Gross, J. J. (2002). Emotion regulation: Affective, cognitive, and social consequences. *Psychophysiology, 39,* 281–291.

Groves, K. S., McEnrue, M. P., & Shen, W. (2008). Developing and measuring the emotional intelligence of leaders. *Journal of Management Development, 27,* 225–250.

Grubb, W. L., & McDaniel, M. A. (2007). The fakability of Bar-On's Emotional Quotient Inventory Short Form: Catch me if you can. *Human Performance, 20,* 43–59.

Grynberg, D., Luminet, O., Corneille, O., Grèzes, J., & Berthoz, S. (2010). Alexithymia in the interpersonal domain: A general deficit of empathy? *Personality and Individual Differences, 49,* 845–850.

Guilford, J. P. (1967). *The nature of human intelligence.* New York: McGraw-Hill.

Guilford, J. P. (1988). Some changes in the structure-of-intellect model. *Educational and Psychological Measurement, 48,* 1–4.

Hall, J. A., Andrzejewski, S. A., & Yopchick, J. E. (2009). Psychosocial correlates of interpersonal sensitivity: A meta-analysis. *Journal of Nonverbal Behavior, 33,* 149–180.

Halpern, D. F. (2006). Introduction: How organizations can alleviate the traffic jam at the intersection of work and family. *American Behavioral Scientist, 49,* 1147–1151.

Hansenne, M., & Bianchi, J. (2009). Emotional intelligence and personality in major depression: Trait versus state effects. *Psychiatry Research, 166,* 63–68.

Hare, R. D., & Neumann, C. S. (2009). Psychopathy and its measurement. In P. L. Corr & G. Matthews (Eds.), *Cambridge handbook of personality* (pp. 660–686). Cambridge, UK: Cambridge University Press.

Harms, P. D., & Credé, M. (2010). Emotional intelligence and transformational and transactional leadership: A meta-analysis. *Journal of Leadership & Organizational Studies, 17,* 5–17.

Hawkins, J. D., Smith, B. H., & Catalano, R. F. (2004). Social development and social and emotional learning. In J. E. Zins, R. P. Weissberg, M. C. Wang, & H. J. Walberg (Eds.), *Building academic success on social and emotional learning. What does the research say?* (pp. 135–150). New York, NY: Teachers College Press.

Hemmati, T., Mills, J. F., & Kroner, D. G. (2004). The validity of the Bar-On emotional intelligence quotient in an offender population. *Personality and Individual Differences, 37*, 695–706.

Hertel, J., Schütz, A., & Lammers, C.-H. (2009). Emotional intelligence and mental disorder. *Journal of Clinical Psychology, 65*, 942–954.

Hogan, M. J., Parker, J. D. A., Wiener, J., Watters, C., Wood, L. M., & Oke, A. (2010). Academic success in adolescence: Relationships among verbal IQ, social support and emotional intelligence. *Australian Journal of Psychology, 62*, 30–41.

Hogarty, G. E., Flesher, S., Ulrich, R., Carter, M., Greenwald, D., Pogue-Geile, M., Kechavan, M., Cooley, S., DiBarry, A. L., Garrett, A., Parepally, H., & Zoretich, R. (2004). Cognitive enhancement therapy for schizophrenia. Effects of a 2-year randomized trial on cognition and behavior. *Archives of General Psychiatry, 61*, 866–876.

Holmen, A., Juuhl-Langseth, M., Thormodsen, R., Melle, I., & Rund, B. R. (2010). Neuropsychological profile in early-onset schizophrenia-spectrum disorders: Measured with the MATRICS battery. *Schizophrenia Bulletin, 36*, 852–859.

Horn, J., & Noll, J. (1994). A system for understanding cognitive capabilities: A theory and the evidence on which it is based. In D. K. Detterman (Ed.), *Current topics in human intelligence: Volume IV.* (pp. 151–203). New York: Springer-Verlag.

Horn, J. L. (2008). Spearman, *g*, expertise, and the nature of human cognitive capability. In P. C. Kyllonen, R. D. Roberts, & L. Stankov (Eds.), *Extending intelligence: Enhancement and new constructs* (pp. 159–194). New York, NY: Taylor & Francis.

Horn, J. L., & Hofer, S. M. (1992). Major abilities and development in the adult period. In R. J. Sternberg & C. Berg (Eds.), *Intellectual development* (pp. 44–99). New York, NY: Cambridge University Press.

Horn, J. L., & Masunaga, H. (2000). New directions for research into aging and intelligence: The development of expertise. In T. J. Perfect & E. A. Maylor (Eds.), *Models of cognitive aging* (pp. 125–159). Oxford, UK: Oxford University Press.

Hughes, J. (2005). Bringing emotion to work: Emotional intelligence, employee resistance and the reinvention of character. *Work, Employment and Society, 19*, 603–625.

Humphrey, N., Curran, A., Morris, E., Farrell, P., & Woods, K. (2007). Emotional intelligence and education: A critical review. *Educational Psychology, 27*, 235–254.

Humphrey, N., Lendrum, A., & Wigelsworth, M. (2010). Social and emotional aspects of learning (SEAL) programme in secondary schools: National evaluation. Retrieved September 21, 2011, from http://www.education.gov.uk/research

Jaušovec, N., & Jaušovec, K. (2010). Emotional intelligence and gender: A neurophysiological perspective. In A. Gruszka, G. Matthews, & B. Szymura (Eds.), *Handbook of individual differences in cognition: Attention, memory and executive control* (pp. 109–126). New York, NY: Springer.

Jensen-Campbell, L. A., Knack, J. M., & Rex-Lear, M. (2009). Personality and social relations. In P. L. Corr & G. Matthews (Eds.), *Cambridge handbook of personality* (pp. 506–523). Cambridge, UK: Cambridge University Press.

John, O. P., & Gross, J. J. (2007). Individual differences in emotion regulation. In J. J. Gross (Ed.), *Handbook of emotion regulation* (pp. 351–372). New York, NY: Guilford Press.

Johnson, S. J., Batey, M., & Holdsworth, L. (2009). Personality and health: The mediating role of trait emotional intelligence and work locus of control. *Personality and Individual Differences, 47,* 470–475.

Jones, A. P., Happ, F. G. E., Gilbert, F., Burnett, S., & Viding, E. (2010). Feeling, caring, knowing: Different types of empathy deficit in boys with psychopathic tendencies and autism spectrum disorder. *Journal of Child Psychology and Psychiatry, 51,* 1188–1197.

Jordan, P. J., Ashkanasy, N. M., & Ascough, K. (2007). Emotional intelligence in organizational behavior and industrial-organizational psychology. In G. Matthews, M. Zeidner, & R. D. Roberts (Eds.), *Emotional intelligence: Knowns and unknowns* (pp. 356–375). New York, NY: Oxford University Press.

Jordan, P. J., & Troth, A. C. (2002). Emotional intelligence and conflict resolution: Implications for human resource development. *Advances in Developing Human Resources, 4,* 62–79.

Jordan, P. J., Murray, J. P., & Lawrence, S. A. (2009). The application of emotional intelligence in industrial and organizational psychology. In C. Stough, D. H. Saklofske, & J. D. A. Parker (Eds.), *Assessing emotional intelligence: Theory, research, and applications* (pp. 171–190). New York, NY: Springer Science and Business Media.

Joseph, D. L., & Newman, D. A. (2010). Emotional intelligence: An integrative meta-analysis and cascading model. *Journal of Applied Psychology, 95,* 54–78.

Kafetsios, K., & Zampetakis, L. A. (2008). Emotional intelligence and job satisfaction: Testing the mediatory role of positive and negative affect at work. *Personality and Individual Differences, 44,* 712–722.

Kahneman, D., Krueger, A. B., Schkade, D. A., Schwarz, N., & Stone, A. A. (2004). A survey method for characterizing daily life experience: The Day Reconstruction Method. *Science, 306,* 1776–1780.

Kam, C., Greenberg, M. T., & Kusché, C. A. (2004). Sustained effects of the PATHS curriculum on the social and psychological adjustment of children in special education. *Journal of Emotional and Behavioral Disorders, 12,* 66–78.

Kaufman, A. S. (2009). *IQ testing 101.* New York, NY: Springer Publishing Company.

Kazdin, A. E. (1995). *Conduct disorders in childhood and adolescence* (2nd ed.). Thousand Oaks, CA: Sage.

Kee, K. S., Horan, W. P., Salovey, P., Kern, R. S., Sergi, M. J., Fiske, A. P., Lee, J., Subotnik, K. L., Nuechterlein, K., Sugar, C. A., & Green, M. F. (2009). Emotional intelligence in schizophrenia. *Schizophrenia Research, 107,* 61–68.

Keefe, R. S. E., Fox, K. H., Harvey, P. D., Cucchiaro, J., Siu, C.,& Loebel, A. (2011). Characteristics of the MATRICS Consensus Cognitive Battery in a 29-site antipsychotic schizophrenia clinical trial. *Schizophrenia Research, 125,* 161–168.

Keefer, K. V., Parker, J. D. A., & Saklofske, D. H. (2009). Emotional intelligence and physical health. In C. Stough, D. H. Saklofske, & J. D. A. Parker (Eds.), *Assessing emotional intelligence: Theory, research, and applications* (pp. 191–218). New York, NY: Springer Science and Business Media.

Kelly, B., Longbottom, J., Potts, F., & Williamson, J. (2004). Applying emotional intelligence: Exploring the Promoting Alternative Thinking Strategies curriculum. *Educational Psychology in Practice, 20,* 221–240.

Keltner, D., & Haidt, J. (2001). Social functions of emotions. In T. J. Mayne & G. A. Bonanno (Eds.), *Emotions: Current issues and future directions* (pp.192–213). New York, NY: Guilford Press.

Kennedy-Moore, E., & Watson, J. C. (1999). *Expressing emotion: Myths, realities, and therapeutic strategies.* New York, NY: Guilford Press.

Kerlinger, F. N. (1973). *Foundations of behavioral research* (2nd ed.). New York, NY: Holt, Rinehart, and Winston.

Killgore, W. D. S., & Yurgelun-Todd, D. A. (2007). Neural correlates of emotional intelligence in adolescent children. *Cognitive, Affective, and Behavioral Neuroscience, 7*, 140–151.

Kluemper, D. H. (2008). Trait emotional intelligence: The impact of core-self evaluations and social desirability. *Personality and Individual Differences, 44*, 1402–1412.

Koenen, K. C., Moffitt, T. E., Poulton, R., Martin, J., & Caspi, A. (2007). Early childhood factors associated with the development of post-traumatic stress disorder: Results from a longitudinal birth cohort. *Psychological Medicine, 37*, 181–192.

Koriat, A., Melkman, R., Averill, J. R., & Lazarus, R. S. (1972). The self-control of emotional reactions to a stressful film. *Journal of Personality, 40*, 601–619.

Kyllonen, P. C., & Christal, R. E. (1990). Reasoning ability is (little more than) working memory capacity?! *Intelligence, 14*, 389–433.

Kyllonen, P. C., Roberts, R. D., & Stankov, L. (Eds.) (2008). *Extending intelligence: Enhancement and new constructs.* New York, NY: Routledge.

Landy, F. J. (2006). The long, frustrating, and fruitless search for social intelligence: A cautionary tale. In K. R. Murphy (Ed.), *A critique of emotional intelligence: What are the problems and how can they be fixed?* (pp. 81–123). Mahwah, NJ: Erlbaum.

Landy, F. J. (2005). Some historical and scientific issues related to research on emotional intelligence. *Journal of Organizational Behavior, 26*, 411–424.

Lane, R. D. (2000). Levels of emotional awareness: Neurological, psychological, and social perspectives. In R. Bar-On & J. D. A. Parker, (Eds.), *The handbook of emotional intelligence: Theory, development, assessment, and application at home, school, and in the workplace.* (pp. 171–191). San Francisco, CA: Jossey-Bass.

Lane, R. D., Quinlan, D. M., Schwartz, G. E., Walker, P. A., & Zeitlin, S. B. (1990). The Levels of Emotional Awareness Scale: A cognitive-development measure of emotion. *Journal of Personality Assessment, 55*, 124–134.

Lane, R.D., Reiman, E.M., Axelrod, B., Yun, L-S., Holmes, A., & Schwartz, G.E. (1998.) Neural correlates of levels of emotional awareness: Evidence of an interaction between emotion and attention in the anterior cingulate cortex. *Journal of Cognitive Neuroscience, 10*, 525–535.

Lantieri, L., & Patti, J. (1996). *Waging peace in our schools.* Boston: Beacon Press.

Law, K. S., Wong, C. S., & Song, L. J. (2004). The construct and criterion validity of emotional intelligence and its potential utility for management studies. *Journal of Applied Psychology, 89*, 483–496.

Lazarus, R. S. (1999). *Stress and emotion: A new synthesis.* New York, NY: Springer Publishing.

Lazarus, R. S. (1991). *Emotion and adaptation.* New York, NY: Oxford University Press.

Lazarus, R. S. (1990). Theory-based stress measurement. *Psychological Inquiry, 1*, 3–13.

Lazarus, R. S., & Folkman, S. (1984). *Stress, appraisal, and coping.* New York, NY: Springer.

LeDoux, J. E. (1996). *The emotional brain: The mysterious underpinnings of emotional life.* New York, NY: Simon & Schuster.

Lee, S. H. (2008). Working memory and intelligence in children: What develops? *Journal of Educational Psychology, 100*, 581–602.

Legree, P. J., Psotka, J., Tremble, T., & Bourne, D. R. (2005). Using consensus based measurement to assess emotional intelligence. In R. Schulze & R. D. Roberts (Eds.), *Emotional intelligence: An international handbook* (pp. 155–179). Cambridge, MA: Hogrefe & Huber.

Lenaghan, J. A., Buda, R., & Eisner, A. B. (2007). An examination of the role of emotional intelligence in work and family conflict. *Journal of Managerial Issues, 19*, 76–94.

Lewis, M. (2001). Issues in the study of personality development. *Psychological Inquiry, 12*, 67–83.

Libbrecht, N., & Lievens, F. (2011). *Further validity evidence for the situational judgment test paradigm to emotional intelligence measurement.* Unpublished manuscript submitted for publication.

Lilienfeld, S. O., Lynn, S. J., Ruscio, J., & Beyerstein, B. L. (2009). *Fifty great myths of popular psychology: Shattering widespread misconceptions about human behavior.* Chichester, England: Wiley-Blackwell.

Lindqvist, E., & Vestman, R. (2011). The labor market returns to cognitive and noncognitive ability: Evidence from the Swedish Enlistment Study. *American Economic Journal: Applied Economics, 3*, 101–128.

Lischetzke, T., & Eid, M. (2006). Why extraverts are happier than introverts: The role of mood regulation. *Journal of Personality, 74*, 1127–1162.

Livesley, W. J., & Larstone, R. M. (2008). The Dimensional Assessment of Personality Pathology (DAPP). In G. J. Boyle, G. Matthews, & D.H. Saklofske, (Eds.), *The SAGE handbook of personality theory and assessment, Vol 2: Personality measurement and testing* (pp. 608–625). Thousand Oaks, CA: Sage Publications.

Lopes, P. N., Brackett, M. A., Nezlek, J. B., Schutz, A., Sellin, I., & Salovey, P. (2004). Emotional intelligence and social interaction. *Personality and Social Psychology Bulletin, 30*, 1018–1034.

Lopes, P. N., Salovey, P., & Straus, R. (2003). Emotional intelligence, personality, and the perceived quality of social relationships. *Personality and Individual Differences, 35*, 641–658.

Lopes, P. N., Salovey, P., Côté, S., &. Beers, M. (2005). Emotion regulation abilities and the quality of social interaction. *Emotion, 5*, 113–118.

Losh, M., & Capps, L. (2006). Understanding of emotional experience in autism: Insights from the personal accounts of high-functioning children with autism. *Developmental Psychology, 42*, 809–818.

Lucas, R. E., & Diener, E. (2000). Personality and subjective well-being across the life span. In V. J. Molfese & D. L. Molfese (Eds.) *Temperament and personality development across the life span* (pp. 211–234). Mahwah, NJ: Lawrence Erlbaum.

Lucas, R. E., Le, K., & Dyrenforth, P. S. (2008). Explaining the extraversion/positive affect relation: Sociability cannot account for extraverts' greater happiness. *Journal of Personality, 76*, 385–414.

Luminet, O., Bagby, R. M., Wagner, H., Taylor, G. J., & Parker, J. D. A. (1999). Relation between alexithymia and the five-factor model of personality: A facet-level analysis. *Journal of Personality Assessment, 73*, 345–358.

Lumley, M. A., Gustavson, B. J., Partridge, T., & Labouvie-Vief, G. (2005). Assessing alexithymia and related emotional ability constructs via multiple methods: Interrelationships among measures. *Emotion, 5*, 329–342.

Lumley, M. A., Neely, L. C., & Burger, A. J. (2007). The assessment of alexithymia in medical settings: Implications for understanding and treating health problems. *Journal of Personality Assessment, 89*, 230–246.

Lynn, A. B. (2007). *Quick emotional intelligence activities for busy managers: 50 exercises that get results in just 15 minutes.* New York: AMACOM.

MacCann, C., Fogarty, G. J., Zeidner, M., & Roberts, R. D. (2011). Coping mediates the relationship between emotional intelligence (EI) and academic achievement. *Contemporary Educational Psychology, 36,* 60–70.

MacCann, C., Joseph, D., Newman, D., & Roberts, R. D. (in press). Emotional intelligence within the structure of human cognitive abilities: Psychometric evidence from hierarchical and bifactor models. *Intelligence.*

MacCann, C., & Roberts, R. D. (2008). New paradigms for assessing emotional intelligence: Theory and data. *Emotion, 8,* 540–551.

MacCann, C., Roberts, R. D., Matthews, G., & Zeidner, M. (2004). Consensus scoring and empirical option weighting of performance-based Emotional Intelligence (EI) tests. *Personality and Individual Differences, 36,* 645–662.

MacCann, C., Wang, P., Matthews, G., & Roberts, R. D. (2010). Examining self-report versus other reports in a situational judgment test of emotional abilities. *Journal for Research in Personality, 44,* 673–676.

Malecki, C. K., & Elliot, S. N. (2002). Children's social behaviors as predictors of academic achievement: A longitudinal analysis. *School Psychology Quarterly, 17,* 1–23.

Mancuso, F., Horan, W. P., Kern, R. S., & Green, M. F. (2011). Social cognition in psychosis: Multidimensional structure, clinical correlates, and relationship with functional outcome. *Schizophrenia Research, 125,* 143–151.

Márquez, P. G.-O., Martín, R. P., & Brackett, M. A. (2006). Relating emotional intelligence to social competence and academic achievement in high school students. *Psicothema, 18(Suppl),* 118–123.

Martins, A., Ramalho, N., & Morin, E. (2010). A comprehensive meta-analysis of the relationship between emotional intelligence and health. *Personality and Individual Differences, 49,* 554–564.

Matsumoto, D., LeRoux, J., Wilson-Cohn, C., Raroque, J., Kooken, K., Ekman, P., et al. (2000). A new test to measure emotion recognition ability: Matsumoto and Ekman's Japanese and Caucasian Brief Affect Recognition Test (JACBART). *Journal of Nonverbal Behavior, 24,* 179–209.

Matthews, G. (2009). Cognitive processes and models. In P. L. Corr & G. Matthews (Eds.), *Cambridge handbook of personality* (pp. 400–426). Cambridge, UK: Cambridge University Press.

Matthews, G. (2005). The design of emotionally intelligent machines. *American Journal of Psychology, 118*, 287–322.

Matthews, G., Deary, I. J., & Whiteman, M. C. (2009). *Personality traits* (3rd ed.). Cambridge, MA: Cambridge University Press.

Matthews, G., Emo, A. K., Funke, G., Zeidner, M., Roberts, R. D., Costa, P. T., Jr., & Schulze, R. (2006). Emotional intelligence, personality, and task-induced stress. *Journal of Experimental Psychology: Applied, 12*, 96–107.

Matthews, G., & Funke, G. J. (2006). Worry and information-processing. In G. C. L. Davey & A. Wells (Eds.), *Worry and its psychological disorders: Theory, assessment and treatment* (pp. 51–67). Chichester, UK: Wiley.

Matthews, G., Zeidner, M., & Roberts, R. D. (2006). Measuring emotional intelligence: Promises, pitfalls, solutions? In A. D. Ong & M. H. Van Dulmen (Eds.), *Oxford handbook of methods in positive psychology* (pp. 189–204). Oxford, UK: Oxford University Press.

Matthews, G., Zeidner, M., & Roberts, R. D. (2005). Emotional intelligence: An elusive ability? In O. Wilhelm & R. Engle (Eds.), *Handbook of understanding and measuring intelligence* (pp. 79–99). Thousand Oaks, CA: Sage.

Matthews, G., Zeidner, M., & Roberts, R. D. (2004). Seven myths of emotional intelligence. *Psychological Inquiry, 15*, 179–196.

Matthews, G., Zeidner, M., & Roberts, R. D. (2002). *Emotional intelligence: Science or myth?* Cambridge, MA: MIT Press.

Mauss, I. B., Evers, C., Wilhelm, F. H., & Gross, J. J. (2006). How to bite your tongue without blowing your top: Implicit evaluation of emotion regulation predicts affective responding to anger provocation. *Personality and Social Psychology Bulletin, 32*, 589–602.

Mavroveli, S., Petrides, K. V., Rieffe, C., & Bakker, F. (2007). Trait emotional intelligence, psychological well-being and peer-rated social competence in adolescence. *British Journal of Developmental Psychology, 25*, 263–275.

Mavroveli, S., Petrides, K. V., Sangareau, Y., & Furnham, A. (2009). Exploring the relationships between trait emotional intelligence and objective socio-emotional outcomes in childhood. *British Journal of Educational Psychology, 79*, 259–272.

Mayer, J. D., Caruso, D. R., & Salovey, P. (1999). Emotional intelligence meets traditional standards for an intelligence. *Intelligence, 27,* 267–298.

Mayer, J. D., Caruso, D. R., Salovey, P., & Siterenios, G. (2001). Emotional intelligence as a standard intelligence. *Emotions, 1,* 232–242.

Mayer, J. D., Perkins, D. M., Caruso, D. R., & Salovey, P. (2001). Emotional intelligence and giftedness. *Roeper Review: A Journal on Gifted Education, 23,* 131–137.

Mayer, J. D., Roberts, R. D., & Barsade, S. G. (2008). Human abilities: Emotional intelligence. *Annual Review of Psychology, 59,* 507–536.

Mayer, J. D., & Salovey, P. (1997). What is emotional intelligence? In P. Salovey & D. J. Sluyter (Eds.), *Emotional development and emotional intelligence: Educational implications* (pp. 3–34). New York, NY: Basic Books.

Mayer, J. D., Salovey, P., & Caruso, D. R. (in press). *Mayer-Salovey-Caruso Emotional Intelligence Test: Youth Version (MSCEIT: YV)*: Item Booklet. Toronto, Canada: Multi-Health Systems.

Mayer, J. D., Salovey, P., & Caruso, D. R. (2002). *Mayer-Salovey-Caruso Emotional Intelligence Test (MSCEIT) User's Manual.* Toronto, Canada: Multi-Health Systems.

Mayer, J. D., Salovey, P., & Caruso, D. R. (2000). Models of emotional intelligence. In R. J. Sternberg (Ed.), *Handbook of intelligence* (pp. 396–420). New York, NY: Cambridge University Press.

Mayer, J. D., Salovey, P., Caruso, D. R., & Sitarenios, G. (2003). Measuring emotional intelligence with the MSCEIT V2.0. *Emotion, 3,* 97–105.

Mayne, T. J. (1999). Negative affect and health: The importance of being earnest. *Cognition & Emotion, 13,* 601–635.

McAdams, D. P., & Pals, J. L. (2006). A new Big Five: Fundamental principles for an integrative science of personality. *American Psychologist, 61,* 204–217.

McCrae, R. R. (2000). Emotional intelligence from the perspective of the five-factor model of personality. In R. Bar-On & J. D. A. Parker (Eds.), *The handbook of emotional intelligence: Theory, development, assessment, and application at home, school, and in the workplace* (pp. 263–276). San Francisco, CA: Jossey-Bass.

McCrae, R. R., & Costa, P. T. (2008). Empirical and theoretical status of the five-factor model of personality traits. In G. J. Boyle, G. Matthews, & D. H. Saklofske (Eds.), *Sage handbook of personality theory and testing: Volume 1: Personality theories and models* (pp. 273–294). Thousand Oaks, CA: Sage.

McDaniel, M. A., Hartman, N. S., Whetzel, D. L., & Grubb, W. L. (2006). Situational judgment tests: Validity and an integrative model. In R. Ployhart & J. Weekley (Eds.), *Situational judgment tests: Theory, measurement, and application* (pp. 183–204). New York, NY: Jossey-Bass.

McDaniel, M. A., Morgeson, F. P., Finnegan, E. B., Campion, M. A., & Braverman, E. P. (2001). Use of situational judgment tests to predict job performance: A clarification of the literature. *Journal of Applied Psychology, 86*, 730–740.

McGrew, K. S. (2005). The Cattell-Horn-Carroll (CHC) theory of cognitive abilities: Past, present, and future. In D. P. Flanagan & Harrison, P. L. (Eds.), *Contemporary intellectual assessment: Theories, test, and issues (2nd edition)* (pp. 136–202). New York: Guilford Press.

Mierke, J., & Klauer, K. C. (2003). Method-specific variance in the implicit association test. *Journal of Personality and Social Psychology, 85*, 1180–1192.

Mikolajczak, M., & Luminet, O. (2008). Trait emotional intelligence and the cognitive appraisal of stressful events: An exploratory study. *Personality and Individual Differences, 44*, 1445–1453.

Mikolajczak, M., Luminet, O., Leroy, C., & Roy, E. (2007). Psychometric properties of the Trait Emotional Intelligence Questionnaire: Factor structure, reliability, construct, and incremental validity in a French-speaking population. *Journal of Personality Assessment, 88*, 338–353.

Mikolajczak, M., Luminet, O., & Menil, C. (2006). Predicting resistance to stress: Incremental validity of trait emotional intelligence over alexithymia and optimism. *Psicothema, 18(Suppl)*, 79–88.

Mikolajczak, M., Menil, C., & Luminet, O. (2007). Explaining the protective effect of trait emotional intelligence regarding occupational stress: Exploration of emotional labour processes. *Journal of Research in Personality, 41*, 1107–1117.

Mikolajczak, M., Nelis, D., Hansenne, M., & Quoidbach, J. (2008). If you can regulate sadness, you can probably regulate shame: Associations between trait emotional intelligence, emotion regulation and coping efficiency across discrete emotions. *Personality and Individual Differences, 44*, 1356–1368.

Mikolajczak, M., Roy, E., Luminet, O., Fille, C., & de Timary, P. (2007). The moderating impact of emotional intelligence on free cortisol responses to stress. *Psychoneuroendocrinology, 32*, 1000–1012.

Mikolajczak, M., Roy, E., Verstrynge, V., & Luminet, O. (2009). An exploration of the moderating effect of trait emotional intelligence on memory and attention in neutral and stressful conditions. *British Journal of Psychology, 100*, 699–715.

Mischel, W. (1996). From good intentions to willpower. In P. M. Gollwitzer & J. A. Bargh, (Eds.), *The psychology of action: Linking cognition and motivation to behavior* (pp. 197–218). New York, NY: Guilford Press.

Mischel, W., & Ebbesen, E. B. (1970). Attention in delay of gratification. *Journal of Personality and Social Psychology, 16*, 329–337.

Mischel, W., Shoda, Y., & Rodriguez, L. M. (1989). Delay of gratification in children. *Science, 244*, 933–938.

Montgomery, J. M., McCrimmon, A. W., Schwean, V. L., & Saklofske, D. H. (2010). Emotional intelligence in Asperger syndrome: Implications of dissonance between intellect and affect. *Education and Training in Autism and Developmental Disabilities, 45*, 566–582.

Morrone-Strupinsky, J. V., & Lane, R. D. (2007). Parsing positive emotion in relation to agentic and affiliative components of extraversion. *Personality and Individual Differences, 42*, 1267–1278.

Motowidlo, S. J., Borman, W. C., & Schmit, M. J. (1997). A theory of individual differences in task and contextual performance. *Human Performance, 10*, 71–83.

Mullin, B. C., & Hinshaw, S. P. (2007). Emotion regulation and externalizing disorders in children and adolescents. In J. J. Gross (Ed.). *Handbook of emotion regulation* (pp. 523–541). New York, NY: Guilford Press.

Murphy, K. R., & Sideman, L. (2006). The fadification of emotional intelligence. In K. R. Murphy (Ed.), *A critique of emotional intelligence: What are the problems and how can they be fixed?* (pp. 283–299). Mahwah, NJ: Lawrence Erlbaum Associates.

Murray, J. P., Jordan, P. J., & Ashkanasy, N. M. (2006). Training to improve emotional intelligence and performance: What interventions work? Paper presented at the *20th annual conference of the annual meeting of the Australian and New Zealand Academy of Management*, Rockhamptom, Australia.

Muyia, H. M., & Kacirek, K. (2009). An empirical study of a leadership development training program and its impact on emotional intelligence quotient (EQ) scores. *Advances in Developing Human Resources, 11*, 703–718.

Nastasi, B. K., Moore, R. B., & Varjas, K. M. (2004). *School-based mental health services: Creating comprehensive and culturally specific programs.* Washington, DC: American Psychological Association.

Newsome, S., Day, A. L., & Catano, V. M. (2000). Assessing the predictive validity of emotional intelligence. *Personality & Individual Differences, 29*, 1005–1016.

Nigg, J. T. (2006). Temperament and developmental psychopathology. *Journal of Child Psychology and Psychiatry, 47*, 395–422.

Nolen-Hoeksema, S., Wisco, B. E., & Lyubomirsky, S. (2008). Rethinking rumination. *Perspectives on Psychological Science, 3*, 400–424.

Nowicki, S., & Carton, J. (1993). The measurement of emotional intensity from facial expressions. *Journal of Social Psychology, 133*, 749–750.

Nunnally, J. C. (1978). *Psychometric theory* (2nd ed.). New York, NY: McGraw Hill.

Oatley, K. (2004). Emotional intelligence and the intelligence of emotions. *Psychological Inquiry, 15*, 216–221.

Oatley, K., & Bolton, W. (1985). A social-cognitive theory of depression in reaction to life events. *Psychological Review, 92*, 372–388.

Oatley, K., & Johnson-Laird, P. N. (1996). The communicative theory of emotion: Empirical tests, mental models, and implications for social interaction. In L. L. Martin & A. Tesser (Eds.), *Striving and feeling: Interactions among goals, affect, and self-regulation* (pp. 363–393). Hillsdale, NJ: Lawrence Erlbaum.

Ormel, J., & Wohlfarth, T. (1991). How neuroticism, long-term difficulties, and life situation change influence psychological distress: a longitudinal model. *Journal of Personality and Social Psychology, 60*, 744–755.

O'Sullivan, M. (2007). Trolling for trout, trawling for tuna: The methodological morass in measuring emotional intelligence. In G. Matthews, M. Zeidner, & R. D. Roberts (Eds.), *The science of emotional intelligence: Knowns and unknowns* (pp. 258–287). New York, NY: Oxford University Press.

O'Toole, B. I., & Stankov, L. (1992). Ultimate validity of psychological tests. *Personality and Individual Differences, 13*, 699–716.

Palmer, B. R., Donaldson, C., & Stough, C. (2002). Emotional intelligence and life satisfaction. *Personality and Individual Differences, 33,* 1091–1100.

Palmer, B. R., Walls, M., Burgess, Z., & Stough, C. (2001). Emotional intelligence and effective leadership. *Leadership and Organisational Development Journal, 22,* 5–10.

Parker, J. D. A. (2005). The relevance of emotional intelligence for clinical psychology. In R. Schulze & R. D. Roberts (Eds.), *Emotional intelligence: An international handbook* (pp. 271–287). Ashland, OH: Hogrefe & Huber.

Parker, J. D. A. (2000). Emotional intelligence: Clinical and therapeutic implications. In R. Bar-On & J. D. A. Parker (Eds.), *The handbook of emotional intelligence: Theory, development, assessment, and application at home, school, and in the workplace* (pp. 490–504). San Francisco, CA: Jossey-Bass.

Parker, J. D. A., Hogan, M. J., Eastabrook, J. M., Oke, A., & Wood, L. M. (2006). Emotional intelligence and student retention: Predicting the successful transition from high school to university. *Personality and Individual Differences, 41,* 1329–1336.

Parker, J. D. A., Keefer, K. V., Taylor, G. J., & Bagby, R. M. (2008). Latent structure of the alexithymia construct: A taxometric investigation. *Psychological Assessment, 20,* 385–396.

Parker, J. D. A., Saklofske, D. H., Wood, L. M., & Collin, T. (2009). The role of emotional intelligence in education. In C. Stough, D. H. Saklofske, & J. D. A. Parker (Eds.), *Assessing emotional intelligence: Theory, research, and applications* (pp. 239–255). New York, NY: Springer Science and Business Media.

Parker, J. D. A., Summerfeldt, L. J., Hogan, M. J., & Majeski, S. A. (2004). Emotional intelligence and academic success: examining the transition from high school to university. *Personality and Individual Differences, 36,* 163–172.

Parker, J. D. A., Taylor, G. J., & Bagby, R. M. (2003). The 20-Item Toronto Alexithymia Scale III. Reliability and factorial validity in a community population. *Journal of Psychosomatic Research, 55,* 269–275.

Parrott, W. G. (2002). The functional utility of negative emotions. In L. Feldman-Barrett & P. Salovey (Eds.), *The wisdom in feeling: Psychological processes in emotional intelligence* (pp.341–359). New York, NY: Guilford Press.

Paulhus, D. L. (2002). Socially desirable responding: the evolution of a construct. In H. I. Braun & D. N. Jackson (Eds.), *The role of constructs in psychological and educational measurement* (pp. 49–69). Mahwah, NJ: Erlbaum.

Paulhus, D. L., Lysy, D. C., & Yik, M. S. M. (1998). Self-report measures of intelligence: Are they useful proxies as IQ tests? *Journal of Personality, 66,* 525–554.

Pekrun, R., & Frese, M. (1992). Emotions in work and achievement. *International Review of Industrial and Organizational Psychology, 7,* 154–200.

Pennebaker, J. W. (1997). Writing about emotional experiences as a therapeutic process. *Psychological Science, 8,* 162–166.

Peters, C., Kranzler, J. H., & Rossen, E. (2009). Validity of the Mayer-Salovey-Caruso Emotional Intelligence Test: Youth Version-Research Edition. *Canadian Journal of School Psychology, 24,* 76–81.

Petrides, K. V., Fredrickson, N., & Furnham, A. (2004). The role of trait emotional intelligence in academic performance and deviant behavior at school. *Personality and Individual Differences, 36,* 277–293.

Petrides, K. V., & Furnham, A. (2003). Trait emotional intelligence: Behavioural validation in two studies of emotion recognition and reactivity to mood induction. *European Journal of Personality, 17,* 39–57.

Petrides, K. V., Furnham, A., & Mavroveli, S. (2007). Trait emotional intelligence: Moving forward in the field of EI. In G. Matthews, M. Zeidner, & R. D. Roberts (Eds.), *The science of emotional intelligence: Knowns and unknowns* (pp. 151–166). New York, NY: Oxford University Press.

Petrides, K. V., Pérez-González, J. C., & Furnham, A. (2007). On the criterion and incremental validity of trait emotional intelligence. *Cognition and Emotion, 21,* 26–55.

Petrides, K. V., Sangareau, Y., Furnham, A., & Frederickson, N. (2006). Trait emotional intelligence and children's peer relations at school. *Social Development, 15,* 537–547.

Petrides, K. V., Vernon, P. A., Schermer, J. A., Ligthart, L., Boomsma, D. I., & Veselka, L. (2010). Relationships between trait emotional intelligence and the Big Five in the Netherlands. *Personality and Individual Differences, 48,* 906–910.

Picard, R. W. (2007). Toward machines with emotional intelligence. In G. Matthews, M. Zeidner, & R. D. Roberts (Eds.), *The science of emotional intelligence: Knowns and unknowns* (pp. 396–416). New York, NY: Oxford University Press.

Pitterman, H., & Nowicki, S. J. (2004). A test of the ability to identify emotion in human standing and sitting postures: The Diagnostic Analysis of Nonverbal Accuracy-2 Posture Test (DANVA2-POS). *Genetic, Social, and General Psychology Monographs, 130,* 146–162.

Popper, K. R. (1963). *Conjectures and refutations.* London: Routledge and Keagan Paul.

Prati, L. M., Douglas, C., Ferris, G. R., Ammeter, A. P., & Buckley, M. R. (2003). Emotional intelligence, leadership effectiveness, and team outcomes. *International Journal of Organizational Analysis, 11,* 21–40.

Quick, J. C., Quick, J. D., Nelson, D. L., & Hurrell, J. J. (1997). *Preventive stress management in organizations.* Washington, DC: American Psychological Association.

Riggs, N. R., Greeberg, M. T., Kusché, C. A., & Pentz, M. A. (2006). The meditational role of neurocogniton in the behavior outcomes of a social-emotional program in elementary school students: Effects of the PATHS curriculum. *Prevention Science, 7,* 91–102.

Riley, H., & Schutte, N. S. (2003). Low emotional intelligence as a predictor of substance-use problems. *Journal of Drug Education, 33,* 391–398.

Rivers, S. E., Brackett, M. A., Reyes, M. R., Mayer, J. D., Caruso, D. R., & Salovey, P. (in press). Measuring emotional intelligence in early adolescence with the MSCEIT-YV: Psychometric properties and relationship with academic performance and psychosocial functioning. *Journal of Psychoeducational Assessment.*

Rivers, S. E., Brackett, M. A., Salovey, P., & Mayer, J. D. (2007). Measuring emotional intelligence as a set of mental abilities. In G. Matthews, M. Zeidner, & R. D. Roberts (Eds.), *The science of emotional intelligence: Knowns and unknowns* (pp. 230–257). New York, NY: Oxford University Press.

Roberts, B. W., Kuncel, N. R., Shiner, R., Caspi, A., & Goldberg, L. R. (2007). The power of personality: The comparative validity of personality traits, socioeconomic status, and cognitive ability for predicting important life outcomes. *Perspectives on Psychological Science, 2,* 313–345.

Roberts, R. D., Betancourt, A. C., Burrus, J., Holtzman, S., Libbrecht, N., MacCann, C., Matthews, G., Minsky, J., Naemi, B., & Schulze, R.

(in press). *Multimedia assessment of emotional abilities: Development and validation*. ETS Research Report Series. Princeton, NJ: ETS.

Roberts, R. D., Goff, G. N., Anjoul, F., Kyllonen, P. C., Pallier, G., & Stankov, L. (2000). The Armed Services Vocational Aptitude Battery: Not much more than acculturated learning (Gc)!? *Learning and Individual Differences, 12*, 81–103.

Roberts, R. D., & Lipnevich, A. A. (in press). From general intelligence to multiple intelligences: Meanings, models, and measures. In T. Urdan (Ed.), *APA educational psychology handbook, Volume 2*. Washington, DC: American Psychological Association.

Roberts, R. D., MacCann, C., Matthews, G., & Zeidner, M. (2010). Emotional intelligence: Towards a consensus of models and measures. *Social & Personality Psychology Compass, 4*, 821–840.

Roberts, R. D., Mason, A., & MacCann, C. (April, 2011). The management of emotion using the Situational Test of Emotion Management: Expanding the nomological net. In S. Kaplan & J. Cortina (Chairs), Understanding and managing workplace emotions: Measures, predictors, processes, and outcomes. *26th Annual Society for Industrial and Organizational Psychology Conference*, Chicago, IL.

Roberts, R. D., Schulze, R., & MacCann, C. (2008). The measurement of emotional intelligence: A decade of progress? In G. Boyle, G. Matthews, & D. Saklofske (Eds.), *The Sage handbook of personality theory and assessment* (pp. 461–482). New York, NY: Sage.

Roberts, R. D., Schulze, R., O'Brien, K., MacCann, C., Reid, J., & Maul, A. (2006). Exploring the validity of the Mayer-Salovey-Caruso Emotional Intelligence Test (MSCEIT) with established emotions measures. *Emotion, 6*, 663–669.

Roberts, R. D., Schulze, R., Zeidner, M., & Matthews, G. (2005). Understanding, measuring, and applying emotional intelligence: What have we learned? What have we missed? In R. Schulze & R. D. Roberts (Eds.), *International handbook of emotional intelligence* (pp. 311–341). Cambridge, MA: Hogrefe & Huber.

Roberts, R. D., & Stankov, L. (1999). Individual differences in speed of mental processing and human cognitive abilities: Towards a taxonomic model. *Learning and Individual Differences, 11*, 1–120.

Roberts, R. D., Zeidner, M., & Matthews, G. (2007). Emotional intelligence: Knowns and unknowns. In G. Matthews, M. Zeidner, & R. D. Roberts (Eds.), *The science of emotional intelligence: Knowns and unknowns* (pp. 419–474). New York, NY: Oxford University Press.

Roberts, R. D., Zeidner, M., & Matthews, G. (2001). Does emotional intelligence meet traditional standards for an "intelligence"? Some new data and conclusions. *Emotion, 1,* 196–231.

Rode, J. C., Arthaud-Day, M. L., Mooney, C. H., Near, J. P., & Baldwin, T. T. (2008). Ability and personality predictors of salary, perceived job success, and perceived career success in the initial career stage. *International Journal of Selection and Assessment, 16,* 292–299.

Rode, J. C., Mooney, C. H., Arthaud-day, M. L., Near, J. P., Rubin, R. S., Baldwin, T. T., & Bommer, W. H. (2008). An examination of the structural, discriminant, nomological, and incremental predictive validity of the MSCEIT© V2.0. *Intelligence, 36,* 350–366.

Romasz, T. E., Kantor, J. H., & Elias, M. J. (2004). Implementation and evaluation of urban school-wide social-emotional learning programs. *Evaluation and Program Planning, 27,* 89–103.

Rossen, E., & Kranzler, J. H. (2009). Incremental validity of the Mayer-Salovey-Caruso Emotional Intelligence Test Version 2.0 (MSCEIT) after controlling for personality and intelligence. *Journal of Research in Personality, 43,* 60–65.

Rossen, E., Kranzler, J. H., & Algina, J. (2008). Confirmatory factor analysis of the Mayer-Salovey-Caruso Emotional Intelligence Test V 2.0 (MSCEIT). *Personality and Individual Differences, 44,* 1258–1269.

Rothbart, M. K., Sheese, B. E., & Conradt, E. D. (2009). Childhood temperament. In P. L. Corr & G. Matthews (Eds.), *Cambridge handbook of personality* (pp. 177–190). Cambridge, UK: Cambridge University Press.

Rozell, E. J., Pettijohn, C. E., & Parker, R. S. (2004). Customer-oriented selling: Exploring the roles of emotional intelligence and organizational commitment. *Psychology and Marketing, 21,* 405–424.

Ryle, G. (1949). *The concept of mind.* London, UK: Hutchinson.

Saklofske, D. H., Austin, E. J., Galloway, J., & Davidson, K. (2007). Individual difference correlates of health-related behaviours: Preliminary evidence for links between emotional intelligence and coping. *Personality and Individual Differences, 42,* 491–502.

Saklofske, D. H., Austin, E. J., Mastoras, S. M., Beaton, L., & Osborne, S. E. (2011). Relationships of personality, affect, emotional intelligence and coping with student stress and academic success: Different patterns of association for stress and success. *Learning and Individual Differences.* doi: 10.1016/j.lindif.2011.02.010.

Saklofske, D. H., Austin, E. J., & Minski, P. S. (2003). Factor structure and validity of a trait emotional intelligence measure. *Personality and Individual Differences, 34,* 707–721.

Sala, F. (2002). *Emotional Competence Inventory (ECI): Technical Manual.* Boston: Hay/Mcber Group.

Salovey, P. (2001). Applied emotional intelligence: Regulating emotions to become healthy, wealthy, and wise. In J. V. Ciarrochi, J. P. Forgas, & J. D. Mayer (Eds.), *Emotional intelligence in everyday life: A scientific inquiry* (pp. 168–184). New York, NY: Psychology Press.

Salovey, P., Bedell, B. T., Detweiler, J. B., & Mayer, J. D. (1999). Coping intelligently: Emotional intelligence and the coping process. In C. R. Snyder (Ed.), *Coping: The psychology of what works* (pp. 141–164). New York, NY: Oxford University Press.

Salovey, P., Bedell, B. T., Detweiler, J. B., & Mayer, J. D. (2000). Current directions in emotional intelligence research. In M. Lewis & J. M. Haviland-Jones (Eds.), *Handbook of emotions* (pp. 504–520). New York, NY: Guilford Press.

Salovey, P., Caruso, D., & Mayer, J. D. (2004). Emotional intelligence in practice. In P. A. Linley & S. Joseph (Eds.), *Positive psychology in practice* (pp. 447–463). Hoboken, NJ: John Wiley.

Salovey, P., & Mayer, J. D. (1990). Emotional intelligence. *Imagination, Cognition and Personality, 9,* 185–211.

Salovey, P., Mayer, J. D., Goldman, S., Turvey, C., & Palfai, T. (1995). Emotional attention, clarity, and repair: Exploring emotional intelligence using the Trait Meta-Mood Scale. In J. W. Pennebaker (Ed.), *Emotion, disclosure, and health* (pp. 125–154). Washington, DC: American Psychological Association.

Salovey, P., Stroud, L. R., Woolery, A., & Epel, E. S. (2002). Perceived emotional intelligence, stress reactivity, and symptom reports: Further explorations using the trait meta-mood scale. *Psychology and Health, 17,* 611–627.

Santesso, D. L., Reker, D. L., Schmidt, L. A., & Segalowitz, S. J. (2006). Frontal electroencephalogram activation asymmetry, emotional intelligence, and externalizing behaviors in 10-year-old children. *Child Psychiatry and Human Development, 36,* 311–328.

Scherer, K. R. (2007). Componential emotion theory can inform models of emotional competence. In G. Matthews, M. Zeidner,

& R. D. Roberts (Eds.), *The science of emotional intelligence: Knowns and unknowns* (pp. 101–126). New York, NY: Oxford University Press.

Scherer, K. R., Banse, R., & Wallbott, H. G. (2001). Emotion inferences from vocal expression correlate across languages and cultures. *Journal of Cross Cultural Psychology, 32,* 76–92.

Schmidt, F. L., & Hunter, J. (2004). General mental ability in the world of work: Occupational attainment and job performance. *Journal of Personality and Social Psychology, 86,* 162–173.

Schmidt-Atzert, L. & Bühner, M. (2002). Entwicklung eines Leistungstests zur Emotionalen Intelligenz: 43 (pp. 9, 22–26). *Kongress der Deutschen Gesellschaft für Psychologie,* Berlin, 2002.

Schnabel, K., Asendorpf, J. B., & Greenwald, A. G. (2008). Using Implicit Association Tests for the assessment of implicit personality self-concept. In G. J. Boyle, G. Matthews, & D. H. Saklofske (Eds.), *The SAGE handbook of personality theory and testing: Volume 2: Personality measurement and testing* (pp. 508–528). Thousand Oaks, CA: Sage.

Schroeder, M. L., Wormsworth, J. A., & Livesley, W. J. (1992). Dimensions of personality disorder and their relationships to the big five dimensions of personality. *Psychological Assessment, 4,* 47–53.

Schulze, R., Wilhelm, O., & Kyllonen, P. C. (2007). Approaches to the assessment of emotional intelligence. In G. Matthews, M. Zeidner, & R. D. Roberts (Eds.), *The science of emotional intelligence: Knowns and unknowns* (pp. 199–229). New York, NY: Oxford University Press.

Schutte, N. S., Malouff, J. M., Bobik, C., Coston, T. D., Greeson, C., Jedlicka, C., & Rhodes, E. W. G. (2001). Emotional intelligence and interpersonal relations. *Journal of Social Psychology, 141,* 523–536.

Schutte, N. S., Malouff, J. M., Hall, L. E., Haggerty, D. J., Cooper, J. T., Golden, C. J., & Dornheim, L. (1998). Development and validation of a measure of emotional intelligence. *Personality and Individual Differences, 25,* 167–177.

Schutte, N. S., Malouff, J. M., Thorsteinsson, E. B., Bhullar, N., & Rooke, S. E. (2007). A meta-analytic investigation of the relationship between emotional intelligence and health. *Personality and Individual Differences, 42,* 921–933.

Seghers, J. P., McCleery, A., & Docherty, N. M. (2011). Schizotypy, alexithymia, and socioemotional outcomes. *Journal of Nervous and Mental Disease, 199,* 117–121.

Sevdalis, N., Petrides, K. V., & Harvey, N. (2007). Trait emotional intelligence and decision-related emotions. *Personality and Individual Differences, 42,* 1347–1358.

Shadish, W. R., Jr., Cook, T. D., & Campbell, D. T. (2002). *Experimental and quasi-experimental designs for generalized causal inference.* Boston, MA: Houghton-Mifflin.

Shaw, T. H., Matthews, G., Warm, J. S., Finomore, V., Silverman, L., & Costa, P. T., Jr. (2010). Individual differences in vigilance: Personality, ability, and states of stress. *Journal of Research in Personality, 44,* 297–308.

Sifneos, P. E. (1973). The prevalence of "alexithymic" characteristics in psychosomatic patients. *Psychotherapy and Psychosomatics, 22,* 255–262.

Skinner, C., & Spurgeon, P. (2005). Valuing empathy and emotional intelligence in health leadership: A study of empathy, leadership behavior and outcome effectiveness. *Health Services Management Research, 18,* 1–12.

Slaski, N. (2001). An investigation into emotional intelligence, managerial stress and performance in a UK supermarket chain. Unpublished paper.

Slaski, M., & Cartwright, S. (2003). Emotional intelligence training and its implications for stress, health and performance. *Stress and Health: Journal of the International Society for the Investigation of Stress, 19,* 233–239.

Slaski, M., & Cartwright, S. (2002). Health, performance, and emotional intelligence: An exploratory study of retail managers. *Stress and Health, 18,* 63–68.

Smith, L., Ciarrochi, J. V., & Heaven, P. C. L. (2008). The stability and change of trait emotional intelligence, conflict communication patterns, and relationship satisfaction: A one-year longitudinal study. *Personality and Individual Differences, 45,* 738–743.

Spearman, C. (1927). *The abilities of man.* New York, NY: MacMillan.

Spearman, C. (1923). *The nature of intelligence and the principles of cognition.* London: MacMillan.

Stankov, L. (1986). Kvashchev's experiment: Can we boost intelligence? *Intelligence, 10,* 209–230.

Stankov, L., Danthiir, V., Williams, L., Gordon, E., Pallier, G., & Roberts, R. D. (2006). Intelligence and the tuning-in of brain networks. *Learning and Individual Differences, 16,* 217–233.

Sternberg, R. J. (2000). The concept of intelligence. In R. J. Sternberg (Ed.), *Handbook of intelligence* (pp. 3–15). New York, NY: Cambridge University Press.

Sternberg, R. J., Conway, B. E., Ketron, J. L., & Bernstein, M. (1981). People's conceptions of intelligence. *Journal of Personality and Social Psychology, 41*, 37–55.

Stokes, T. L., & Bors, D. A. (2001). The development of a same-different inspection time paradigm and the effects of practice. *Intelligence, 29*, 247–261.

Summerfeldt, L. J., Kloosterman, P. H., Antony, M., & Parker, J. D. A. (2006). Social anxiety, emotional intelligence, and interpersonal adjustment. *Journal of Psychopathology and Behavioral Assessment, 28*, 57–68.

Sy, T., Tram, S., & O'Hara, L. A. (2006). Relation of employee and manager emotional intelligence to job satisfaction and performance. *Journal of Vocational Behavior, 68*, 461–473.

Taub, G. E., & McGrew, K. S. (2004). A confirmatory factor analysis of Cattell-Horn-Carroll theory and cross-age invariance of the Woodcock-Johnson Tests of Cognitive Abilities III. *School Psychology Quarterly, 19*, 72–87.

Taylor, G. J., Bagby, R. M., & Parker, J. D. A. (1997). *Disorders of affect regulation: Alexithymia in medical and psychiatric illness.* Cambridge, UK: Cambridge University Press.

Temoshok, L. R., Waldstein, S. R., Wald, R. L., Garzino-Demo, A., Synowski, S. J., Sun, L.,& Wiley, J. A. (2008). Type C coping, alexithymia, and heart rate reactivity are associated independently and differentially with specific immune mechanisms linked to HIV progression. *Brain, Behavior, and Immunity, 22*, 781–792.

Tett, R. P., Fox, K. E., & Wang, A. (2005). Development and validation of a self-report measure of emotional intelligence as a multidimensional trait domain. *Personality and Social Psychology Bulletin, 31*, 859–888.

Thayer, R. E., Newman, J. R., & McClain, T. M. (1994). Self-regulation of mood: strategies for changing a bad mood, raising energy, and reducing tension. *Journal of Personality and Social Psychology, 67*, 910–925.

Thurstone, L. L. (1938). *Primary mental abilities.* Chicago: University of Chicago Press.

Tirre, W. C., & Field, K. A. (2002). Structural models of abilities measured by the Ball Aptitude Battery. *Educational and Psychological Measurement, 62*, 830–856.

Tok, S., & Morali, S. L. (2009). Trait emotional intelligence, the Big Five personality dimensions and academic success in physical education teacher candidates. *Social Behavior and Personality, 37*, 921–932.

Topping, K. J., Holmes, E. A., & Bremner, W. G. (2000). The effectiveness of school-based programs: For the promotion of social competence. In R. Bar-On & J. D. A. Parker (Eds.), *The handbook of emotional intelligence* (pp. 411–432). San Francisco, CA: Jossey-Bass.

Tranel, D., & Bechara, A. (2009). Sex-related functional asymmetry of the amygdala: Preliminary evidence using a case-matched lesion approach. *Neurocase, 15*, 217–234.

Trinidad, D. R., & Johnson, C. A. (2002). The association between emotional intelligence and early adolescent tobacco and alcohol use. *Personality and Individual Differences, 32*, 95–105.

Trinidad, D. R., Unger, J. B., Chou, C.-P., & Johnson, C. (2005). Emotional intelligence and acculturation to the United States: Interactions on the perceived social consequences of smoking in early adolescents. *Substance Use and Misuse, 40*, 1697–1706.

Tulsky, D. S., & Price, L. R. (2003). The joint WAIS-III and WMS-III factor structure: Development and cross-validation of a six-factor model of cognitive functioning. *Psychological Assessment, 15*, 149–162.

Twenge, J. M., & Campbell, W. K. (2009). *The narcissism epidemic: Living in the age of enlightenment.* New York, NY: Free Press.

Uziel, L. (2007). Individual differences in the social facilitation effect: A review and meta-analysis. *Journal of Research in Personality, 41*, 579–601.

Vachon, D. D., & Bagby, R. M. (2007). The clinical utility of emotional intelligence: Association with related constructs, treatment, and psychopathology. In G. Matthews, M. Zeidner, & R. D. Roberts (Eds.), *The science of emotional intelligence: Knowns and unknowns* (pp. 339–355). New York, NY: Oxford University Press.

Vakola, M., Tsaousis, I., & Nikolaou, I. (2004). The role of emotional intelligence and personality variables on attitudes toward organizational change. *Journal of Managerial Psychology, 19*, 88–110.

Van der Zee, K., Thijs, M., & Schakel, L. (2002). The relationship of emotional intelligence with academic intelligence and the Big Five. *European Journal of Personality, 16*, 103–125.

Van Rooy, D. L., Whitman, D. S., Viswesvaran, C., & Pluta, P. (2010). Emotional intelligence: Additional questions still unanswered. *Industrial and Organizational Psychology, 3*, 149–153.

Van Rooy, D. L., & Viswesvaran, C. (2004). Emotional intelligence: A meta-analytic investigation of predictive validity and nomological net. *Journal of Vocational Behavior, 65*, 71–95.

Van Rooy, D. L., Viswesvaran, C., & Pluta, P. (2005). An evaluation of construct validity: What is this thing called emotional intelligence? *Human Performance, 18*, 445–462.

Vernon, P. A., Villani, V. C., Schermer, J. A., & Petrides, K. V. (2008). Phenotypic and genetic associations between the big five and trait emotional intelligence. *Twin Research and Human Genetics, 11*, 524–530.

Vigoda-Gadot, E., & Meisler, G. (2010). Emotions in management and the management of emotions: The impact of emotional intelligence and organizational politics on public sector employees. *Public Administration Review, 70*, 72–86.

Watson, D., & Pennebaker, J. W. (1989). Health complaints, stress, and distress: Exploring the central role of negative affectivity. *Psychological Review, 96*, 234–254.

Wechsler, D. (1974). The IQ is an intelligent test. In A. J. Edwards (Ed.), *Selected papers of David Wechsler.* New York: Academic Press.

Wedeck, J. (1947). The relationship between personality and "psychological ability." *British Journal of Psychology, 37*, 133–151.

Weisinger, H. (1998). *Emotional intelligence at work: The untapped edge for success.* San Francisco, CA: Jossey-Bass.

Weissberg, R. P., & Greenberg, M. T. (1998). School and community competence-enhancement and prevention programs. In I. E. Siegel & K. A. Renninger (Eds.), *Handbook of child psychology: Vol. 4. Child psychology in practice* (5th ed., pp. 877–954). New York, NY: Wiley.

Weist, M., Stiegler, K., Stephan, S., Cox, J., & Vaughan, C. (2010). School mental health and prevention science in the Baltimore City schools. *Psychology in the Schools, 47*, 89–100.

Wells, A. (2000). *Emotional disorders and metacognition: Innovative cognitive therapy.* Chichester, UK: Wiley.

Wells, A., & Cartwright-Hatton, S. (2004). A short form of the Metacognitions Questionnaire: Properties of the MCQ-30. *Behaviour Research and Therapy, 42*, 385–396.

Wells, A., & Davies, M. I. (1994). The Thought Control Questionnaire: A measure of individual differences in the control of unwanted thoughts. *Behaviour Research and Therapy, 32*, 871–878.

Wells, A., & Matthews, G. (1994). *Attention and emotion: A clinical perspective.* Hove: Erlbaum.

Welsh, M., Park, R. D., Widaman, K., & O'Neil, R. (2001). Linkages between children's social and academic competence: A longitudinal analysis. *Journal of School Psychology, 39*, 463–481.

Wharton, A. S. (2009). The sociology of emotional labor. *Annual Review of Sociology, 35*, 147–165.

Widiger, T. A., & Mullins-Sweatt, S. N. (2009). Five-factor model of personality disorder: A proposal for DSM-V. *Annual Review of Clinical Psychology, 5*, 197–220.

Wiggins, J. S. (2003). Paradigms of personality assessment: An interpersonal odyssey. *Journal of Personality Assessment, 80*, 11–18.

Yammarino, F. J., & Bass, B. M. (1990). Long-term forecasting of transformational leadership and its effects among naval officers: some preliminary findings. In K. E. Clark & M. B. Clark (Eds.), *Measures of leadership.* West Orange, NJ: Leadership Library of America, Inc.

Yang, S-Y., & Sternberg, R. J. (1997). Taiwanese Chinese people's conceptions of intelligence. *Intelligence, 25*, 21–36.

Youngmee, K., Schulz, R., & Carver, CS. (2007). Benefit finding in the cancer caregiving experience. *Psychosomatic Medicine, 69*, 283–291.

Zeidner, M. (2005). Emotional intelligence and coping with occupational stress. In A. G. Antoniou & C. L. Cooper (Ed.), *New perspectives in occupational health psychology* (pp. 218–239). Cheltenham, UK: Edward Elgar Publishing.

Zeidner, M., & Kaluda, I. (2008). Romantic love: What's emotional intelligence (EI) got to do with it? *Personality and Individual Differences, 44*, 1684–1695.

Zeidner, M., & Matthews, G. (in press). Personality. In T. Urdan (Ed.), *APA educational psychology handbook* (Vol. 2). Washington, DC: American Psychological Association.

Zeidner, M., & Matthews, G. (2011). *Anxiety 101.* New York, NY: Springer Publishing Company.

Zeidner, M., Matthews, G., & Roberts, R. D. (2011). The emotional intelligence, health, and well-being nexus; What have we learned and what have we missed?. Working Paper. Laboratory for Research on Personality, Emotions, and Individual Differences, University of Haifa.

Zeidner, M., Matthews, G., & Roberts, R. D. (2009). *What we know about emotional intelligence: How it affects learning, work, relationships and our mental health*. Cambridge, MA: MIT Press.

Zeidner, M., Matthews, G., & Roberts, R. D. (2006). Emotional intelligence, coping, and adaptation. In J. Ciarrochi, J. Forgas, & J. D. Mayer (Eds.), *Emotional intelligence in everyday life: A scientific inquiry* (2nd ed., pp. 100–125). Philadelphia, PA: Psychology Press.

Zeidner, M., Matthews, G., & Roberts, R. D. (2001). Slow down, you move too fast: Emotional intelligence remains an "elusive" intelligence. *Emotion, 1*, 265–275.

Zeidner, M., Matthews, G., Roberts, R. D., & MacCann, C. (2003). Development of emotional intelligence: Towards a multi-level investment model. *Human Development, 46*, 69–96.

Zeidner, M., Matthews, G., & Roberts, R. D., & (in press). The emotional intelligence, health, and well-being nexus: What have we learned and what have we missed? *Applied Psychology: Health and Well-being*.

Zeidner, M., & Olnick-Shemesh, D. (2010). Emotional intelligence and subjective well-being revisited. *Personality and Individual Differences, 48*, 431–435.

Zeidner, M., Roberts, R. D., & Matthews, G. (2009). *What we know about emotional intelligence: How it affects learning, work, relationships and our mental health*. Cambridge, MA: MIT Press.

Zeidner, M., Roberts, R. D., & Matthews, G. (2004). The emotional intelligence bandwagon: Too fast to live, too young to die. *Psychological Inquiry, 15*, 239–248.

Zeidner, M., Roberts, R. D., & Matthews, G. (2002). Can emotional intelligence be schooled? A critical review. *Educational Psychologist, 37*, 215–231.

Zeidner, M., & Saklofske, D. S. (1996). Adaptive and maladaptive coping. In M. Zeidner & N. S. Endler (Eds.), *Handbook of coping* (pp. 505–531). New York, NY: John Wiley and Sons.

Zeidner, M., Shani-Zinovich, I., Matthews, G., & Roberts, R. D. (2005). Assessing emotional intelligence in gifted and non-gifted high school students: Outcomes depend on the measure. *Intelligence, 33*, 369–391.

Ziegler, M., MacCann, C., & Roberts, R. D. (Eds.) (2011). *New perspectives on faking in personality assessment.* New York, NY: Oxford University Press.

Zins, J. E., Payton, J. W., Weissberg, R. P., & O'Brien, M. U. (2007). Social and emotional learning for successful school performance. In G. Matthews, M. Zeidner, & R. D. Roberts (Eds.), *Emotional intelligence: Knowns and unknowns* (pp. 376–395). New York, NY: Oxford University Press.

Zins, J. E., Weissberg, R. P., Wang, M. C., & Walberg, H. J. (Eds.) (2004). *Building academic success on social and emotional learning: What does the research say?* New York, NY: Teachers College Press.

Index